HUNGRY?

NEW YORK CITY

THE LOWDOWN ON

WHERE THE

REAL

PEOPLE

EAT!

Edited by
Joe Cleemann & Marie Estrada

Los Angeles, California

First Printing: April, 2002

10 9 8 7 6 5 4 3 2 1

Library of Congress Cataloging-in-Publication Data
Hungry? New York City: The Lowdown on Where
the Real People Eat!
by Glove Box Guides, an imprint of Really Great Books
Edited by Joe Cleemann & Marie Estrada
272 p. 8.89 x 22.86 cm.
ISBN 1-893329-09-7
I. Title II. Food Guides III. New York City IV. Joe Cleemann &
Marie Estrada

Production by Wendy Staroba Loreen
Illustrations by Ingrid Olson, Tülbox Creative Group

Visit our Web site at www.HungryCity.com

To order Hungry? or our other Glove Box Guides, or for
information on using them as corporate gifts, e-mail us at
Sales@HungryCity.com or write to:

Glove Box Guides
P.O. Box 861302
Los Angeles, CA 90086

THANKS

. . . **To our contributors**

Emma Berndt, Melissa Contreras, Michael Connor, Philip Curry, Peter Davis, Andrew Eastwick, Laramie Flick, Shannon Godwin, Jeff Gomez, Scott Benjamin Gross, Matthew Gurwitz, John Hartz, Esti Iturralde, Joanna Jacobs, Mayu Kanno, Tanya Laplante, Nemo Librizzi, Anikah McLaren, Julie Mente, Sarah Mente, Jessica Nepomuceno, Larry Ogrodnek, Julia Pastore, Jeremy Poreca, Steve Powers, Laura Ann Russo, Lindy Settevendemie, Jill Sieracki, Teresa Theophano, Rebecca Wendler, Sarah Winkeller, Brad Wood, and Andrew Yang

. . . **To people who lent suggestions and support**

Nichole Argyres, Elizabeth Beier, Brian Callaghan, Andrea Estrada, Reanne Estrada, Keith Kahla, Nina Wiener, and Wayne Yang

. . . **To the Glove Box Guides Staff**

The interns: Janelle Herrick, Zoltan Majdik, and Janna Kuntz. Susan Jonaitis, proofreader and editorial assistant. Ingrid Olson, Graphic Designer. Wendy Staroba Loreen, interior book production and, by our account, Quark guru. Mari Florence and Deborah Churchill Luster, for making the Glove Box Guides possible. And most especially, Kristin L. Petersen, our longsuffering editor who—perhaps more than any other editor in recent memory—deserves praise for her guidance, encouragement, and particularly (we can't stress this enough) her patience.

—*Joe Cleemann & Marie Estrada,*
Editors

CONTENTS

KEY TO THE BOOK

Icons

 Breakfast is the specialty

 Midday Nourishment

 Feast the night away

From the sea to your plate

Eat on the street

Food on the run

It's late and you're hungry

 Sleep is for the weak

 Nice places to dine solo

 Get cozy with a date

 Have a fresh air experience

 In business since 1969 or before

 Eateries that best embody the Hungry? spirit

Cost

While *Hungry?* is limited to eateries where you can get a meal for $10 or less, there are some super cheap spots, as well as some pricier joints that we made an exception for (only going over $10 by a few bucks) based on fabulous atmosphere or a unique menu.

    $ **Supacheap!** ($5 and under)
    $$ **Just right!** ($6–8)
    $$$ **Live a little!** ($9–12)
    $$$$ **Go whole hog!** (over $13)

Payment

Note that most places that take *all* the plastic we've listed also take Diner's Club, Carte Blanche, and the like.

Cash only   Benjamins, bills, bread, dough, green.... you get it!

    VISA   Visa

    Master Card

    American Express

    Discover

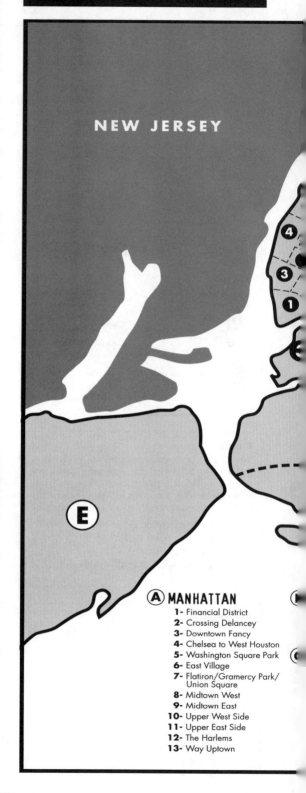

NEW JERSEY

4

3

1

E

E

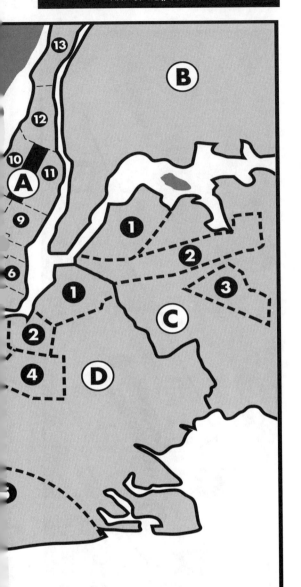

RONX/WAY UPTOWN
Washington Heights/The Hub/
Riverdale/Outer Bronx

UEENS
1- Astoria/Long Island City
2- Ride the 7
3- Central Queens

(D) BROOKLYN
1- Williamsburg/Greenpoint
2- Downtown Brooklyn East
3- Downtown Brooklyn West
4- Prospect Park
5- South Brooklyn

(E) STATEN ISLAND

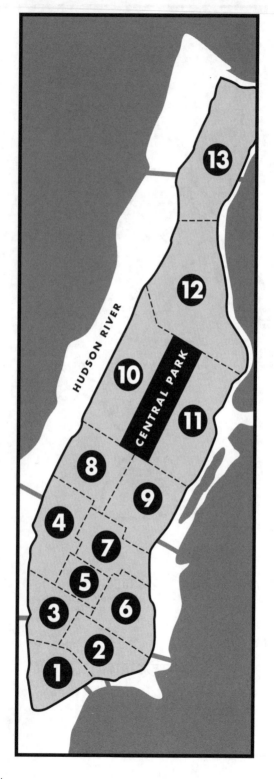

HUDSON RIVER

CENTRAL PARK

MANHATTAN

PLEASE READ

 The only sure thing in life is change. We've tried to be as up-to-date as possible, but places change owners, hours and menus as often as they open up a new location or go out of business. Call ahead so you don't end up wasting a time crossing town and arrive after closing time.

 Every place in *Hungry?* is recommended, for something. Each reviewer has tried to be honest about his/her experience of the place, and sometimes a jab or two makes its way into the mix. If your favorite spot is slammed for something you think is unfair, it's just one person's opinion! And remember, under the Fair Use Doctrine, some statements about the establishments in this book are intended to be humorous as parodies. Whew! Got the legal stuff out of the way.

 While we list over 350 eateries in the book, that's just the beginning of cheap and delicious eats in NYC. Visit hungrycity.com for more reviews, updates, and all the information you need for your next eating adventures.

 If you can't afford to tip you can't afford to eat out. In the United States, most servers make minimum wage or less, and depend on tips to pay the rent. Tip fairly, and not only will you get better service when you come back, but you'll start believing in karma (if you don't already).

 Too busy to go out? Or too tired? Many of the eateries offer take out or delivery in the local area. Call ahead—this is when the fax number comes in handy.

 Know about a place we missed? Willing to divulge your secrets? Send your ideas for the next edition to "Hungry? New York City Update" c/o Glove Box Guides, P.O. Box 861302, Los Angeles, CA 90013 or e-mail update@hungrycity.com. There's no guarantee we'll use your idea, but if it sounds right for us we'll let you know.

INTRODUCTION

"Where the real people eat . . ."

We felt uneasy searching for places where *the* real people eat. Who, after all, are *the* real people? Real people, we could have understood. By virtue of simplicity, complexity, vibrancy, or stupidity, most of us can make a case for inclusion in these ranks. But then comes that article—*the*—and suddenly we're dealing with an entirely different can of worms. Now some are in and others are out. And we (representatives of the media) would seem such unlikely arbitrators of sincerity. Surely we owe some kind of explanation.

Who are they?

Are the real people workaday slobs who grab a bag of McDonalds on their ways home? Are they life-affirming thrill-seekers who slam Mountain Dew and Power Bars en route to their next stupid stunts? Are they polished sophistos who have cultivated appreciation for what is truly worthwhile in life? Do they value entertainment or edification? Cold comfort or change? Walk-on parts in the war to . . . you get the idea.

Who knows?

But you can say this much: just about any claimant to the title, *the real people,* can appreciate the allure of good food at reasonable prices. And that's what we went after: varied and delicious meals that require the breaking of twenties. Five dollar meals. Eight dollar meals. Ten dollar meals. Meals from Greece, Jordan, Japan, Malaysia, Italy, the Dominican Republic. Meals for vegetarians, Vegans, meat-eaters, Jews and Muslims, businesspersons and students, the sane and the insane.

Specious reasoning . . .

So that's what we've come up with: these are the places that the real people ought to like. Function follows form, or vice versa. Are we right? You decide: if you've read this far, you either consider yourself one of the real people or you're aghast at our attempt to define who they are. Whichever is the case, know that we didn't (indeed, we couldn't) do it alone.

On method . . .

Here's what we did: we went to as many people as we could find—friends, co-workers, friends of friends, obscure contacts, chat room lingerers, utter strangers—and we asked them for help. What places do you know, we asked, where a person can eat well for loose change?

What's a place that deserves credit but doesn't always get it? What places would, in a just universe, have a few glowing reviews posted on their walls or in their front windows? Would you like to help them to be recognized?

Filling in the blanks . . .

Sometimes we found a deserving neighborhood left out in the cold. Occasionally we'd come across a great culinary institution that, by some shortcoming in our survey techniques, was missed altogether. When these situations came up, either one of us, or someone in our employ, set out to see that justice was done. So, in addition to what we initially collected, you'll find sidebars on places like Belmont and Koreatown. You'll find sidebars that cover the city's Filipino offerings, or its better options for pizza and hot dogs. You'll also find reviews for places in Staten Island and the Bronx that few outside their surrounding neighborhoods ever visit.

Complete?

No. With a city New York's size, never. But it's a start . . .

And what does the future hold?

Hopefully, second and third editions of *Hungry? New York City* will cover the places we missed, or the places we mentioned in passing. Places in Brooklyn and Queens, even places in Manhattan, that deserve attention. But on a more practical note, the future holds subway service changes, openings and closings, change of hours, change of payment methods. We try to be thorough, but with what seems like half the subway lines in the city temporarily rerouted after the attacks, you never know when normalcy will return and our directions will become inaccurate. So a piece of advice: consult a subway map.

Enjoy!

—*Joe Cleemann & Marie Estrada*
New York City

MANHATTAN

Re-exploring Lower Manhattan

Over 200 years ago, New York primarily consisted of Lower Manhattan south of Canal St., with Pearl, Front, and South streets forming its urban center. Shippers and merchants lived on the Battery, Bowling Green, Greenwich St. (where the World Trade Center once stood), and Broadway, while Artisans lived in present-day TriBeCa.

By the mid-1800s, a grid system of streets and avenues was imposed on the entire island. Rivers and streams were filled in and built over. By 1850, commerce had polluted the area and the gentry moved out and up to the quiet suburbs of today's Greenwich Village, while the poorer German and Irish immigrants remained. Along Wall St. and Broadway, the once single family homes of shippers and merchants were replaced by banks and office buildings. In 1883, the Brooklyn Bridge was built, transferring thousands of workers daily into Lower Manhattan. Skyscrapers twelve stories high were erected on Wall St. and Broadway. From Broadway to the Hudson River was the Washington Market, the city's wholesale food market, and the Hudson River was bustling with freighters delivering goods and ships delivering passengers.

In 1898, after the consolidation of what are now the five boroughs into one single entity, New York's population was a staggering three million, making it the second largest city in the world, surpassed only by London. By 1945, after the Great Depression and two World Wars, the American dollar had become the world's standard currency. New York was an international city, with Wall St. its financial center. And to this today, even as it recovers from incredible loss, Lower Manhattan remains the financial, political, and judicial heart of New York City.

•••

Around the Courts and the Civic Center

For "a touch of traditional" Pakistani cuisine until the wee hours of the morning, cruise on over to Church St. between Duane and Reade Sts. to the ever popular **Pakistan Tea House** for frighteningly generous four to six dollar vegetarian, meat, or *dale chawal* (yellow lentils and white rice) combination platters, fresh *naan*, fabulously creamy, non-iced mango *lassi*, and impressive dessert choices from *gulab jamon* and *ras malai* to homemade *kulfi*. Serve yourself water from one of the pitchers in the icebox. *176 Church St., Manhattan, 10013, (212) 240-9800. Daily: 11 AM–4 AM. Cash only.*

Head one block east onto Broadway, New York's oldest and longest street, and walk south toward John Street where **Tokyo Lunch, Maggie's Cajun Grill, Roxy Food Shop**, and **Seh Ja Meh Korean Restaurant** are located. On the way you'll pass numerous landmarks including the deliciously ornate Woolworth Building, which between 1913 and 1930 was the world's tallest (233 Broadway between Park Pl. and Barclay St.), the original site of Columbia University (previously King's College) at Broadway and Murray St., and St. Paul Chapel's at Vesey St., the city's only existing pre-Revolutionary brownstone church.

At **Tokyo Lunch** be prepared for cramped quarters and the scent of fried food in the air. Choose from various soups, noodles, curry, *donburi* (over rice dishes), and sushi. Especially tasty is the fried fish (changes day to day from salmon to whiting to red bass), served over rice with a thick barbecue sauce tasting faintly of wasabi, and an iceberg lettuce salad with carrot ginger dressing. After you order, take a seat in the back, where business suits and shoppers sit on medium and super-low stools hunkering over their food at counters. *10 John St., Manhattan, 10038, (212) 608-1394. Mon–Fri: 11 AM–4 PM. Cash only.*

Next door is **Maggie's Cajun Grill** where you can get any of seven Louisiana specialties like Maggie's famous flame-broiled bourbon chicken, shrimp *étouffe* (stir-fried with tomato sauce), or blackened fish. The dishes come with rice and two vegetables—all for under six bucks. Or, try the vegetarian platter with choice of carrots, beans, sweet corn, string beans, steamed cabbage, or fried potatoes with onion, and a side of rice for under four bucks. *12 John St., Manhattan, 10038, (212) 577-2668. Mon–Fri: 11 AM–5:30pm. Cash only.*

While **Roxy Food Shop** doesn't look like much, this All-American joint, established in 1948, serves a mean grilled cheese on rye and a darn good egg cream from the fountain. Roxy Lunch Box Special includes a sandwich, French fries, and a fountain soda. *20 John St., Manhattan, 10038, (212) 349-4704/5. Mon–Fri: 24 hours, Sat: midnight–4 PM. Cash only.*

If you feel like some *kimchi* or barbecue and can afford to splurge a little, hit **Seh Jah Meh Korean Restaurant.** Here you can sit in an open dining area with 40 others and chomp on tasty *kimchi* pancakes or *bim bim bop* sizzling in a stone bowl. Korean Citrus drink and OB beer are particularly good at cooling the tongue. *26 John St., Manhattan, 10038, (212) 766-5825. Mon–Fri: 11:30 AM–9 PM. Visa MC Amex.*

Continue south on Broadway toward Trinity Church (built in 1846) and its 2.5 acre graveyard, which houses 300-year-old tombstones. Famous Americans buried in the graveyard include Alexander Hamilton and William Bradford, publisher of New York's first newspaper, the *Gazette*. Near the Trinity Church, on the shadowed Thames St., between Broadway and Trinity Pl. you'll find **Big Al's,** where a Chicago style slice of Neopolitan or lasagna pizza comes with a cute threat: "Big Al says you better like it or else!!!" Big Al's is a brightly lit classically decorated pizzeria with about twenty polished stools. *9 Thames St., Manhattan, 10006, (212) 964-3269/70. Mon–Fri: 7 AM–6:30 PM. Visa MC Amex Discover.*

If you're not craving pizza, head west on Rector St. and get yourself to **George's Restaurant,** established in 1951. Order a sandwich—Philly beef steak or any one of the overstuffed variety such as meat loaf, smoked turkey, steak, or chicken meatloaf. Health conscious? There's a decent "Weight Watcher's Specials" section of the menu, which includes the Slenderell: tuna or salmon with cottage cheese, lettuce and tomato, or fruit salad. Or have a big baked stuffed potato—choice of tuna, chicken salad, bacon, chili, broccoli, spinach, or mushrooms, with melted cheese. And wash it all down with a two-scoop banana split and a shot of espresso or a cold beer. Seats 50 at tables, including counter. *89 Greenwich St., Manhattan, 10006, (212) 269-8026. Mon–Fri: 6 AM–9 PM, Sat: 6 AM–4 PM. Visa MC Amex Discover.*

Or are you in the mood for some Mexican food? Next door at **Tajin Restaurant,** a lovely space with pink walls that seats about 50 at tables, sink your teeth into a nice spinach mushroom, cheese, chicken, or beef enchilada or a Texas burrito stuffed with steak, *chorizo,* mushrooms, onions, and potatoes. Have it with a Mexican or Domestic beer or some refreshing home made lemonade. *85 Greenwich St., Manhattan, 10006, (212) 509-5017. Mon–Fri: 7 AM–9 PM, Sat: 11 AM–8 PM. Visa MC Amex.*

Across the street, and next door to a topless bar that has smut written all over it, you'll find **Cordato's,** a bright pizzeria—with a bar in the back. Here, you can have a wholesome submarine special (genoa salami, cappicolla ham, and provolone with tomato, onion, and hot pepper dashed with oil and vinegar) or the Giakoumo's Special American Style (made with ham, bologna, cheese, and liverwurst with lettuce and tomato on wheat). Salads and pizza-by-the-slice also available. *94 ½ Greenwich St., Manhattan, 10006, (212) 233-1573. Mon–Fri: 24 hours, Sat: closes at midnight. Visa MC Amex.*

•••

Around Wall St. and the Stone Street Historic District

Head east on Broadway toward Wall St., so named for the five foot wall built here in 1653 by Governor Peter Stuyvesant to shield the then Dutch colony from British invasion (and to keep the Native Americans out and the cows in). You'll pass Bankers Trust Building, The Federal Hall National Memorial (with the statue of George Washington in front), The New York Stock Exchange. The Stone Street Historic District covers Stone St. between William and Pearl streets, Coenties Alley and S. William St. The majority of the buildings in this district are four and five-story commercial structures that replaced those leveled by the Great Fire of 1835.

Imagine your favorite small Chinese takeout, a hundred times bigger, with two levels of seating and even cheaper prices, and you've got **Yip's Restaurant.** Daily specials with choice of various rice dishes or noodles—none exceeding five bucks. None. The Hot Bar Buffet is a steal ($3.89 per pound 11 AM–1:45 PM and an incredible $2.99 per pound 1:45 PM–3:30 PM). *18 Beaver St., Manhattan, 10004, (212) 480-9010. Mon–Fri: 10:30 AM–8:30 PM, Sat: 11 AM– 3 PM. Cash only.*

Giuliano's Pizzeria and Deli, at the corner of Stone and Broad Streets, has a vast menu from pizza to burgers to sandwiches to seafood dishes and soups. Seating upstairs for over a hundred. But if the options are too overwhelming, the friendly staff will help you create your own salad from both hot and cold items such as Thai chicken or smoked turkey with a base of spinach, romaine, and mesclun. Don't miss the spicy fries and strawberry banana piña colada shake. *88 Broad St., Manhattan, 10004, (212) 344-0220. Mon–Fri: 6 AM–9 PM, Sat: 6 AM–5 PM. Visa MC Amex Discover.*

For a slightly corporate, Ikea-like adventure, have a zucchini and melted tomato quiche from the Hot and Crispy section of **Pax Wholesome Foods.** Also available are *quesadillas,* pizza, wraps, various soups, sandwiches, desserts, and coffee. *90 Broad St., Manhattan, 10004, (212) 483-8100. Mon–Fri: 6 AM–6 PM, Sat: 7 AM–3 PM. Visa MC Amex Discover.*

Next door to Pax, is **Imperial Chinese,** which has a very ornamented waiting room and a banquet room in which you'd imagine a Chinese wedding could take place. Too expensive, folks, but interesting eye-candy.

A few shops over is **Amazing Japanese & Thai Restaurant.** Just like the name says, two cuisines are available under one roof—and there are two separate menus as well. Unless you want to eat in a relatively dark space, order one of the Amazing Thai-Japanese Lunch Combos, such as the sushi, *pad* Thai, and *maki* in one box. It is only available for take-out, so find a bench or walk south to the Seaport and lunch outside. *11 Stone St., Manhattan, 10004, (212) 742-0088/ 9720. Mon–Fri: 11 AM–9:30 PM. Visa MC Amex Discover.*

Are you ready for the fabulously sparkling, tasty but cheap eating experience known as **Prêt a Manger?** Decked out in shiny metal everywhere— including stylish ultra modern stools—this expansive eatery runs like a well-oiled machine. Tasty, tasty, tasty sandwiches and cakes. See review p. 104. *60 Broad St., Manhattan, 10004, (212) 825-0412. Mon–Fri: 7 AM–5 PM. Visa MC Amex.*

At the famed intersection of Broad St. and Exchange Pl. is the modern and chic **Vine Market Café** (next to the much pricier Vine Restaurant). One of the only restaurants in this area open on Sunday, here you can get great salmon, sandwiches, make your own salad at the buffet bar, or have some sushi in a pleasant casual setting. *25 Broad St., Manhattan, 10004, (212) 344-8463. Mon–Fri: noon– 9:45 PM. Visa MC Amex Discover. www. vinefood.com.*

• • •

Pearl St. and
The Historic Fraunces Tavern Block

Where Pearl St. currently runs, docks filled with oyster harvesters once lined the water. Sometimes, after workers removed the meat from the oyster and tossed the waste on the streets, sideliners found pearls in the shells or lying in the cracks in the road.

And, northeast of Pearl St., around Broad St., the Dutch colonists dug a large canal in an effort to recreate the surroundings of their homeland. The water quickly turned putrid and the disappointed Dutch filled in the filthy canal to create the present street. The marriage of muck and money characterizes the financial district to this day.

Located next to historical Fraunces Tavern (where General Washington gave his farewell address to his Revolutionary War officers in 1783), **Pearl Palace Restaurant** serves Pakistani and Indian favorites such as chicken *tikka masala.* Weekdays 11 AM–3 PM there is an all-you-can eat lunch buffet, which includes dessert. *60 Pearl St., Manhattan, 10004, (212) 482-0771. Daily: 11 AM–2:30 AM. Visa MC Amex Discover.*

Feel like you've stepped into Old World Italy at charming **Zigolini's Famiglia** where you can get traditional spaghetti or wonderful sandwiches such as the Sabino (grilled salmon, capers, dill, scallion, romaine lettuce, and lemon juice on black olive bread) or brie cheese, roasted eggplant, and roasted peppers on sourdough. Check for daily specials.

66 Pearl St., Manhattan, 10004, (212) 425-7171. Mon–Fri: 6 AM–5pm. Visa MC Amex Discover.

Kyoto of Japan is always packed during lunch, when the $5.95 special lunch box is available (with 17 items to chose from, such as sashimi, sushi, tempura, and teriyaki). With a sushi bar and seating for 48, you'd do well to also come here in the evening, when the atmosphere is relaxed and the helpful and friendly owner and staff may be able to chat with you while you sip your sake. *76 Pearl St., Manhattan, 10004, (212) 363-1668. Mon–Fri: 11 AM–9:30 PM. Visa MC Amex Discover.*

Situated in the midst of giant restaurants that can seat over 200, **Terrace Fish & Chip** is a tiny hole-in-the wall that manages to hold its own by providing fresh, simple fried fare at ultracheap prices. Try the double whiting sandwich with French fries or shrimp with seafood rice. Seating for four at the counter. *77 Pearl St., Manhattan, 10004, (212) 809-4604. Mon–Fri: 11 AM–5 PM. Cash only.*

A few doors away, the friendly, no-nonsense **Pearlstone Chinese Restaurant** serves plenty of vegetarian options and alternatives to usual Chinese entrées. Particularly popular here is sesame chicken and the vegetarian dishes made with bean curd. Seating for over 200. *81 Pearl St., Manhattan, 10004, (212) 509-0312. Mon–Fri: 10:30 AM–10 PM, Sat: 10:30 AM–3 PM. Visa MC Amex.*

Across from 85 Broad St., **Diwan-E-Khaas** serves up fine Northern Indian cuisine in a pleasant casual setting that seats about 50. Have the *dal makhani* or chicken *vindaloo* with a vegtable *samosa* (filled with spiced potatoes and green peas). Wash it down with a sweet or mango *lassi*. Top it off with *rasmalai* and you'll be ready for your afternoon nap instantly. *26 S. William St., Manhattan, 10004, (212) 248-2361. Mon–Sat: 11 AM–10 PM. Visa MC Amex.*

Head south toward Water St. and you'll find **Soprano's.** Across the street from the expansive 1 New York Plaza, this is where to get a good slice of Margarita pizza (made with fresh mozzarella and basil). *30 Water St., Manhattan, 10004, (212) 809-0999/6666. Mon–Fri: 8 AM–6 PM. Visa MC Amex.*

•••

The Fulton Fish Market in the South Street Seaport

Located on South St., between Beeckman and Fulton Sts., the **Fulton Fish Market** is the nation's largest wholesale fish market. It was established in 1821 as a retail market for the purpose of supplying common people with the necessities of life at reasonable prices. Between midnight and 8 AM, you can see restaurateurs and retailers making their picks from the gasping catch. The city, for years, has unsuccessfully tried to move it next to the wholesale vegetable market at Hunts Point in the Bronx. In the wee hours of the morning between May and October, there's a behind-the-scenes tour (if you can stomach the sight and stench of wriggling fish!). Call (212) 748-8786 for tour information.

Before September 11ᵗʰ, Lower Manhattan was, to the majority of New Yorkers, a mysterious place—a landscape of ominous buildings towering incongruously over curvy cobblestoned streets and antiquated edifices—visited for no other reason than for jury duty, to renew a drivers license, or to meet with a lawyer or broker. But this area is so much more. It's filled with incredible history, architecture, and, of course, amazing food. We encourage you, beyond civic duty, financial or legal affairs, to visit and support and most importantly, eat your way through Lower Manhattan.

—*Marie Estrada*

Burritoville
(see p. 31)
Mexican
20 John St., Manhattan 10038
Phone (212) 766-2020
and
36 Water St., Manhattan 10004
Phone (212) 757-1100

Prêt a Manger
(see p. 104)
British Sandwich Shop
60 Broad St., Manhattan 10004
Phone (212) 825-8825

Teriyaki Boy
(see p. 91)
Japanese Fast Food/Sushi
22 Maiden Ln., Manhattan 10038
Phone (212) 385-8585

"What I say is that, if a man really likes potatoes,
he must be a pretty decent
sort of fellow."

—*A.A. Milne*

CROSSING DELANCEY
(CHINATOWN AND THE LOWER EAST SIDE)

Dragon Land Bakery

(see p. 17)
Chinese Bakery
125 Walker St., Manhattan 10013
Phone (212) 219-2012

Dumpling House

*If we had such a thing as half a dollar sign,
we'd use it for this unbelievably cheap,
terrifically tasty dumpling, porridge, and noodle joint.*

$

118 A Eldridge St.
(south of Broome St.)
Phone (212) 625-8008

CATEGORY	Chinese Dumpling and Noodle House
HOURS	Daily: 8 AM–10 PM
SUBWAY	4, 5, 6, J, M, Z to Brooklyn Bridge/ City Hall
PAYMENT	Cash only
POPULAR FOOD	Made-in front of you dumplings—have the vegetable steamed dumplings (eight per order); also several dollar breakfast specials, pork noodle soup, *lo mein, chow fun,* and hot and sour soup
UNIQUE FOOD	Try the sweet *mung* bean porridge with a chive and egg steamed bun—very filling
DRINKS	Soda, juice, tea
SEATING	Seats about six at a counter
AMBIENCE	Narrow space not for those prone to claustrophobia; bring patience—the staff is friendly, but speaks very little English
EXTRAS/NOTES	Some items on the menu may not be available. Then again, a slew of non-listed treats are. So, look around and see what the neighborhood folk are munching on and do a lot of pointing and smiling.

—*Marie Estrada*

Fong Da Bakery, Inc.

(see p. 17)
Chinese Bakery
83 Essex St., Manhattan 10013
Phone (212) 353-0166

Didjaknow?

To distinguish between sweet buns filled with sweetened
bean paste and seasoned buns filled with vegetables and
meat, a red dot is painted at the center of the sweet buns,
so that it resembles a woman's breast.

Tea Houses

Bubble Tea, pearl milk tea, *boba* milk tea, tapioca milk tea, pearl tea drink, *boba* ice tea, *boba nai cha, zhen zhou nai cha,* pearl ice tea, black pearl tea, pearl shake . . .

As Chinatown gobbles up adjacent neighborhoods, New York's retail economy, is witnessing an invigorating infusion of East Asian immigration, talent, ideas, and now capital investment. Joining the district's traditional red and gold storefronts and oft-gaudy dining halls, a new breed of sleek, modern, and aesthetically subdued refreshment counters (answering to corporate offices in Taiwan and Hong Kong) is finding an appreciative—and growing—clientele in the city: enter the tea houses.

Not your Granny's idea of a tea house, maybe. These recent arrivals offer remarkable varieties of refreshing and colorful tea drinks, often in tall cups or mugs, and often as not sporting triple-wide straws through which customers inhale marble-sized pellets of gooey tapioca. The more ordinary teas demand respect—green, jasmine, oolong, herbal, ginseng, the list goes on—but it's the more gimmicky, more photogenic, and certainly more exotic tapioca versions that pack in the crowds. A recent Taiwanese invention, these are alternately known as Bubble Tea, pearl milk tea, *boba* milk tea, tapioca milk tea, pearl tea drink, *boba* ice tea, *boba nai cha, zhen zhou nai cha,* pearl ice tea, black pearl tea, pearl shake . . .

Served as iced teas, or as thick, frothy milkshakes, the tapioca concoctions come in dozens of flavors. The milkshakes are the more interesting: try Taro Milk Tea or Sesame Milk Tea if you're a beginner. While not everyone goes home happy the first time, the typical range of options all but promises that you'll find something to keep you coming back.

Here are just a few of the places where you can get started:

Green Tea Café
- *Crossing Delancey: 45 Mott St., Manhattan, 10013, (212) 693-2888. Sun–Thurs: 10 AM–midnight, Fri/Sat: 10 AM–2 AM. www.greenteacafe.com*

Saint's Alp Tea House
- *Crossing Delancey: 51 Mott St., Manhattan, 10013, (212) 766-9889. Daily: 11 AM–11:30 PM.*
- *East Village/Alphabet City: 39 Third Ave., Manhattan, 10013, (212) 598-1890. Mon–Thurs: 1 PM–midnight, Fri/Sat: 1 PM–1 AM, Sun: 1 PM–11 PM.*

- *South Brooklyn: 5801 Eighth Ave., Brooklyn, 11220, (718) 437-6622. Daily: noon–11 PM. www.saints-alp.com.hk*

Ten Ren
- *Crossing Delancey: 75 Mott St., Manhattan, 10013, (212) 349-2286. Daily: 10 AM–8 PM.*
- *South Brooklyn: 5817 Eighth Ave., Brooklyn, 11220, (718) 853-0660. Daily: 10 AM–8 PM.*
- *Ride the 7: 135-18 Roosevelt Ave., Queens, 11354, (718) 461-9305. Daily: 10 AM–8 PM. www.tenren.com*

—Joe Cleemann & Mayu Kanno

Fried Dumpling

No-frills dumpling kitchen.
$

106 Mosco St., Manhattan 10013
(at Mott St.)
Phone (212) 693-1060

CATEGORY	Chinese Dumpling House
HOURS	Daily: 8:30 AM–8:30 PM
SUBWAY	J, M, N, Q, R, W, Z, 6 to Canal Street
PAYMENT	Cash only
POPULAR FOOD	Dumplings! Dumplings! Dumplings! As the name implies (by the way, we don't know if there's more to the name than Fried Dumpling—those were the only English words on the sign), this place specializes in fried dumplings—get five of the juicy dough pockets for $1, or, if you sold your Enron stock in time, opt for the pricier fried pork buns (four for $1)
UNIQUE FOOD	It's hard to say what's unique about dumplings, but the price is singularly low; you can take home 30 frozen dumplings for small change, then cook them yourself, but you'll miss out on Fried Dumpling's dipping sauce
DRINKS	A couple varieties of tea and soda
SEATING	Five at the counter
AMBIENCE	Not much to look at in terms of decoration, but you can follow the entire life cycle of a fried dumpling: from the meat mixer, to the fryer, to your stomach; if it's conversation you're after—and you're not already fluent in the appropriate dialect of Chinese—bring a phrase book
OTHER ONES	• Crossing Delancey: 99 Allen St., Manhattan, 10002, (212) 941-9975 (slightly more spacious location)

—Joe Cleemann

Green Tea Café

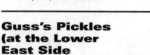

(see p. 10)
Tea House
45 Mott St., Manhattan 10013
Phone (212) 693-2888

Guss's Pickles (at the Lower East Side Tenement Museum)

(see p. 16)
Kosher Pickles
90 Orchard St., Manhattan 10002
Phone (212) 431-0233

Hop Kee Restaurant

*Basement location is easy to miss, but the
food sure isn't.*
$$$
21 Mott St., Manhattan 10013
(between Mosco St. and Bowery)
Phone: (212) 964-8365

CATEGORY	Cantonese Chinese
HOURS	Sun–Thurs: 11 AM–midnight Fri/Sat: 11 AM–4 AM
SUBWAY	4, 5, 6, J, M, Z to Brooklyn Bridge/ City Hall
PAYMENT	Cash only
POPULAR FOOD	Chinese broccoli with oyster sauce; steamed sea bass; boneless steamed chicken; salted pork chop with hot peppers; the wildly popular house special, seafood combination Cantonese *chow mein* or *lo mein,* feeds two to three—studded with fresh, sweet shrimp, cuttlefish, and scallops—this dish, like most of the food here, never needs extra salting
UNIQUE FOOD	Roast duck wonton soup; watercress with pork; winter melon with chicken; seaweed with pork and corn with chicken; also, snails Cantonese style
DRINKS	Soda, juice
SEATING	Seats about 150
AMBIENCE	Pay no mind to the chaos or the harshly lit basement space—this may look like a factory cafeteria, but your taste buds will tell you otherwise
EXTRAS/NOTES	Cutlery for the table comes in stainless steel columns, to better serve the huge delegations of Chinese and Filipinos who flock here on weekends. Service is admirably attentive, even if you're stuck in one of the far-off corner tables, as will often be the case when the place is full. Chinese tea sets and Jasmine tea for sale.

—*Melissa Contreras*

House of Vegetarian

(see p. 99)
Chinese/Vegan
68 Mott St., Manhattan 10013
Phone (212) 226-6572

K and D Bakery

(see p. 17)
Chinese Bakery
143 A Mott St., Manhattan 10013
Phone (212) 226-8988

King Wah Bakery

(see p. 18)
Chinese Bakery
25 E. Broadway, Manhattan 10013
Phone (212) 513-7107

Maria's Bakery

(see p. 18)
Chinese Bakery
42 Mott St., Manhattan 10013
Phone (212) 732-3888

May May Chinese Gourmet and Bakery

(see p. 17)
Chinese Bakery
35 Pell St., Manhattan 10013
Phone (212) 267-0733

Mei-Ju Vege Gourmet

I'd eat here every day if I lived in the area.
$$
154 Mott St., Manhattan 10013
(between Broome and Grand Sts.)
Phone (646) 613-0643

CATEGORY	Chinese Vegetarian Buffet
HOURS	Daily: 8 AM–8 PM
SUBWAY	4, 5, 6, J, M, Z to Brooklyn Bridge/ City Hall
PAYMENT	Cash only
POPULAR FOOD	With over 20 choices to heap on your plate, leave room for the savory sweet and sour gluten and the vermicelli noodles
UNIQUE FOOD	You won't have room, so take the wrapped rice roll with sautéed onion or the mushroom and *seitan* steamed bun to go
DRINKS	Soda, juice, tea

SEATING	Seats three at stools and a counter
AMBIENCE	Not a large operation, the food buffet (as it should) monopolizes the space—friendly service and very happy customers

—*Marie Estrada*

New Pasteur

No pretense here, just good, solid, Vietnamese food.
$$

85 Baxter St., Manhattan 10013
(at Canal St.)
Phone (212) 608-3656 or 608-4838

CATEGORY	Vietnamese
HOURS	Daily: 11 AM–9:30 PM
SUBWAY	6, Q, W, N, R, J, M, Z to Canal St.
PAYMENT	Cash only
POPULAR FOOD	*Muc chien don* (crispy squid in a little salt and pepper) is the most popular dish, according to the waiter; also try the piping-hot, ever-popular Vietnamese staple *pho,* available with beef, seafood, shrimp, chicken, or vegetables—enormous portions; or have the simple but fantastic rice vermicelli with curried chicken—if chicken's not your thing, try the barbecued shrimp, pork, beef, or vegetables; or the steamed shrimp rolls served with peanut dipping sauce
UNIQUE FOOD	If you're feeling adventurous, try the *ech um xa ot* (frog legs with curry sauce in casserole, served with various vegetables, all drowned in a delicious and spicy curry sauce)—one of the pricier items on the menu, but well worth it
DRINKS	You can get everything from soda to green bean with coconut milk; hot coffee with condensed milk is a tasty treat
SEATING	Four tables of four, three tables of six, and two round tables (which can seat four to six)
AMBIENCE	Situated directly across from a juvenile detention facility, New Pasteur is not a restaurant you go to for the atmosphere (i.e., it's not the place for a romantic first date), but it's not without charm—white muslin curtains on the window hide the view of the corrections facility
EXTRAS/NOTES	The white sign outside is rimmed with blinking colored lights—and its straightforward lack of pretense weeds out the tourists and the snooty upper crust. New Pasteur is filled with neighborhood folk, students complaining vocally about their love lives, and New Yorkers who know good, cheap Vietnamese food when they see it. Here you can sit for hours

without being bothered. The waiter assures me that there are a lot of regulars and no tourists—a feature he clearly doesn't want to change.

—Sarah Winkeller

Pho Bang Restaurant

Modest appearance hides cunning contender for best Vietnamese food in NYC.

$$

157 Mott St., Manhattan 10013

(between Grand and Broome Sts.)

Phone (212) 966-3797

CATEGORY	Vietnamese
HOURS	Daily: 10 AM–10 PM
SUBWAY	J, M, N, Q, R, W, Z, 6 to Canal St.; S to Grand St.; J, M to Bowery
PAYMENT	Cash only
POPULAR FOOD	Your buck gets a bang with the *pho* (rice noodle beef soup); choice of extra large bowl or regular bowl—regular should satisfy most appetites; it's always delicious, but read the menu descriptions carefully if any of the following terms make you uneasy: brisket, tendon, *omosa* (we don't know what this is), navel—but you're bound to find something that won't offend your sensibilities
UNIQUE FOOD	The *bún* (rice vermicelli) dishes are awfully good
DRINKS	Beer, tea, soda
SEATING	Thirty-five at tables
AMBIENCE	Straddles conventional take-out and relaxed sit-down motifs; Vietnamese beer ads, depicting the country's stunning geography and its pretty (traditionally dressed) models, line the walls—nothing fancy, but comfortable, and the largely Vietnamese clientele (not to mention the brisket, tendon, *omasa,* and navel) suggests that you're dealing with the real thing here

—Joe Cleemann

Saint's Alp Tea House

(see p. 10)

Tea House

51 Mott St., Manhattan 10013

Phone (212) 766-9889

"Almost every person has something secret he likes to eat."
—M.F.K. Fisher

One-Handed Jobs On-the-Go!

When you need one hand free, grab one of these: pickles, knishes, fist-sized sandwiches, fried rice balls, Chinese tamales, or sweet and savory buns.

Pickles!
Guss's Pickles—A Landmark Since 1920

Head on over to the Lower East Side Tenement Museum on Sunday afternoon for one of Guss's glorious kosher gherkins, and while you're at it, learn all about the history of pickles and the Lower East Side pickle business. Did you know that America consumes over five million pounds of pickles a year? That pickles are mentioned at least twice in the Bible (11:5 and Isaiah 1:8)? That 17th century Dutch dealers sold pickled Brooklyn cucumbers at markets on Fulton, Washington, and Canal Streets in Manhattan?

Guss's pickles are available on Sundays after 11:30 AM at the Lower East Side Tenement Museum. *Crossing Delancey/Chinatown: 90 Orchard St., Manhattan, 10002, (212) 431-0233. Sun–Thurs: noon–6 PM. Fri: 10 AM–3 PM. Cash only. www.tenement.org*

Knishes!
Yonah Schimmel Knishery—A Landmark Since 1910

One look, one sniff, one nosh of a world famous handmade baked (not fried), round-shaped, and extremely filling Yonah knish, and you'll know why this great grandmama of knisheries has been around since 1910. Over a dozen varieties of potato or cheese knishes available. Eat the red cabbage (vinegary) as you go, and brown bag one spinach (with scallions) and one sweet potato—directions on the menu for heating them up at home. Follow with a cup of yogurt, which is made from a ninety-year-old strain and rumored to have a calming effect on the stomach. *East Village: 137 E. Houston St., Manhattan, 10002, (212) 477-2858. Daily: 9 AM–7 PM. Visa MC Amex Discover.*

Fist-sized Sandwiches!
Soup & Smoothie Heaven

Slide over Whitecastle! The fist-sized sandwiches at S & S Heaven are made with sesame seed buns and come in a variety of choices such as tuna, turkey, and ham, dressed with tomato and lettuce, and wrapped in cellophane—for 99¢ a pop, why not have three! See review p. 90. *Midtown East: 316 Fifth Ave., Manhattan, 10001, (212) 279-5444. Mon–Fri: 8:30 AM–7 PM. Sat: 10 AM–5 PM. Cash only.*

Fried Rice Balls!
Rosario's Pizza

Established in 1963, Rosario's is known for an incredible slice, but eating a slice on the go is not as easy as some New Yorkers make it look. So pass on the slice and grab a fried rice ball or two—your outfit will thank you for it. *East Village: 173 Orchard St., Manhattan, 10002, (212) 777-9813. Mon–Fri: 10 AM–3 PM. Sat/Sun: 10 AM–5 PM.*

Chinese Tamales! (Zongzi)
May May Chinese Gourmet and Bakery

In Chinatown, you see them everywhere—*zongzi*—glutinous rice wrapped in green bamboo leaves in the shape of a triangle or—you guessed it, a rectangular Mexican tamale, and bundled with string. Generally, a layer of pork and vegetables is imbedded in the glutinous rice (glutinous rice is considered a luxury in China and is eaten on special occasions; it's grown and harvested under the same conditions as regular long or short grain rice, but contains more sugar and fat). At **May May,** in addition to the pork and veg variety, you can find meatless *zongzi* filled with mung bean, mushroom, and marinated *seitan* or wheat gluten. *Crossing Delancey/Chinatown: 35 Pell St., Manhattan, 10013, (212) 267-0733. Daily: 8 AM–7 PM. Cash only.*

No muffins. Just Buns! Buns! And More Buns!

They look plain, even boring, and maybe that's why they don't enjoy top billing in most Chinese bakeries. But don't be deceived by appearances—mouth-watering secrets lie in wait within these globular, slightly shiny hunks of dough. Joining ubiquitous entries like red bean paste and roast pork, dozens of new and inventive flavors (and combinations of flavors) are filling Chinatown's buns: ham and cheese, ham and egg, beef curry, tuna, dried pork, dried pork and egg, ham and corn—even hot dogs! And they're cheap (considerably less than a dollar!). A few of the many, many places where you can get buns:

Dragon Land Bakery

Crossing Delancey/Chinatown: 125 Walker St., Manhattan, 10013, (212) 219-2012. Daily: 7:30 AM–8 PM. Cash only.

Fong Da Bakery, Inc.

Crossing Delancey/Chinatown: 83 Essex St., Manhattan, 10013, (212) 353-0166. Mon–Sat: 6 AM–8 PM. Sun: 7 AM–7 PM. Cash only.

K and D Bakery

Crossing Delancey/Chinatown: 143 A Mott St., Manhattan, 10013, (212) 226-8988. Daily: 7 AM–8:30 PM. Cash only.

King Wah Bakery
*Crossing Delancey/Chinatown: 25 E. Broadway,
Manhattan, 10013, (212) 513-7107. Daily: 6:30 AM–
8 PM. Cash only.*

Maria's Bakery
*Crossing Delancey/Chinatown: 42 Mott St.,
Manhattan, 10013, (212)732-3888. Daily: 7:30
AM–7:30 PM. Cash only.*

So grab something and go. Next time you're
running late for a show, let your stomach purr
with satisfaction and leave the growling to the cats
onstage.

—Marie Estrada

Sweet-n-Tart Restaurant

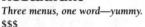

Three menus, one word—yummy.
$$$
20 Mott St., Manhattan 10013
(at Mosco St.)
Phone (212) 964-0380 • Fax (212) 571-7697

CATEGORY	Chinese
HOURS	Daily: 9 AM–midnight
SUBWAY	4, 5, 6, J, M, Z to Brooklyn Bridge/ City Hall
PAYMENT	Cash only
POPULAR FOOD	*Har gaw* (steamed shrimp dumpling); fried turnip cake; Chinese vegetable in oyster sauce; *congee;* salt-baked scallops and cuttlefish—good for two
UNIQUE FOOD	The house specials are *tong shui*— medicinal soups that don't taste medicinal at all; hot black sesame paste soup has all the sweet, sticky lusciousness of peanut butter; nut-filled glutinous dumplings are similarly decadent for dessert, but order them at the beginning of the meal, (they take 15 minutes to prepare); various rice dishes—studded with frog, quail, eel, or other tasty morsels—are flavorfully steamed in wooden casseroles just right for two; once in a while, the kitchen brings out surprise trays; be sure to hoard the sweet rolls filled with mango cream, or you may never see them again
DRINKS	Tapioca pearl drinks, fresh juices and shakes, assorted teas, soda
SEATING	Over 200
AMBIENCE	Chinese teenagers come here all hours to flirt over bubble drinks, as they still do a few blocks away at the first and much smaller Chinatown branch, Sweet-n-Tart Café; even so, both levels of this semi-new restaurant fill up quickly at weekend

lunch with both locals and savvy foodies looking for dim sum as good as any you would get in Hong Kong

EXTRAS/NOTES Despite the risqué names (First Love, With Your Kiss), ultra-fresh juices are a serious business here. The staff will gladly steer you through the intricacies of three exhaustive menus—one for dim sum, another for regular entrees, and another for drinks and *tong shui*. And that's not counting the specials listed on the walls. Not to worry—nearly everything's yummy anyway. Probably one of the first places in Manhattan to serve bubble drinks.

OTHER ONES • Crossing Delancey: 76 Mott St., Manhattan, 10013, (212) 334-8088
• Ride the 7: 136-11 38th Ave., Queens, 11354, (718) 661-3380

—Melissa Contreras

Ten Ren
(see p. 11)
Tea House
75 Mott St., Manhattan 10013
Phone (212) 349-2286

Vegecyber
(see p. 101)
Chinese Vegetarian/Vegan
210 Center St., Manhattan 10013
Phone (212) 625-3980

Vegetarian Dim Sum House
(see p. 101)
Chinese Vegetarian/Vegan
24 Pell St., Manhattan 10013
Phone (212) 577-7176

Vegetarian Paradise 3 (VP3)
(see p. 101)
Chinese/Vegan
33 Mott St., Manhattan 10013
Phone (212) 406-6988

Wo-Hop Restaurant
In the basement; cheap Chinese.
Since 1938
$$
17 Mott St., Manhattan 10013
(at Mosco St., just south of Bayard St.)
Phone (212) 962-8617

CATEGORY Chinese
HOURS 24/7

SUBWAY	4, 5, 6, J, M, Z to Brooklyn Bridge/City Hall
PAYMENT	Cash only
POPULAR FOOD	Famous for wonton soup, *chow fun,* and all kinds of noodle dishes—but I go for the world class cold sesame noodles
UNIQUE FOOD	All your favorite and familiar dishes are here, but some of the lesser known such as noodles with pickled cabbage and spicy meat sauce or the fried squid with salt and pepper are worth a try
SEATING	Forty at tables
AMBIENCE	This place is just right after a long night drinking or policing, as the 4 AM crowd is equal parts cops and tipsy civilians—expect no frills décor and attentive service
EXTRAS/NOTES	Buy a Wo-Hop dragon T-shirt on the way out (white for hipster, black for mod or hesher or sound guy) and your wardrobe is complete.

—Steve Powers

DOWNTOWN FANCY

Amin
(see p. 30)
Indian
110 Reade St., Manhattan 10013
Phone (212) 285-2466

Baluchi's Indian Food
(see p. 176)
Northern Indian
193 Spring St., Manhattan 10012
Phone (212) 226-2828

Brisas del Caribe
A little delicioso Santo Domingo among SoHo chichi.
$
489 Broadway, Manhattan 10012
(at Broome St.)

CATEGORY	Caribbean
HOURS	Daily: 7 AM–6 PM
SUBWAY	N, R to Prince St.
PAYMENT	Cash only
POPULAR FOOD	Delicious helpings of roast pork and plantains ordered from the counter
UNIQUE FOOD	American hamburgers and french fries round out the quick-and-greasy fare
DRINKS	Soda, juice
SEATING	About 15, some at the counter.

AMBIENCE	A lunchtime dive usually skipped by the Armani crowd, this is a place where some Spanish might help and pointing works fine
EXTRAS/NOTES	Closes earlier than most stores, so grab a cheap meal here first and blow the money you saved on shoes.

—Esti Iturralde

Buffa's Deli and Coffee Shop

A perfect diner and true relic of a forgotten era.
Since 1928
$$

54 Prince St., Manhattan 10012
(between Lafayette and Mulberry Sts.)
Phone (212) 226-0211

CATEGORY	Diner
HOURS	Mon–Fri: 6 AM–3:45 PM
SUBWAY	F, V, S, 6 to Broadway/Lafayette; N, R to Prince St.
PAYMENT	Cash only
POPULAR FOOD	Get the tuna on pumpernickel and a pickle; or, try any one of their Hero sandwiches—Superman/Lex Luther (grilled Virginia ham and cheese), Silence of the Lambs (corned beef and pastrami), Headless Body in a Topless Bar (grilled chicken breast), or Night on Earth (Swiss cheese bacon burger)
UNIQUE FOOD	Try the Pink Flamingo sandwich (egg salad, bacon, and anchovies)
DRINKS	Espresso machine turns out lattes and mochas, tea, beer, soda, milkshakes, fresh-squeezed juices, and Fresh Samantha Juices
SEATING	About 50 at tables and counter
AMBIENCE	White Formica tables, brown leather stools against a long counter—charmingly grumpy and very New York to some, weathered and ornery to others—see for yourself
EXTRAS/NOTES	Breakfast and lunch specials, chili, and fresh homemade soups. And pay for the newspaper you snagged on the way in, because I never do.

—Steve Powers

Burritoville

(see p. 31)
Mexican
144 Chambers St., Manhattan 10007
Phone (212) 964-5048

French Fries

Americans eat an average of four servings of french fries per week. So, you'd think we would have come up with something better than the abysmal specimens of starch doused in oil that pass for your average fry these days. Sure, we can manipulate the potato into any shape imaginable—from krinkle cut to curlycue—but few fries amount to more than a stick of soggy blandness barely able to deliver ketchup, salt, and grease to our waiting mouths. Enter the Belgians who have raised the frying of the potato to an art form. Only Americans mistakenly attribute fries to our friends in France. The "french" in "french-fried potatoes" comes from the culinary verb "to french," meaning to cut into thin strips.

Understanding that potatoes are difficult to cook through without scorching the outside, the Belgians have perfected the double cooking method: The first oil bath cooks the inside while keeping it moist. And a second dunking, at a higher temperature, perfectly crisps, goldens, and even slightly puffs, the outside. Debates rage about the best type of potato to use, the ideal length between baths, the most flavorful oil (in Europe, horse tallow seems to be a favorite), even the type and timing of the salt sprinkle. More obsessive minds can tackle those questions—my bottom line is taste. Luckily in New York, there are plenty of great places to get your fry fix.

Pommes Frites

If the brilliant fries didn't keep me coming back, the Dickensian atmosphere certainly would. All golden crsipiness on the outside, and perfectly moist on the inside, these are fries to go out of your way for. The basic toppings (ketchup, malt vinegar, mayo, and mustard) are free, but only the confirmed purist should pass on the other 30 dipping sauces, like sweet mango chutney mayo, Thai peanut sauce, roasted garlic mayo, or the special (layers of Belgian mayo, diced onion, and ketchup). Don't be shy—ask for a free sample. Then, squeeze onto a bench and munch away. *East Village: 123 Second Ave., Manhattan, 10003, (212) 674-1234. Sun–Thurs: 11:30 AM–midnight, Fri/Sat: 11:30 AM–1 AM.*

B. Frites

From the specially grown potatoes to the imported Belgian mayo and high-tech, top-of-the-line Rubbens fryer, B. Frites pays attention to detail—and it pays off. Although this well-ordered, cheerful shop has only a few awkward places to stand, they have invented a quaint paper cone with a built-in dipping well. Most of their specialty sauces like mango tango, *americaine,* and pesto perfecto, are made with that addictive Belgian mayo. You won't be disappointed if you get it plain.

If for some reason the *frites* aren't enough, B.Frites offers a wide selection of fruit smoothies, soups and salads to round out your meal. *Midtown West: 1657 Broadway, Manhattan, 10019, (212) 767-0858. Mon–Thurs: 11 AM–11:30 PM, Fri/Sat: 11 AM– midnight, Sun: noon–10 PM. www.Bfrites.com.*

Le Frite Kot

Compared to the sleek, denuded *frites* sold at most shops, the potatoes here are wonderfully rustic with little flakes of skin still clinging to them. Once you have your generous portion of *frites* and some of the exceptional aioli-garlic dipping sauce, climb up the steep staircase and hunker down at one the wooden tables or benches. With classic rock on the radio, beer on tap, and a few NYU students trying to look studious, it's a comfortable cross between your parents' basement and a neighborhood bar—only without the bathroom. The same owners run adjoining Vol de Nuit (see review p. 53). *Around Washington Park: 148 W. Fourth St., Manhattan, 10012, (212) 979-2616. Daily: noon–midnight.*

F&B

Beignets, belgian waffles, and beer are fast foods I can get into. This chic and friendly European import also serves nicely salted, if sometimes limp, *pommes frites*. If their lively selection of dips and flavors (Thai chili, curry sundried tomato, and truffle oil among others) don't sufficiently mix it up for you, try their sweet potato *frites* or a mixed bag of onion, sweet potato and *pommes frites* (see review p. 36). *From Chelsea to West Houston: 269 W. 23rd St., Manhattan, 10011, (646) 486-4441. Mon–Fri: 11 AM–11 PM, Sat: 9 AM–midnight, Sun: 9 AM–11 PM.*

And for when you just can't help yourself, **American Fast Food…**

Far and away, **McDonald's** seems to boast the fast food fry of choice. These are generally, hot, crispy, and have that unique flavor only a bit of lingering beef fat can provide. While **Ranch One** does not quite have "the best fries on the planet" in my book, these thicker cut fries with slivers of skin have a genuine homemade feel. And then there's **Nathan's**. Nothing quite brings me back to the food courts of my youth than Nathan's krinkle cut fries drowning in melted cheese. A touch greasy, but only in the best comfort food sort of way.

Now, if you're in the mood for a slab of meat and a glass of merlot with your *frites*, the city has sprouted a bistro on nearly every corner. Most pride themselves on their *frites* but **Pastis, Les Halles** (run by Anthony Bourdain of *Kitchen Confidential* fame) and **Petite Abeille** are particularly splurge-worthy. **Pastis:** *From Chelsea to West Houston: 9 Ninth Ave., Manhattan, 10014,*

*(212) 929-4844. Sun–Thurs: 9 AM–2 AM,
Fri/Sat: 9 AM–2:30 AM.* **Les Halles:** *Midtown East:
411 Park Ave. South., Manhattan, 10016,
(212) 679-4111. Daily: noon–midnight.* **Petite
Abeille:** *From Chelsea to West Houston: 400 W. 14ᵗʰ
St., Manhattan, 10014, (212) 727-1505. Daily:
7 AM–midnight; and 134 W. Broadway, Manhattan,
10014, (212) 791-1360. Daily: 7 AM–10 PM.*

—Julia Pastore

Café le Gamin

(see p. 44)
Brunch/French Café
50 MacDougal St., Manhattan 10012
Phone (212) 254-4678

Cendrillon

(see p. 120)
Filipino
45 Mercer St., Manhattan 10013
Phone (212) 343-9012

Crêpe Café

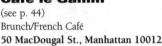

Oh yeah, I'll eat a crêpe on the street.
$
Corner of Prince St. and Broadway
(in front of the Swatch Watch store)

CATEGORY	Crêpe Cart
HOURS	Sat/Sun: 11 AM–6 PM
SUBWAY	N, R to Prince St.
PAYMENT	Cash only
POPULAR FOOD	Sweet and savory crêpes of all kinds—try the super-filling *Italienne* made with mozzarella, marinara, and ricotta cheese; or the *champignon* made with fresh mushroom; for the ultra sweet lover, *dulce de leche* made with caramel milk and sugar
UNIQUE FOOD	Argentinian *empanadas* stuffed with meat and fresh herbs
DRINKS	Juice, soda, bottled water
SEATING	Two can eat at the cart while standing, otherwise walk with it
AMBIENCE	In the heart of one of the busiest corners of SoHo, a welcome addition to the hot dog, pretzel, and roasted nut street family
OTHER ONES	• Midtown West: W. 53ʳᵈ St. (between Fifth and Sixth Aves.), Manhattan. Mon–Fri: 11 AM–6 PM (this is the Crêpe Café Cart's weekday location).

—Marie Estrada

Ear Inn

Everyone should know about the Ear Inn...your mom, pop, grandmother, great grandfather, great-great grandfather...
Since 1817
$$

326 Spring St., Manhattan 10013
(between Washington St. and Greenwich Ave.)
Phone (212) 226-9060

CATEGORY	American Pub
HOURS	Daily: noon–4 AM
SUBWAY	C, E to Canal St.
PAYMENT	VISA MasterCard American
POPULAR FOOD	Order a great burger, fresh fish, or chicken, with the perfectly poured pint of Guinness
DRINKS	Full bar (Guinness, Harp, and Bass on tap), coffee, tea
SEATING	About 75 at tables and booths
AMBIENCE	Mellow, some say, haunted space with a friendly staff and mixed clientele; on Monday you may see Dan Hovey and Fausto play their guitars and sing songs about love and electric guitars
EXTRAS/NOTES	Located in the 200 year old James Brown House, the Ear Inn has been one of THE hangouts for rock and jazz musicians over the past 50 years. The list of famous regulars and visitors is impressive: Salvador Dalí, John Lennon, Tom Waits, Philip Glass, John Cage, and Pete Seeger. An apartment above Ear Inn supposedly served as a home away from home for those customers, who may have enjoyed their night out a bit too much. Before there were celebs, the Ear Inn's clientele was smugglers, prostitutes, and sailors. It's believed that Ear Inn is haunted by a seaman named Mickey who was killed by a car out front. Impress your friends with this factoid: The Ear Inn became "Ear" after part of the neon "B" in the "Bar" sign burned out. Occasional poetry or music performances in the evenings.

—Steve Powers

Hampton Chutney Co.

Out-of-this-world Indian flavors, by way of Long Island.
$$$

68 Prince St., Manhattan 10012
(at Broadway)
Phone (212) 226-9996 • Fax (212) 226-7278
www.hamptonchutney.com

CATEGORY	Indian Sandwich Shop
HOURS	Daily: 11 AM–8 PM

SUBWAY	N, R to Houston St.
PAYMENT	
POPULAR FOOD	Specialties are *dosas* and *uttapas,* enormous savory sandwich crepes made from an out-of-this-world sourdough rice pancake (*dosas* are thin; *uttapas* are thicker), stuffed with all manner of delicious Indian and American goodies such as *kalamata* olives, Indian-spiced potato, asparagus, goat cheese, grilled portabello, and curry chutney chicken, and served with your choice of six chutneys in flavors like pumpkin, curry, cilantro, and peanut
DRINKS	Try their very special cardamom coffee, a spiced hot milk and coffee concoction that is at once exotic and comforting; BYO for alcohol
SEATING	Three tables and seats at the counter make room for about 19
AMBIENCE	Very informal; mostly caters to the neighborhood
EXTRAS/NOTES	Any of the *dosas* or *uttapas* is huge enough to share with a friend. I highly recommend the curry chutney chicken, spinach, and balsamic roasted onion *dosa*. As the name indicates, they started as an actual chutney company in Amangansett, Long Island, and opened their first restaurant there. If you plan to be in the neighborhood, call ahead for details: (631) 267-3131.

—Joanna Jacobs

Jerry's Restaurant

(see p. 45)
Brunch
101 Prince St., Manhattan 10012
Phone (212) 966-9464

Karahi Indian Cuisine

Chicken tikka masala so good you'll order it three times a week for a year.
$$$
508 Broome St., Manhattan 10013
(between W. Broadway and Thompson St.)
Phone (212) 965-1515 • Fax (212) 219-9766
www.karahi.com

CATEGORY	Northern Indian
HOURS	Mon–Sun: noon–3 PM (all-you-can-eat buffet lunch) Sun–Thurs: 5 PM–10:15 PM Fri/Sat: 5 PM –10:45 PM
SUBWAY	A, C, E to Canal St.
PAYMENT	
POPULAR FOOD	Curry, lamb *vindaloo, moiley,* and tandoori chicken; 11-course buffet lunch (entrees change daily)

UNIQUE FOOD	*Murg tikka masala; kulfi* (specialty from India: thickened milk, cooked for several hours, then frozen, which has nutty taste of almonds and pistachios)
DRINKS	Full bar, lassi (sweet, salty, mango), coffee, tea, juices (orange, mango, cranberry), soda
SEATING	Tables for 65
AMBIENCE	As different from Sixth St. Christmas lights and tinsel as you can get—tastefully decorated, warm woods inflected with bright colors—and authentic Indian ornamentation
EXTRAS/NOTES	Karahi earns high marks for its perfect presentation of any and all Indian delicacies. A newcomer with the determination to prove itself in a field crowded with old-timers resting on their laurels.

—Steve Powers

Lucky's Juice Joint

(see p. 99)
Vegetarian/Vegan
75 W. Houston St., Manhattan 10012
Phone (212) 388-0300

Lupe's East L.A. Kitchen

It's tough to find good Mexican food in New York, but Lupe's comes through strong.
$$
110 Sixth Ave., Manhattan 10013
(corner of Watts St.)
Phone (212) 966-1326

CATEGORY	Mexican Diner
HOURS	Sun–Tue: 11:30 AM–11 PM Wed–Sat: 11:30 AM–midnight
SUBWAY	A, C, E, to Canal St.
PAYMENT	Cash only
POPULAR FOOD	Those in the know go for the chili *relleno* (mild green chili stuffed with cheese and served with two sauces) or the *pollo norteño* (pieces of marinated chicken breast grilled with onions, tomatoes, and grilled chilis); all entrees served with rice, beans, and salad
UNIQUE FOOD	Staple Mexican fare prepared uniquely; enchiladas *suizas* (chicken, cheese, sour cream in a green chili sauce); enchiladas *mole* (chicken in a dark chili sauce of 20 ingredients—including chocolate)
DRINKS	Domestic and Mexican beer, tequila, *café con leche,* Mexican hot chocolate, Mexican soda, *agua frescas*
SEATING	About 50 at tables

AMBIENCE	All the elements of East LA are subtley displayed in this clean diner with wonderful Mexican music lingering with the chatter of customers
EXTRAS/NOTES	Can't-believe-it, super-cheap weekend brunch menu (Sat/Sun: 11:30 AM–4 PM). Plenty of fat burritos, quesadillas, tamales, and tacos for vegetarians and non-vegetarians as well. This is legit East LA Mexican food—down to the freshly made *horchata*.

—*Steve Powers*

M & O Grocery & Imported & Domestic Products

This is where to get a great sandwich on Portuguese bread.

$$

124 Thompson St., Manhattan 10012
(corner of Prince St.)

Phone (212) 477-8222

CATEGORY	Deli
HOURS	Daily: 7:30 AM–1:30 AM
SUBWAY	C, E to Prince St.
PAYMENT	Cash only
POPULAR FOOD	Go on Tuesday or Friday and get the perfectly prepared turkey sandwich; otherwise, sandwiches of all kinds made with freshly baked meats are available every day of the week (salami, roast beef, pork loin, meatloaf, pastrami, or spiced ham); meatballs
UNIQUE FOOD	BLT with M & O's special tangy fresh herb dressing; M & O potato and spinach knishes
DRINKS	Sodas, vitamin waters, juices, coffee, tea
SEATING	Carry out only—eat the sandwich while window shopping at the never-ending row upon row of SoHo boutiques
AMBIENCE	Larger than an average deli, smaller than a big grocery—expect lunch lines ten deep, but the staff is fast and friendly

—*Steve Powers*

Palacinka

You do and you don't want to tell everybody about this crêperia.

$$$

28 Grand St., Manhattan 10013
(between Thompson St. and Sixth Ave.)

Phone (212) 625-0362

CATEGORY	Café and Bar
HOURS	Sun–Wed: 10:30 AM–11 PM
	Thurs–Sat: 10:30 AM–midnight
SUBWAY	A, C, E to Canal St.

PAYMENT	Cash only
POPULAR FOOD	For breakfast, popular sandwiches are the ham with *gruyére* and Dijon mustard and the Colombian steak sandwich with roasted shallots and melted Roquefort cheese; for lunch, it's crêpes all the way; combine savory and sweet: sautéed spinach, feta, and lemon crêpe, grilled portabello mushroom with roasted potato, mozzarella, and pesto, and the Nutella or fresh lemon or lime crepe; *crème de marron* (chestnut paste with *crème fraîche*) is particularly delicious and decadent
UNIQUE FOOD	Be a chef and create your own very special savory crepe from a choice of ham, egg, potato, *gruyére,* tomato, mushrooms, and peppers
DRINKS	Mimosa with fresh squeezed juice, Kir Royal, Bellini, Sake Bloody Mary, espresso, hot chocolate, fresh-squeezed lemonade, Orangina, San Pellegrino, and Martinelli's sparkling apple cider
SEATING	Seats 32 at tables and a leather bench with round bar tables
AMBIENCE	Intimate space blending unpolished chrome with dark wood—warm, welcoming, and many members of the staff are fluent in French
EXTRAS/NOTES	During peak eating hours, expect a slightly longer wait for the on the spot, freshly made crêpes.

—*Marie Estrada*

Uptown Juice Bar

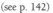

(see p. 142)
Vegetarian/Juice Bar
116 Chambers St., Manhattan 10007
Phone (212) 964-4316

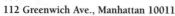
FROM CHELSEA TO WEST HOUSTON

A Salt and Battery

"In Cod We Trust."
$$$
112 Greenwich Ave., Manhattan 10011
(at Jane St.)
Phone (212) 691-2713
www.asaltandbattery.com

CATEGORY	Fish and Chip Shop
HOURS	Daily: noon–10 PM
SUBWAY	A, C, E, 1, 2, 3 to 14th St.
PAYMENT	
POPULAR FOOD	Fish (cod, haddock, tilapia, or whiting) and chips—hold the chips and pay less

UNIQUE FOOD	Chip butty (French fries in a buttered roll), mushy peas, deep-fried Mars bar
DRINKS	British and American beer, sodas
SEATING	Seats seven at the counter
AMBIENCE	A mix of British expatriates craving a taste of home and Village locals looking for a quick and satisfying meal
EXTRAS/NOTES	The restaurant's motto is "In Cod We Trust," and the tender, flaky fish and chips—fried by an authentic ex-British Navy cook (tattoos add authenticity)—are the reason to be here. It's even more British than Britain, where they've abandoned the practice of wrapping their fish and chips in newspaper. Not so here: you can read bits of the *Observer* after your meal, if you don't mind a little grease and malt vinegar blotting the headlines. Owned by Tea and Sympathy, the English restaurant next door.

—Phil Curry

Amin

Shamefully overlooked (and wonderfully inexpensive) neighborhood Indian haunt.

$$$

155 Eighth Ave., Manhattan 10013
(between W. 17th and W. 18th Sts.)
Phone (212) 929-7020

CATEGORY	Indian
HOURS	Daily: noon–10:30 PM
SUBWAY	A, C, E to 14th St.
PAYMENT	VISA
POPULAR FOOD	All the standards done well, especially creamy curry sauces; *kurma* (light cream, almond, and tomato sauce) with lamb, beef, chicken, *keema* (Indian sausage), or vegetables; delicious *malai* (slightly spicy coconut sauce) with same choice of meats or vegetables; for vegetarians, *bindi bhajee* (okra with tomatoes and onions) is melt-in-your-mouth wonderful; even if it's not on the menu, you can ask for the terrific *mottor ponir* (fried mild cheese in a pea sauce); generous portions of rice, *dal,* and condiments included for entrée price
UNIQUE FOOD	*Pakhee* (marinated quail stuffed with meat and almonds, as an appetizer or as a main course)
DRINKS	Domestic and imported beers including a few Indian varieties, house red and white wines, mango or plain sweet *lassi,* soda, tea, and coffee
SEATING	Table seating for about 40
AMBIENCE	Low-key and very low lighting; however, the wallpaper is a fabulous patterned red velvet; friendly wait staff occasionally throws in complementary rice pudding for

	dessert
OTHER ONES	• Downtown Fancy: 110 Reade St., Manhattan, 10013, (212) 285-2466
	• Downtown Brooklyn West: 140 Montague St., Brooklyn, 11201, (718) 855-4791

—Joanna Jacobs

Bright Food Shop

(see p. 44)
Mexican/American Diner
218 Eighth St., Manhattan 10009
Phone (212) 243-4433

Burritoville

Enlightened caudillo *of Manhattan's burrito scene tailors to all tastes, preferences, and diets.*

$$

264 W. 23ʳᵈ St., Manhattan 10011
(between Seventh and Eighth Aves.)
Phone (212) 367-9844
www.burritoville.com

CATEGORY	Mexican
HOURS	Sun–Thurs: 11 AM–midnight Fri/Sat: 11 AM–1 AM
SUBWAY	C, E to 23ʳᵈ St.
PAYMENT	VISA MasterCard AMERICAN DISCOVER
POPULAR FOOD	Innovative burritos for consumers of white, dark, and no meat; the Bob Marley's Last Burrito (jerk chicken spiced with chilies, cloves, and cinnamon); chili *con carne* (spicy ground beef, chili, and two beans), the Lost in Austin (steamed spinach and mushrooms); the 13 inch tortilla wrappers sometimes overwhelm the filling, so tear away excess starch
UNIQUE FOOD	Wraps, salads, soups, stews, and more vegetarian options than you'd expect (Burritoville shares ownership with Veg City Diner, see p. 41); better yet are the tortilla chips which, with a variety of salsas, are free while you wait
DRINKS	"Bottomless" fountain sodas, Burritoville's own line of bottled drinks: lemonade, fruit juice, tea, *horchata;* beer
SEATING	Seats about 75
AMBIENCE	Clean; old maps, old Mexican movie posters, and old photos of rail-riding revolutionaries; Burritoville's secret is out—so even this deep-in-the-heart-of-Chelsea location attracts those who aren't
EXTRAS/NOTES	The first Burritoville opened on the Upper East Side ten years ago. Since then, this hamlet has expanded into a Burritoempire, with 13 locations across Manhattan and outposts as far flung as

New Jersey and Connecticut. Plays
Charley the Gent to lower-rent Fresco
Tortilla's Terry Malloy, except without
the crookedness.

OTHER ONES
- Financial District: 36 Water St.,
  Manhattan, 10004, (212) 757-1100
- Financial District: 20 John St.,
  Manhattan, 10038, (212) 766-2020
- Downtown Fancy: 144 Chambers St.,
  Manhattan, 10007, (212) 964-5048
- East Village: 141 Second Ave.,
  Manhattan, 10003, (212) 260-3300
- Midtown West: 352 W. 39th St.,
  Manhattan, 10018, (212) 563-9088
- Midtown West: 652 Ninth Ave.,
  Manhattan, 10036, (212) 333-5352
- Midtown East: 866 Third Ave.,
  Manhattan, 10022, (212) 980-4111
- Upper West Side: 166 W. 72nd St.,
  Manhattan, 10023, (212) 580-7700
- Upper West Side: 451 Amsterdam Ave.,
  Manhattan, 10024, (212) 787-8181
- Upper East Side: 1606 Third Ave.,
  Manhattan, 10128, (212) 410-2255
- Upper East Side: 1489 First Ave.,
  Manhattan, 10021, (212) 472-8800

—Joe Cleemann

Café le Gamin

(see p. 44)
French Café/Crêpes
183 Ninth Ave., Manhattan 10003
Phone (212) 486-3000

Cafeteria

(see p. 44)
Comfort Food
119 Seventh Ave., Manhattan 10014
Phone (212) 414-1717

Chez Brigitte

*Continental cuisine on
a counter.*
Since 1958
$$$
77 Greenwich Ave., Manhattan 10014
(at Seventh Ave.)
Phone (212) 929-6736

CATEGORY	French
HOURS	Daily: noon–10 PM
SUBWAY	1, 2, 3 to 14th St.
PAYMENT	Cash only
POPULAR FOOD	Simple, homey food with a French country twist: daily specials inc. beef, veal, chicken, and fish standbys; *côtes de poulet*—chicken breast sautéed with

mushrooms in brown sauce—is especially
good and comes with a healthy selection
of side vegetables and starches (roast
potatoes, yellow rice, peas, and salad)

UNIQUE FOOD	You'll find *boeuf bourgignon* or *ragoût de veau* at other French restaurants in the city, but never so well prepared in so short a time and in such a charming setting
DRINKS	Iced and hot tea and coffee; juice, milk, soft drinks; no wine, but feel free to bring your own
SEATING	As the sign on the wall says, "Chez Brigitte will serve 250 people 11 at a time—two narrow rows of stools at counters
AMBIENCE	Just a slice of a room, really, but this welcoming lunch counter is perfect for when you can't make it home for your *mere's* cooking
EXTRAS/NOTES	According to the menu, Marseilles-born Brigitte Catapano opened Chez Brigitte in 1958. Since her retirement in the mid-1980s, the restaurant has been run by Rosa Santos, who had been an employee. Great prices. Slide into the counter, place your order, and one of the very pleasant chefs/waiters will cook right in front of you.

—*Joanna Jacobs*

Corner Bistro

*Vegetarians beware: the burgers
could convert the most committed
of you.*
Since the "Early 20th Century"
$$

331 W. Fourth St., Manhattan 10014
(at Jane St.)
Phone (212) 242-9502 • Fax (212) 242-9502

CATEGORY	Burger Joint
HOURS	Mon–Sat: 11:30 AM–4 AM
	Sun: noon–4 AM
SUBWAY	A, C, E, L to W. 14th; 1, 2 to Christopher St./Sheridan Sq.
PAYMENT	Cash only
POPULAR FOOD	Burgers, from the plain ham-variety to the impressive bacon/chili/cheese-class, and fries
DRINKS	Full bar
SEATING	Thirty-four at tables and more at the bar, always crowded
AMBIENCE	From neighborhood regulars to the midtown crowd, word has gotten out and lines start forming at 7 PM
EXTRAS/NOTES	Jukebox plays tunes, as long as you speak nicely to it.

—*Tanya Laplante*

Meet Me at Chelsea Market

Chelsea Market, the "largest wholesale and retail food concourse in Manhattan," has become a New York City institution. Housed on the ground floor of a former bakery for the National Biscuit Company (Nabisco, bing!), the market opened in April 1997. The market is a collection of mostly single-genre stores, all down one long, oddly-decorated corridor. It is considered a godsend, a great convenience, and a symbol of encroaching high rents and yuppie gentrification (sometimes all three at once). Some may decry "it's just a glorified food court," but oh, the glory!

Although buying a large, or even a moderate, quantity of goods from many of these individual stores will probably strain your wallet, this is a great place to pick up a grab-bag meal or a picnic lunch by skipping from one place to the next.

As you enter the market from Ninth Avenue, the first food store on your left is **Eleni's Cookies**, a bakery offering a pleasing variety of cookies and muffins both individually, in bulk, and in gift tins. Try the snickerdoodles and enjoy a free cup of coffee. Stop in just before the market closes and you can sometimes get deals on that day's cookies. *(212) 255-7990. Daily: 10 AM–6 PM.*

You can smell the **Fat Witch** brownies before you see them—the rich, fudgey brownies are fragrant and glorious, if pricey. The witches come in daily rotating flavors. I heartily recommend trying the Red Witch (with dried cherries), the Breakfast Witch (with a layer of walnuts, oatmeal and coffee), and the old standby, the original Fat Witch. Check out www.fatwitch.com for a whimsically illustrated "true" story about the origin of the brownies. *(888) 41-WITCH. Mon–Fri: 10 AM–7 PM, Sun: 10 AM–6 PM.*

Mosey on down the hall to **Ruthy's Bakery & Café**, a bagel shop/deli with a separate store next door devoted to sweets, especially cheesecakes and their amazing rugelach (flavors include apricot, chocolate raspberry, sugar-free, and the traditional cinnamon and raisin). *(888) 729-8800. Mon–Sat: 7 AM–7 PM, Sun: 10 AM–6 PM. www.ruthys.com.*

For Chelsea Market's true baked goods event, walk next door to **Amy's Breads**. The bread here is justly famous—all of the many varieties are invariably fresh and delicious. I particularly recommend the savory black olive loaf, the crusty and springy sourdough, the organic whole wheat with walnuts, and the wonderfully yeasty and gooey pecan sticky bun. But many Chelsea Marketeers enjoy Amy's Bread without ever setting foot inside, joining those stopping to stare at Amy's kitchen through its large plate glass window to witness the bread being kneaded, rolled, braided, and cut by the line of breadmakers. Truly one of the highlights of the market. *(212) 462-4338. Mon–Fri: 7:30 AM–7 PM, Sat: 8 AM–6 PM, Sun: 9 AM–4 PM. www.amysbread.com.*

Wash the baked goods down with some **Ronnybrook Farm Dairy** milk, which is always fresh and wholesome. Farmed and bottled by a family in New York's Dutchess County, the milk manages to be richer than its corporate competition while not being a whole lot more expensive, since much of the register price is a deposit that gets returned after the bottle does. This milk is pleasingly sweet and creamy—even the skim— and don't miss what could be the chocolate milk experience of your life. The containers are appealing thick-lipped, old-fashioned glass milk bottles. Don't miss their ice creams, ranging from traditional vanilla to creative flavors like ginger crème brûlée, or their cheese. *(212) 741-6455. Daily: 8:30 AM–7 PM. www.ronnybrook.com*

Passing one of the market's more interesting interior sculptures (a large, high fountain fashioned from what looks to be salvaged plumbing equipment), stop in at **The Lobster Place.** A fish market, this is not exactly a place to grab take-out for a picnic (although they have just opened an adjacent sushi take-out bar), but the fish here is wonderfully fresh and often an excellent bargain. Check out their daily specials. *(212) 255-5872. Daily: 9:30 AM–7 PM.*

Chelsea Thai Wholesale is one of the jewels in Chelsea Market's crown. One of the market's few sit-down restaurants, they still cultivate a take-out atmosphere with disposable plates and chop sticks. The meals are skillfully prepared and intensely flavorful, with fresh ingredients in both familiar and creative combinations. Some must-tries include the *pad woon sen* (glass noodle stir fried with chicken, pork, beef, shrimp or tofu and red bell pepper, scallion, bean sprouts and egg—under seven bucks and a delicious change of pace for *pad* Thai fans), and the very spicy *pad kee mow* (rice noodles with garlic, chili, basil, onion, red and green pepper, scallion, tomato, and your choice of meat or tofu). They also sell a small quantity of Thai groceries and gift baskets. *(212) 924-2999. Mon–Fri: 9 AM–7 PM, Sat: 11 AM–7 PM, Sun: 11 AM–6:30 PM.*

Buon Italia sells imported Italian groceries from the prosaic (dried beans, canned tomatoes, crackers) to the sublime (a full complement of cheeses, pastas, olives, and much more). They also have a café in the front corridor with coffees and light prepared foods, including lasagna, salads, and sweets. And don't stop there—another café, hidden in the back, offers more elaborate prepared foods in a case and two or three cozy tables with high-backed armchairs. One of the Market's truly hidden treasures. *(212) 633-9090. Daily: 8 AM–7 PM.*

Pass through a large arch that, during the holiday season, gets covered with so many tiny white lights that you can feel the heat they create, and you will have arrived at **Manhattan Fruit Exchange**, where the produce is both better and cheaper than any of the neighborhood supermarkets. The fruits and veggies are impeccably fresh. And though they stock with an emphasis on seasons and what's locally available, the variety and quality of produce is always impressive. Anyone who loves cooking will get a kick out of going just to see how many different varieties of, say, beans, or apples, or squashes, they stock.

There are a few stores further down the hall that are really worth a look, including **Bowery Kitchen Supply**, and **Imports from Marrakesh, Ltd.**

Rumor has it Chelsea Market will soon be open 24/7! See you there!

From Chelsea to West Houston: 75 Ninth Ave., Manhattan, 10011. Mon–Sat: 9 AM–7 PM, Sun: 9 AM– 6 PM. www.chelseamarket.com

—*Joanna Jacobs*

EJ's Luncheonette
(see p. 124)
Diner
432 Sixth Ave., Manhattan 10011
Phone (212) 473-5555

F&B
Glorified fast food joint: Euro-dogs—a wide selection of unique hot dog variations, and pommes frites.
$$
269 W. 23rd St., Manhattan 10011
(between Seventh and Eighth Aves.)
Phone (646) 486-4441
www.fandbrestaurant.com

CATEGORY	European Street Food
HOURS	Daily: 11 AM–11 PM
SUBWAY	C, E to 23rd St.
PAYMENT	
POPULAR FOOD	The Great Dane combination (an authentic Danish *pølser,* which comes with fried onion flakes and sweet mustard, and

pommes frites with lemonade or iced tea); *pommes frites,* onion *frites,* zucchini *frites,* or sweet potato *frites* with a diverse selection of toppings (garlic aioli, pesto, Thai chili, lemon pepper, etc.); Belgian waffles

UNIQUE FOOD Large selection of unique hot dogs and dressings, including the Farm Dog (smoked chicken and apple hot dog with corn relish), the *Gaucho* Dog (garlic sausage with *chimichurri* sauce), and the Sweet Dog (fried banana on a vanilla waffle bun with strawberry preserves, whipped cream, and chocolate sauce)—many of which can be ordered vegetarian

DRINKS Freshly made lemonade and iced tea, chilled chai tea, limited selection of imported beers, coffee, tea, soft drinks

SEATING Two counters span the length of the narrow location—about 20 seats

AMBIENCE Very pop, and clean—lots of brushed steel and baby blue paint; Euro-retro: the hotdog equivalent of Ikea

EXTRAS/NOTES While F&B hotdogs may seem a little pricier than most, they're not at all your normal hotdogs, and are well worth the scratch. F&B deserves kudos for taking what is traditionally a one-note food and completely reinventing it into various hip, exciting, and extremely delicious variations. The occasionally long lines and limited seating will attest to F&B's popularity (though the good thing about hotdogs is they don't take long to make or eat, so the wait is never too bad). F&B delivers between 33rd and 13th Sts., from Fifth to 11th Aves.

—*Brad Wood*

Famous Famiglia

(see p. 109)
Pizzeria
61 Chelsea Piers, Manhattan 10011
Phone (212) 803-5552

Food Bar

(see p. 45)
Brunch
149 Eighth Ave., Manhattan 10003
Phone (212) 243-2020

Hale and Hearty Soups

(see p. 125)
Soup Shop
75 Ninth St., Manhattan 10011
Phone (212) 255-2400

Moustache

(see p. 62)
Middle Eastern
90 Bedford St., Manhattan 10014
Phone (212) 229-2220

Murray's Bagels

(see p. 85)
Bagels
500 Sixth Ave., Manhattan 10011
Phone: (212) 462-2830
and
242 Eighth Ave., Manhattan 10011
Phone: (646) 638-1335

Nadine's Restaurant

(see p. 45)
American/Brunch
99 Bank St., Manhattan 10014
Phone (212) 924-3165

Paris Commune

(see p. 46)
Café/Brunch
411 Bleecker St., Manhattan 10014
Phone (212) 929-0509

Pastis

(see p. 23)
Bistro/*Frites*
9 Ninth Ave., Manhattan 10014
Phone (212) 929-4844

Petite Abeille

(see p. 23)
Bistro/*Frites*
400 W. 14ᵗʰ St., Manhattan 10014
Phone (212) 727-1505
and
134 W. Broadway, Manhattan 10014
Phone: (212) 791-1360

Ray's Pizza

(see p. 227)
Pizzeria
465 Sixth Ave., Manhattan 10011
Phone (212) 243-2253

REMEMBER THE NEEDIEST!

Rocking Horse Mexican Café

(see p. 46)
Mexican/Brunch
182 Eighth Ave., Manhattan 10003
Phone (212) 463-9511

Rue des Crêpes

*New York's crêpe constituency
finally gets a street name—and,
better yet, a great place to get crêpes.*
$$$
104 Eighth Ave., Manhattan 10011
(between W. 15th and W. 16th Sts.)
Phone (212) 242-9900 • Fax (212) 242-3687
www.ruedescrepes.com

CATEGORY	French Café/Crêpes
HOURS	Mon–Thur: 8 AM–11 PM
	Fri: 8 AM–1 AM
	Sat: 11 AM–1 AM (brunch 11 AM–4 PM)
	Sun: 11 AM–11 PM (brunch 11 AM–4 PM)
SUBWAY	4, 5, 6 to 86th St.
PAYMENT	VISA MasterCard AMERICAN EXPRESS DISCOVER
POPULAR FOOD	Wide variety of creative, meat, cheese, and veggie crêpes; it's hard to top the classic sliced banana and Nutella, but the cinnamon apple crêpe (apples baked with a crispy oatmeal raisin mixture) and the mixed berry (fresh strawberries, blueberries, and raspberries) are certainly contenders
UNIQUE FOOD	American departures from French form: the vegetarian incorporates vegetables, *tabouleh,* white beans, and a *miso* ginger sauce; the wild mushroom crêpe with shallots and tarragon is simple and elegant, while the turkey, fontina cheese, spinach, and mushroom crépe is hearty and satisfying
DRINKS	Full complement of teas and coffees, as well as sodas and seasonal hot and cold drinks, and wine
SEATING	About eight small tables
AMBIENCE	The interior decorator took the name literally, creating an inside outdoor Parisian café, complete with French street signs and cobblestones on the floor

—Joanna Jacobs

Sarabeth's Bakery

(see p. 46)
Brunch
75 Ninth Ave., Manhattan 10003
Phone (212) 989-2424

Spice

Innovative Thai food—grab the lunch specials.

$$$$

199 Eighth Ave., Manhattan 10011
(at 20th St.)

Phone (212) 989-1116

www.spicenyc.com

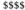

CATEGORY	Modern Thai
HOURS	Sun–Thurs: 11:30 AM–11:30 PM
	Fri/Sat: 11:30 AM–midnight
SUBWAY	A, C, E to 23rd St.
PAYMENT	VISA MasterCard AMERICAN DISCOVER
POPULAR FOOD	Fresh ginger and pineapple, a tangy mix of surprisingly zingy fresh ginger and citrus caramelized in soy; *massaman* curry, a peanut-infused sauce with potatoes; Drunk Man Noodles (a chili-and-basil-spiced noodle concoction with tender shrimp and squid that's miles away from the noodle dishes you find on most Thai menus)
UNIQUE FOOD	A few game and seafood specialties exceed $10 but are well worth it, including the Geyser Shrimp in a Clay Pot (with vegetables and noodles); Chelsea Crispy Duck with sweet and sour sauce gets high marks
DRINKS	Small selection of beers, wine, soft drinks, Thai coffee, and tea
SEATING	Seating for about 40
AMBIENCE	Stylish but not aggressively so; aerodynamic furniture, lovely, low-key décor
EXTRAS/NOTES	Extraordinary lunch specials. Seven days a week, from 11:30 AM–3:30 PM, 15 of Spice's beautifully prepared menu options are available not only at slashed prices ($6–$8) but with one of their creative and tantalizing appetizers free.
OTHER ONES	• East Village: 114 Second Ave., Manhattan, 10003, (212) 988-5348
	• Around Washington Square Park: 60 University Pl., Manhattan, 10003, (212) 982-3758

—Joanna Jacobs & Laramie Flick

Sucelt Coffee Shop

Spanish home-cooking orchestrated by a bevy of most-authentic Colombian matriarchs.

$$

200 W. 14th St., Manhattan 10011
(at Seventh Ave.)

Phone (212) 242-0593

CATEGORY	Latino Diner

HOURS	Mon–Fri: 7 AM–9:30 PM Sat: 7 AM–10 PM Sun: 8 AM–9 PM
SUBWAY	1, 2, 3, F, L, A, C, E to 14th St.
PAYMENT	Cash only
POPULAR FOOD	Take your pick of daily specials; savory stews, never too spicy, opulent soups, fluffy rice, firm beans, caramelized plantains
UNIQUE FOOD	Famous tamales—unwrap the leaf sheath and a whoosh of steam rises from this melt-in-your-mouth dumpling with vegetarian or (Venezuelan, Puerto Rican, Colombian, or Panamanian-style) meat fillings
DRINKS	*Café con leche* is prepared with aplomb, but don't sleep on their fruit shakes, or *batidas,* which may be super-sugary unless you request otherwise
SEATING	Counter seats 10 comfortably, 15 intimately
AMBIENCE	Established in 1977, Sucelt looks like a typical diner but the tastes are dependably extraordinary; not a lot of flummery, just good clean food; look around—all the patrons are Hispanic
EXTRAS/NOTES	I have never been disappointed with Sucelt, though after ordering I have on occasion found myself envious of another customer's plate.

—*Nemo Librizzi*

Tea & Sympathy

(see p. 47)
British Café/Brunch
108-110 Greenwich Ave., Manhattan 10006
Phone (212) 807-8329

Veg City Diner

"No Meat, No Chicken, No Fish—not now—not ever."
$$
55 W. 14th St., Manhattan 10011
(at Sixth Ave.)
Phone (212) 490-6266
www.burritoville.com

CATEGORY	American All-Vegetarian Diner
HOURS	Daily: 10 AM–4 AM
SUBWAY	F, V to 14th St.
PAYMENT	
POPULAR FOOD	Phony Island Corn Dog (even Holden Caulfield couldn't pick out this phony: the dog is topped with mountains of chili and cheese tastes just as good as the meat eater's option); shepherd's pie (lentils, veggies, and garlic mashed potatoes give this dish that just-like-mom-used-to-make

	goodness…minus the minced ham)
UNIQUE FOOD	Vegan meatloaf ("I can't believe it's not meat!") comes with all the fixin's including gravy (not of the Wavy variety); soy ice cream
DRINKS	Full bar, coffee, tea, milk shakes, ice cream sodas, smoothies, veggie juices
SEATING	Seats approximately 85
AMBIENCE	Diner-esque with a modern twist; different personalities convene to chat about music, politics, or just how many selections there are on the menu
EXTRAS/NOTES	Delectable desserts include cakes, rice puddings, pies. Veg City also provides treats for hard-line vegans.

—Jeremy Poreca

The Viceroy

(see p. 47)
Brunch
160 Eighth Ave., Manhattan 10003
Phone (212) 633-8484

Vox

(see p. 47)
Brunch
165 Eighth Ave., Manhattan 10003
Phone (646) 486-3184

AROUND WASHINGTON SQUARE PARK

Bagels on the Square

Great bagels in a great variety with a full line of spreads.
$
7 Carmine St., Manhattan 10014
(between Bleecker St. and Sixth Ave.)
Phone (212) 691-3041

CATEGORY	Bagel Shop
HOURS	24/7
SUBWAY	A, C, E, F, V, S to W. Fourth St.
PAYMENT	Cash only
POPULAR FOOD	With 33 items to choose from, everything is popular—try the sundried tomato Tofutti spread and pat yourself on the back for being so good to yourself
UNIQUE FOOD	Seven types of tofu-based spreads
DRINKS	Soda, juice, coffee, tea, hot chocolate
SEATING	Carry out
AMBIENCE	Efficient service morning noon and night

—Steve Powers

Baluchi's Indian Food

(see p. 176)
Northern Indian
361 Sixth Ave., Manhattan 10014
Phone (212) 929-0456

Caffé Reggio

As seen in Shaft!
Since 1927
$$
119 MacDougal St., Manhattan 10012
(at W. Third St.)
Phone (212) 475-9557

CATEGORY	Italian Café
HOURS	Sun–Thurs: 9 AM–2 AM Fri/Sat: 9 AM–4 AM
SUBWAY	A, C, E, F, V, S to W. Fourth St.
PAYMENT	Cash only
POPULAR FOOD	Italian pastries
UNIQUE FOOD	Anchovies and mozzarella sandwich (hot or cold with pickles, hard-boiled egg, olives, and potato salad on toasted Italian bread, a wicked mix of flavors); *affogato* (assorted ice cream with espresso and fresh whipped cream) is unforgettable
DRINKS	Reggio's Espresso (they also serve American coffee); a nice frothing cappuccino to push you right over the ledge of dangerous self-indulgence; the Reggio, a cup of Irish coffee with liqueur and fresh whipped cream—will pick you up or put your head to bed depending on when you have it and what last night was like
SEATING	Six sidewalk tables and 18 indoor tables can be rearranged and supplied with additional chairs
AMBIENCE	Sultry red and wooden interior, with ornate wooden frames holding Italian Renaissance-style paintings; you'll find students and regular folk alike chatting, meeting, and planning across marble-topped tables while getting their caffeine on
EXTRAS/NOTES	Reggio was a featured locale in the original *Shaft,* and gave its name to an Isaac Hayes-penned musical interlude on the soundtrack. It's been rumored that those dirty Beat poets used to hang around the joint.

—*Matthew Gurwitz*

"New York is a sucked orange."
—*Ralph Waldo Emerson*

Brunch In NYC

What's brunch? As usual, a character from the *Simpsons* explained it best. In this case, bowling alley gigolo Jacques, who said: "You'd love it. It's not quite breakfast, it's not quite lunch, but it comes with a slice of cantaloupe at the end. You don't get completely what you would at breakfast, but you get a good meal."

Here are just a few places to get it in New York . . .

Bright Food Shop

Cute diner serves inventive Mexican-American dishes and alcohol. *From Chelsea to West Houston: 218 Eighth Ave. (at W. 21st St.), Manhattan, 10009, (212) 243-4433. Brunch served daily: 10 AM–4 PM.*

Café le Gamin

Charming French café atmosphere with some of the best crepes in the city—take Mom there. *Downtown Fancy: 50 McDougal St., (at King St.), Manhattan, 10012, (212) 254-4678; From Chelsea to West Houston: 183 Ninth Ave., (at W. 22nd St.), Manhattan, 10003, (212) 486-3000. Sat/Sun: 8 AM–midnight.*

Cafeteria

Just like your high school's cafeteria...if you went to school with the *Beverly Hills 90210* crowd. Upscale American comfort food and booze. *From Chelsea to West Houston: 119 Seventh Ave., (at W. 17th St.), Manhattan, 10014, (212) 414-1717. Brunch served daily: 6 AM–5 PM.*

The Comfort Diner

Comfort food in a comfy setting—great for when friends visit from the Midwest. No alcohol. *Midtown East: 214 E. 45th St., (at Third Ave.), Manhattan, 10017, (212) 867-4555; Upper East Side: 142 E. 86th St., (at Lexington Ave.), Manhattan, 10028, (212) 426-8600. Brunch served Sat/Sun: 9 AM–4 PM.*

EJ's Luncheonette

Diner fare and a child-friendly environment. Beer and wine. See review p. 124. *Upper West Side: 447 Amsterdam Ave., (at 81st St.), Manhattan, 10024, (212) 873-3444. Brunch served Sat/Sun: 8:30 AM–3 PM.*

Fairway Café

Right above the Fairway Market. A truer NYC experience couldn't be had for brunch: it's fun, the food is fabulous—and it's at Fairway. No alcohol. See p. 134. *Upper West Side: 2127 Broadway, (between 74th and 75th Sts.), Manhattan, 10023, (212) 595-1888. Brunch foods served all day, 8 AM–7 PM.*

Flea Market

There's this small café in Paris....wait, we're not in Paris? Alcohol served. *East Village/Alphabet City: 131 Ave. A, (between St. Marks's and Ninth St.), Manhattan, 10009, (212) 358-9280. Brunch served Sat/Sun: 10 AM–4 PM.*

Foodbar

Hot boys, hot wait staff, full on *gay fabulous*— and also full on fun. Skip the mimosa or Bloody Mary and go for the watermelon margarita. *From Chelsea to West Houston: 149 Eighth Ave., (between W. 17th and W. 18th Sts.), Manhattan, 10003, (212) 243-2020. Brunch served Sat/Sun: 11 AM– 4:30 PM, Mon–Fri: 11 AM–4 PM.*

Harvest Restaurant

This place is so good and so popular we haven't been able to get in the last three times we've tried (but we'll keep trying). Think flapjacks bigger than your head. Think steak and eggs. Think I'll order a Bloody Mary. *Downtown Brooklyn West: 218 Court St., (between Baltic and Warren Sts.), Brooklyn, 11201, (718) 624-9267. Brunch served Sat/Sun: 10 AM–3 PM.*

Jerry's Restaurant

You'll expect the cast of *Sex and the City* to be seated next to you—and at this hip, model-packed joint they just might be. Eggs, salads, sandwiches, and a full bar. *Downtown Fancy: 101 Prince St., (between Greene and Mercer Sts.), Manhattan, 10012, (212) 966-9464. Brunch served Sat/Sun: 10:30 AM–5 PM.*

Market Café

Who knew there were such great eats to be had in this corner of Midtown? Steak, salad, salmon, "everything," and beer and wine are more than worth a little hike. *Midtown West: 496 Ninth Ave., (between 37th and 38th Sts.), Manhattan, 10018, (212) 564-7350. Brunch served Sun: 10 AM–4 PM.*

Nadine's Restaurant

Old school Village hangout and one of our faves: friendly food, friendly vibe, American cuisine and a full bar. *From Chelsea to West Houston: 99 Bank St., (at Greenwich St.), Manhattan, 10014, (212) 924-3165. Brunch served Sat/Sun: 10:30 AM–4 PM.*

Old Devil Moon

Showcases the glorious culinary achievements of the "White Trash" culture so many New Yorkers disdain. Southern food with veggie selections. Beer and wine. *East Village/Alphabet City: 511 E 12th St., (between Aves. A and B), Manhattan, 10009, (212) 475-4357. Brunch served Sat/Sun: 10 AM–4 PM.*

One and One

Real Irish breakfast, and a free mimosa or Bloody Mary with your food. So relaxed you could wind up hanging out until dinner. *East Village/Alphabet City: 76 E. First St., (at First Ave.), Manhattan, 10009, (212) 260-9950. Brunch served Sat/Sun: noon–5 PM.*

Oznot's Dish

Cardamom French toast (with raisins, nutmeg, yogurt, and fresh fruit) is just one of the delights that awaits. Full bar. *Williamsburg/ Greenpoint: 79 Berry St., (at N. Ninth St.), Brooklyn, 11211, (718) 599-6596. Brunch served Sat/Sun: 10 AM–4:30 PM, Mon–Fri: 11 AM–4:30 PM.*

Paris Commune

Grab a book and some smokes and experience what brunching is all about. Not quite a French café, and not quite the kind of place Louise Michel would have hung around, but it's a popular hot spot. So be prepared to wait outside. Omelettes, French toast, pancakes, alcohol. *From Chelsea to West Houston: 411 Bleecker St., (between E. 11th and Bank Sts.), Manhattan, 10014, (212) 929-0509. Brunch served Sat/Sun: 10 AM–3 PM.*

Rocking Horse Mexican Café

Inventive Mexican brunch, *huevos rancheros*— yum yum. Full bar. *From Chelsea to West Houston: 182 Eighth Ave., (between W. 19th and W. 20th Sts.), Manhattan, 10003, (212) 463-9511. Brunch served Sat/Sun: 11 AM–3:30 PM.*

Sarabeth's West

Fab omelettes, pancakes and waffles don't necessarily fit our criteria for cheap eats...but it is THE place to go for the lady who brunches. Bar. *Upper West Side: 423 Amsterdam Ave., (between W. 80th and W. 81st Sts.), Manhattan, 10024, (212) 496-6280. Brunch served Sat/Sun: 8 AM–4 PM.*

Other Ones:
- *Sarabeth's Bakery: From Chelsea to West Houston: 75 Ninth Ave., Manhattan, 10003, (212) 989-2424.*
- *Sarabeth's At The Whitney: Upper East Side: 945 Madison Ave., Manhattan, 10021, (212) 570-3670.*
- *Sarabeth's East: Upper East Side: 1295 Madison Ave., New York, 10128, (212) 410-7335.*

7A

Some say it's trendy, some call it a dive, but we say go there for a smoke and one of the best and most leisurely brunches in town. Burgers, vegetarian fare, pasta, burritos—basically everything, and a full bar. *East Village/Alphabet City: 109 Ave. A, (at E. Seventh St.), Manhattan, 10009, (212) 673-6583. Brunch served Sat/Sun: 10 AM–5 PM.*

Sylvia's

A bit out of our price range, but worth a splurge. Go early and beat the after church crowd. Yes, you want everything covered in gravy. Full bar. *The Harlems: 328 Malcolm X Blvd., (between W. 126th and W. 127th Sts.), Manhattan, 10027, (212) 996-0660. Brunch served Sat/Sun: 12:30 PM–4 PM.*

Tea & Sympathy

What is there to say except that this tiny place is a fave? We don't really want you to go 'cause then we won't get in. Standard British fare in a small, bustling café setting. Bring Your Own Bottle. *From Chelsea to West Houston: 108-110 Greenwich Ave., (at Seventh Ave.), Manhattan, 10006, (212) 807-8329. Brunch served Sat/Sun: 9:30 AM–1:30 PM.*

The Viceroy

Great people-watching during brunch and an even better spot to be watched. Scrumptious prixfixe menu and champagne mimosas. *From Chelsea to West Houston: 160 Eighth Ave., (at 18th St.), Manhattan, 10003, (212) 633-8484. Brunch served Sat/Sun: 11:30 AM–5 PM.*

Vox

All I need to say is $9.95 unlimited champagne brunch. But don't miss the food: American infused with South American and Asian flavors. *From Chelsea to West Houston: 165 Eighth Ave., (between W. 18th and W. 19th Sts.), Manhattan, 10003, (646) 486-3184. Brunch served Sat/Sun: 11 AM–4 PM.*

—Michael Connor

Down the Hatch

Get your Suicidal Atomic Wings fix at this college dive, literally.

$$

179 W. Fourth St., Manhattan 10012
(between Sixth and Seventh Aves.)
Phone (212) 627-9747

CATEGORY	American Pub
HOURS	Sun–Thurs: noon–2 AM Fri/Sat: noon–4 AM
SUBWAY	A, C, E, F, V, S to W. Fourth St., 1 to Christopher St.
PAYMENT	VISA MasterCard AMERICAN
POPULAR FOOD	Try some fine buffalo chicken wings by the dozen with plenty of celery to take the edge off, or a veggie or turkey burger topped with jack cheese, jalapeños, grilled onions; don't miss the Smothered Fries—wafer fries topped with cheese, chili, and jalapeños
UNIQUE FOOD	Combo basket of wafer and onion fries is inspired; Chicken Littles—sliced skinless

chicken breast on a bed of lettuce with choice of eight Dipmania! Sauces (Atomic, pepper parmesan, horseradish, sweet and sour, blue cheese, honey mustard, ranch, and barbecue)

DRINKS	Full bar with plenty of beer—five on tap, 16 bottled varieties
SEATING	Seats 20 at booths and stools
AMBIENCE	Completely casual, underground, brick walls, wood, filled with jocks
EXTRAS/NOTES	Play some foosball.

—Steve Powers

Grey Dog's Coffee

Neighborhood spot where the staff is friendly and the vibe is homey.

$$$

33 Carmine St., Manhattan 10014
(between Bleecker and Bedford Sts.)
Phone (212) 462-0041 • Fax (212) 414-1091

CATEGORY	American
HOURS	Sun–Thurs: 6:30 AM–11:30 PM (kitchen closes 10:30 PM) Fri/Sat: 7 AM–12:30 AM (kitchen closes 11:30 PM)
SUBWAY	A, C, E, F, V, S to W. Fourth St.
PAYMENT	Cash only
POPULAR FOOD	Great sandwiches on homemade breads and a dinner menu that includes catfish tacos and truly splurge-worthy seared tuna
UNIQUE FOOD	All homemade desserts to die for—brownies, strawberry shortcakes, pumpkin tarts
SEATING	Seating for about 45
DRINKS	Domestic and foreign beer, extensive and darn good wine offerings—don't miss the hot spiced wine, sodas
AMBIENCE	Homey, homey, homey—homey.

—Steve Powers

Harry's Burritos

Baskin-Robbins variety; burritos the size of your head.

$$

76 W. Third St., Manhattan 10012
(at Thompson St.)
Phone (212) 260-5588
www.harrysburritos.com

CATEGORY	Mexican Cantina
HOURS	Sun–Thurs: 11:30 AM–midnight Fri/Sat: 11:30 AM–1 AM
SUBWAY	A, C, E, F, V, S to W. Fourth St.
PAYMENT	VISA
POPULAR FOOD	Vegetarian chili burrito—you couldn't pack one more ounce of chili, rice, and

	cheese into a tortilla and after you're done the same will go for your stomach
UNIQUE FOOD	Three grain burrito—berries, raisins, and barley may sound like trail mix ingredients, but mixed with beans, rice, and cheese, this burrito is ready for the long haul
DRINKS	Full range of alcohol: liquor, wine, and beer; Boylan's soda
SEATING	Seating for 30
AMBIENCE	Given the location right smack in the middle of New York University, there tends to be a lot of starving students as well as the munchie-craving folk just finishing a stroll through neighboring Washington Square Park
EXTRAS/NOTES	Most of the ingredients from your favorite burrito can be purchased in bulk, so you can take them home and make one EVEN FATTER!
OTHER ONES	• Upper West Side: 241 Columbus Ave., Manhattan, 10023, (212) 580-9494 • East Village: 93 Ave. A, Manhattan, 10009, (212) 254-2054 (Benny's Burrito is owned by the same guy and operated the same way—just named for a different family member)

—Jeremy Poreca

Joe's Pizza

A damn fine slice of pizza…maybe the best in NYC, but why start a fight?

$

233 Bleecker St., Manhattan 10014

(corner of Carmine St.)

Phone (212) 366-1182

CATEGORY	Pizzeria
HOURS	Sun–Thurs: 9 AM–4 AM Fri/Sat: 9 AM–5 AM
SUBWAY	A, B, C, D, E, F, V, S to W. Fourth St., 1 to Carmine
PAYMENT	Cash only
POPULAR FOOD	Get the fresh mozzarella, plain cheese, or pepperoni and walk with it—or sit and have a gyro or salad
DRINKS	Soda, Snapple, juice, water
SEATING	About 30 at tables
AMBIENCE	Not very glamorous or chic— just good pizza
EXTRAS/NOTES	Joe's Pizza around the corner came first (same owners), about 25 years ago, but this is the Joe's to go to.
OTHER ONES	• Around Washington Square Park: 7 Carmine St., Manhattan, 10014, (212) 255-3946

—Steve Powers

John's Pizzeria

(see p. 226)
Pizzeria
408 E. 64th St., Manhattan 10021
Phone (212) 935-2895

Le Frite Kot

(see p. 23)
Frites Stand
148 W. Fourth St., Manhattan 10003
Phone (212) 979-2616

Mamoun's

Best falafel anywhere!
$
119 MacDougal St., Manhattan 10012
(between W. Third and Bleecker Sts.)
Phone (212) 674-8685
www.mamounsfalafel.com

CATEGORY	Middle Eastern
HOURS	Daily: 10 AM–5 AM
SUBWAY	A, C, E, F, V, S to W. Fourth St.
PAYMENT	Cash only
POPULAR FOOD	Do yourself a favor and go for the phenomenal falafel and creamy *baba ganoush* sandwich—and finish with a Turkish Delight, a light (but sweet) flowery-flavored caramel with pistachios
UNIQUE FOOD	*Makdoos*—miniature eggplant stuffed with walnuts, garlic, and marinated with olive oil; Syrian rice made with long grain rice, tomato paste, and a secret spice
DRINKS	Quench your thirst with the mango iced tea—a blend of freshly squeezed mango juice and Mamoun's special iced tea, fresh squeezed homemade lemonade, or tamarind drink; for something hot, try Mamoun's hot tea or Turkish coffee
SEATING	About 15 snuggly at five tables
AMBIENCE	Expect efficient service but always a wait at this small no-frills space with old world charm that's always filled with people from all walks of life
EXTRAS/NOTES	Kindly leave a tip for the three guys packed behind the counter like an overstuffed pita.

—*Steve Powers*

Didjaknow?

New York City restaurants that seat 20 or more customers are required by law to provide bathroom facilities.

Meskerem

Traditional Ethiopian cooking in a communal dining environment.

$$$$

124 MacDougal St., Manhattan 10012
(at W. Fourth St.)

Phone (212) 777-8111

CATEGORY	Ethiopian
HOURS	Daily: 11 AM–11 PM
SUBWAY	A, C, E, F, V, S to W. Fourth St.
PAYMENT	VISA · MasterCard · AMERICAN
POPULAR FOOD	*Doro wat* (chicken seasoned with onions, garlic, sautéed in butter, finished with red wine and ground red pepper); all dishes served with *injera,* a spongy Ethiopian flat bread
UNIQUE FOOD	Meskerem Combo: pan cooked prime beef (sautéed with ground red pepper, prime beef seasoned with garlic, onions, and ginger served with collard greens), lamb (sautéed in butter garlic, ginger, and mild curry, split lentils cooked with ginger, garlic, onions, olive oil, and mild curry), and lentils cooked with garlic, onions, olive oil, topped with ground red pepper
DRINKS	*Bedele* (an Ethiopian beer similar to Heineken), Corona, scotch, whiskey, and cognac, red and white wine, and five kinds of honey wine: some light, one fuller bodied, and more honey-sweet, cranberry and blackberry flavored
SEATING	Seats 34, including four at the bar
AMBIENCE	Cozy garden floor restaurant with view of MacDougal Street through small paned windows; subtle track lighting; Ethiopian panels depicting Mary and Disciples of Christ; photos of Ethiopian people, countryside, mountains
EXTRAS/NOTES	Traditional Ethiopian garments and jewelry, along with popular Ethiopian CDs, are for sale. Meskerem means September; Ethiopian New Year is Sept. 1st.
OTHER ONES	• Midtown West: 468 W. 47th St., Manhattan, 10036, (212) 664-0520

—Matthew Gurwitz

Peanut Butter & Co.

No corners cut, just crusts, honey, crusts.

$$

240 Sullivan St., Manhattan 10012
(at Bleecker St.)

Phone (212) 677-3995

www.ilovepeanutbutter.com

CATEGORY	Peanut Butter Boutique
HOURS	Sun–Thurs: 11 AM–9 PM
	Fri/Sat: 11 AM–10 PM

SUBWAY	A, C, E, F, V, S to W. Fourth St.
PAYMENT	VISA · Mastercard · American Express · Discover
POPULAR FOOD	Peanut butter sandwiches with fluff, jams, jellies, and one with cream cheese and chocolate chips called the Cookie Dough Surprise—all between four and six bucks; crusts on all sandwiches removed upon request
UNIQUE FOOD	Any peanut butter purveyor would be a peon if it didn't bow to the king of Graceland's crowning culinary delight: keep it regal with the Elvis, a banana-stuffed grilled peanut butter sandwich slathered with honey; bring home the bacon for about $1 more
DRINKS	All the usual bottled beverages (water, juices, and pop); old-fashioned root beers and cream sodas, and real cherry lime rickeys; ultimately one of the utterly smooth milks—chocolate, strawberry, and malted—is the perfect match for peanut butter: suck one through a silly straw for an extra quarter
SEATING	Seating for 20
AMBIENCE	Country-kitchen-meets-'50s-soda-shop aesthetic is a throw back to Rockwellian Americana, all except for the moonlighting tattooed-and-pierced NYC bike messengers who deliver take-out orders in brown paper lunch bags
EXTRAS/NOTES	Are you a smoothie, or a crunchy nut? Or maybe you got a feelin' for the flavor: put a white or dark chocolate or cinnamon raisin swirl in your world. You're covered however you like it. PB&C home-blends its own peanut butters to go (in recycled glass containers).

—*Matthew Gurwitz*

Sacred Chow

(see p. 100)
Vegetarian
522 Hudson St., Manhattan 10014
Phone (212) 337-0863

Spice

(see p. 40)
Modern Thai
60 University Pl., Manhattan 10003
Phone (212) 982-3758

> "In Manhattan, every flat surface is a
> potential stage and
> every inattentive waiter an unemployed,
> possibly unemployable actor."
> —*Quentin Crisp*

Temple in the Village

Old World Mom and Pop Eatery increases health, wealth, and wisdom of its clientele.

$$

74 W. Third St., Manhattan 10012

(between LaGuardia Pl. and Thompson St.)

Phone (212) 475-5670

CATEGORY	Vegetarian Buffet
HOURS	Mon–Sat: 11 AM–10 PM
SUBWAY	A, C, E, F, V, S to W. Fourth St.; Q to W. Fourth St.
PAYMENT	Cash only
POPULAR FOOD	Of the endless array of fresh Korean and Japanese dishes, proprietor/Taoist Immortal in disguise says the Tofu Jim is the most popular attraction—although the spinach salad also has a strong following
UNIQUE FOOD	Seven grain rice—a mixture of brown rice, barley, millet, *aduki* beans, brown sweet rice, white and black soy beans
DRINKS	A selection of fresh squeezed juices, bottled all-natural drinks, hot and iced teas
SEATING	Seats 20, take-out available
AMBIENCE	Not the hippy-dippy atmosphere we expect from a health-food joint; serious folks, serious about their bodies, reading books, scribbling notes, listening to the limpid flow of classical music that makes this dining experience all the more enlightening
EXTRAS/NOTES	I know what you're thinking, seven grain rice—big whoop, right? Well, eat it and see the Popeyesque effect it will have on your organism.

—*Nemo Librizzi*

Vegetarian Paradise 2 (VP2)

(see p. 101)

Chinese/Vegan

144 W. Fourth St., Manhattan 10012

Phone (212) 260-7130

Vol de Nuit

Eat your heart out, Time Cop: Belgian beer washes down mussels from Brussels!

$$$$

148 W. Fourth St., Manhattan 10012

(at Sixth Ave.)

Phone (212) 979-2616

www.voldenuitbar.com

CATEGORY	Belgian Beer and *Frite* Joint
HOURS	Daily: 4 PM–2 AM
SUBWAY	A, C, E, F, V, S to W. Fourth St.

PAYMENT	VISA MasterCard AMERICAN DISCOVER
POPULAR FOOD	Heaps of Belgian *frites* served in a paper cone
UNIQUE FOOD	$10 and change gets you mussels served in the kind of pot your mom would use to cook potatoes
DRINKS	World-class selection of beer and wine
SEATING	Seats 50
AMBIENCE	Attracts people who don't count calories
EXTRAS/NOTES	Started out as a mere *frite* stand and grew into a beer and *frite* joint.

—*Jeremy Poreca*

Yatagan Kebab House

Yet again, the döner kebab turns up to entice the Hungry?

$$$

104 MacDougal St., Manhattan 10012
(between Bleecker and W. Third Sts.)
Phone (212) 677-0952

CATEGORY	Turkish/Middle Eastern
HOURS	Daily: 10:30 AM–5 AM
SUBWAY	A, C, E, F, V, S to W. Fourth St.
PAYMENT	Cash only
POPULAR FOOD	Falafel; the *döner* kebab—so named for the Turkish word for "to turn"—is made fresh daily from breast of lamb layered with ground beef and (more) lamb, slow cooked on a rotisserie; just one is stuffed with enough succulent slices of meat, onions, tomatoes, and lettuce to feed you twice
DRINKS	*Ayran,* a traditional Turkish drink made from yogurt, water, and salt (like an unsweetened Indian *lassi*); black tea with cardamom seeds, coffee, soda, water
SEATING	Tables seat 16
AMBIENCE	Village dwellers looking for a bite after the pubs close, taxi drivers in need of fuel, "some belly dancers," not a few speaking Turkish; narrow brick interior, hung with photos of the Blue Mosque in Istanbul, an enormous (and considering his Westernizing agenda, rare) photo of Ataturk in Ottoman dress
EXTRAS/NOTES	Opened in 1983 by Gultekin Ismihanli, a Turkish immigrant, Yatagan is now run by Nedret Akan. Turhan Ismihanli, Gultekin's son, can usually be found behind the counter; he's a fountain of five borough food knowledge. Across the street is a deli that claims to stock 400 exotic beers.

—*Matthew Gurwitz*

EAST VILLAGE

Angelica Kitchen

(see p. 98)
Vegetarian
300 E. 12th St., Manhattan 10003
Phone (212) 228-2909

B & H Dairy Restaurant

From the shtetl to the city.
Since 1938
$$

127 Second Ave., Manhattan 10003
(between St. Mark's Pl. and E. Seventh St.)
Phone (212) 505-8065

CATEGORY	Jewish Dairy Kosher Vegetarian
HOURS	Mon–Sat: 7 AM–10 PM
	Sun: 8 AM–10 PM
SUBWAY	N, R to Eighth St.; 6 to Astor Pl.
PAYMENT	Cash only
POPULAR FOOD	For breakfast, the "famous" challah French toast; for dinner, daily specials of such favorites as blintzes, *pierogies,* smoked whitefish, and potato pancakes all served with a cup of soup; a number of vegetarian entrées
UNIQUE FOOD	Soups (vegetable, mushroom barley, lentil, split pea, cabbage, potato, lima bean, hot borscht, matzo ball, yankee bean), plus delicious buttered challa, make for excellent meals by themselves; as with most kosher Jewish cuisine, the food is hearty but calm to the palate
DRINKS	Fresh-squeezed juices, tea, coffee, soda
SEATING	Twelve at small tables, 10 at counter
AMBIENCE	B & H serves mostly locals in a cramped, unremarkable, diner-like interior, where the countermen are gruff but friendly— just how New Yorkers like it

—*Peter Davis*

Baluchi's Indian Food

(see p. 176)
Northern Indian
104 Second Ave., Manhattan 10003
Phone (212) 780-6000

Burritoville

(see p. 31)
Mexican
141 Second Ave., Manhattan 10003
Phone (212) 260-3300

The Indian Restaurant Row on E. Sixth Street Christmas in July . . . or August . . . or September . . .

The Indian enclave on E. Sixth St. has its detractors. Some call these restaurants "cheesy." Others chime in with "commercial," "touristy," "inauthentic," and "really cheesy." Serious charges, but what crimes against taste have really gone down on E. Sixth?

Champions of authenticity would do well to remember that India—the world's largest democracy, and one of its most vibrant—is hardly subdued or unyieldingly traditionalist. On the contrary, the home of Bollywood cinema has never shied away from entrepreneurial activity. So should an Indian restaurant, or a row of them, be derided as inauthentic for neglecting to recreate the precise tastes and feels and smells of some backwater mess hall? Unless one's idea of authenticity is informed predominantly by *Temple of Doom* (either the village scene or the palace scene) all charges should be dropped. Complaints about E. Sixth St. usually boil down to this: the restaurants hang up too many Christmas lights.

Maybe they do. But the atmosphere is usually enjoyable and the lunch specials—mountains of food for as little as $4.95—can't be beaten anywhere in the city. And, while taste is subjective, the food's pretty good too.

Rose of India, a critical favorite, is decked out like Santa's dining car: long, narrow, and covered in colorful Christmas lights. The comprehensive menu includes nine types of bread, and comprehensive platters featuring the tandoori, vegetable, and Rose of India dinners, all with soup, appetizer, vegetable, desert, and more. These can run in the $10–$13 range, but that's for everything. Cheaper options abound. *308 E. Sixth St., Manhattan, 10003, (212) 533-5011. Daily: noon–midnight. Visa, MasterCard.*

Next door and down a flight of stairs, the **Taj Restaurant** offers scores of Indian dishes, along with an (almost) incomparable $4.95 lunch special from noon–4 PM. *310 E. Sixth St., Manhattan, 10003, (212) 505-8056. Daily: noon–midnight. Visa, MasterCard, AmEx.*

That's not to be confused with nearby **Taj Mahal Indian Restaurant**, which has won endorsements from both Bon Jovi and ZZ-Top. The lunch special here, served noon–5:30 includes

soup, *papadum*, rice, cabbage, *naan*, a choice of appetizer, a choice of appetizer and main course, a soda, tea or coffee, and desert. $4.95 unless you opt for *tandoori*, in which case it's $5.50.
318 E. Sixth St., Manhattan, 10003, (212) 529-2217. Daily: noon–midnight. Visa, MasterCard, AmEx.

And don't confuse either with **Raj Mahal,** where traditional clay (*tandoori*) ovens combine with less traditional beer and wine and a cool name. Once again, you're looking at a $4.95 lunch special. *322 E. Sixth St., Manhattan, 10003, (212) 982-3632. Daily: noon–midnight. Visa, MasterCard, AmEx, Discover.*

Slightly more elegant options can mean slightly more expensive specials, but you're still only likely to be out a few extra bucks. **Calcutta** offers an enormous 12-course combination platter at lunchtime for $6.95, and plenty of full meals around the clock for about as much. *324 E. Sixth St., Manhattan, 10003, (212) 982-8127. Daily: noon–midnight. Visa, MasterCard, AmEx.*

Behind a gold façade, **Mitali** wins disproportionate praise from the city's many critics: a somewhat shorter menu and buffet-style lunches promise considerable attention to the culinary details. You could actually spend a lot of money here, but that's only if you opt for the lobster *tandoori*. *334 E. Sixth St., Manhattan, 10003, (212) 533-2508. Daily: noon–midnight. Visa, MasterCard, AmEx.*

Sonali Indian Restaurant specializes in Bangladeshi-style food and is particularly proud of its *mulligatwany* Soup. Numerous seafood dishes include items like shrimp *tandoori masala* and crabmeat *shobji*, but they're nowhere near as cheap as the salmon specials. *326 E. Sixth St., Manhattan, 10003, (212) 505-7517. Daily: noon–2 AM. Visa, MasterCard, AmEx.*

Not to be forgotten, **Kashmir Tandoori** has a full bar and several *biryani* specialties—an Indo-Pakistani creation served on *basmati* rice.
304 E. Sixth St., Manhattan, 10003, (212) 529-8250. Daily: noon–midnight, Visa, MasterCard, AmEx.

There are more yet. Everyone who's eaten along E. Sixth St. has his or her favorite place to grab a bite. Don't be afraid to try a few—most stay safely within the budget range. We all need a little Christmas once in awhile.

—*Joe Cleemann*

Dawgs on Park

(see p. 112)

Hot Dogs

178 E. Seventh Ave., Manhattan 10009

Phone (212) 598-0667

El Castillo de Jagua Restaurant

The perfect place for comfort food after a night drinking on Ludlow.

$$

113 Rivington St., Manhattan 10002

(corner of Essex St.)

Phone (212) 982-6412/3

CATEGORY	Dominican
HOURS	Sun–Thurs: 8 AM–midnight Fri/Sat: 8 AM–1 AM
SUBWAY	F, V to Second Ave. or Delancey St.
PAYMENT	Cash only
POPULAR FOOD	Rice and beans—fortunately they come with just about everything and go perfectly with popular dishes such as fried chunks of chicken, roast pork, and Dominican style fried beef
UNIQUE FOOD	Why not try the *mofongo* (mashed green plantains with pork skin, seasoned with garlic and salt), or the *pescado en escabeche* (pickled fish), or *pulpo enchilado* (octopus in hot sauce)?
DRINKS	Wash it all down with a papaya milkshake or a *café con leche;* also natural juices, fruit milk shakes, *café con leche,* tea, soda
SEATING	About 65 at tables, including counter seating
AMBIENCE	Always busy, and filled with East Village old timers, new timers, Dominican teens, lone diners, and families—point if you don't speak Spanish
EXTRAS/NOTES	Some seafood specialties of the house can get quite pricey—otherwise you can eat tremendously well for under eight bucks.

—Marie Estrada

Elvie's Turo-Turo

Point and eat till you drop—for under $10.

$$

214 First Ave., Manhattan 10009

(between E. 12th and E. 13th Sts.)

Phone (212) 473-7785

CATEGORY	Filipino
HOURS	Daily: 11 AM–9 PM
SUBWAY	L to First Ave.; 4, 5, 6, N, R to Union Sq.
PAYMENT	VISA · · ·
POPULAR FOOD	*Adobo* (meat simmered in vinegar, garlic, and soy sauce); barbecue; *longanisa* (spicy

pork sausage); *nilaga* (stew); *pinakbet* (sautéed vegetables with fish paste); *halo-halo* (tropical fruits on shaved ice drizzled with milk and topped with yam-flavored ice cream and flan)

UNIQUE FOOD　*Paksiw na lechon* (pig's trotters simmered in vinegar and soy sauce); *dinuguan* (pig's blood stew); assorted rice cakes; *turon* (caramelized bananas fried in spring roll wrappers); *puto bumbong* (sticky rice roll steamed in bamboo and rolled in coconut); *balut* (duck embryos)

DRINKS　*Sarsi* (the native sarsaparilla) and other sodas, *buko* (young coconut) and mango juices

SEATING　Eighteen at tables

AMBIENCE　Filipinos and non-, students, tourists— a generally eclectic bunch typical of the neighborhood—discover the joys of meat and sweet, sticky snacks at this cheerfully decorated, friendly cafeteria

EXTRAS/NOTES　Take a tray, point to what you want (*turo turo* means "point, point"), and pay up. The menu is on the blackboard behind the counter and changes daily. Most entrées are served with a mountain of rice. And yes, you can get vegetables and fish here, too. Die-hard vegetarians can also console themselves with sublimely sticky, rich Filipino desserts, particularly the mountainous *halo-halo,* silky *leche* flan, *ube* (purple yam jam), and vari-colored rice cakes. The cassava cake, baked with coconut milk and sugar, will totally change your perception of root crops.

—*Melissa Contreras*

Flea Market

(see p. 45)
French Café
131 Ave. A, Manhattan 10009
Phone (212) 358-9280

Flor's Kitchen

Don't have a Venezuelan grandmother? Flor's more than makes up for it.
$$$
149 First Ave., Manhattan 10003
(at E. Ninth St.)
Phone (212) 387-8949
www.florskitchen.com

CATEGORY　Venezuelan
HOURS　Mon–Thurs: 11 AM–11 PM
　　　　　Fri/Sat: 11 AM–midnight
　　　　　Sun: 10 AM–11 PM
SUBWAY　6, N, R to Astor Pl.
PAYMENT

POPULAR FOOD	The barbecue gets high marks—look for the magic word: *asado; criollas empanadas,* flaky, fried dough pockets, full of spiced goodies, also keep the crowds coming
UNIQUE FOOD	*Arepas,* Venezuela's answer to the Mexican tortilla: "fried cornmeal" price, *apepas* taste
DRINKS	Beer, wine, Sangria, tea, coffee, fresh juices including pineapple and guava
SEATING	Seats approximately 18
AMBIENCE	Hip Eastsiders, along with others, often form lines; tiny, colorful, cozy seating area makes you feel as though you're in someone's kitchen, the heavenly smells only add to the effect

—Tanya Laplante

Harry's Burritos

(see p. 48)
Mexican Cantina
93 Ave. A, Manhattan 10009
Phone (212) 254-2054

Kate's Joint

(see p. 99)
Vegetarian/Vegan Comfort Food
58 Ave. B, Manhattan 10009
Phone (212) 777-7059

Katz's Delicatessen   [landmark]

"Send a Salami to Your Boy in the Army."
Since 1888
$$

205 E. Houston St., Manhattan 10002
(corner of Ludlow St.)
Phone (212) 254-2246, or 1-800-4-HOT-DOG
Fax (212) 674-3270
www.katzdeli.com

CATEGORY	Delicatessen
HOURS	Sun–Tues: 8 AM–10 PM Wed/Thurs: 8 AM–11 PM Fri/Sat: 8 AM–3 AM
SUBWAY	F to Second Ave.
PAYMENT	[VISA] [MasterCard] [AMERICAN EXPRESS]
POPULAR FOOD	Frankfurters and chili dogs to die for, gargantuan pastrami and corned beef sandwiches, delicious Katz salami sandwiches, New York egg cream, and traditional potato *latkes* and blintzes
UNIQUE FOOD	Everything at Katz's is unique in that quintessentially New York way—mountains of fresh meats piled high on rye or whole-wheat or whatever you desire; salami is homemade; also of note and not to be missed are Katz's tongue sandwich, cured in house

DRINKS	Don't miss the New York egg cream—this is as real as it gets; Katz's also has a line of specialty beers, plus a million other standard restaurant beverages
SEATING	Plenty of table seating in a cafeteria-like setting
AMBIENCE	Worn and cluttered, but somehow bright and open at the same time, here's where the fun starts: get a green piece of paper when you walk in the door, and it's literally your meal ticket (whatever you do, for God's sake, don't lose your ticket!!!) and once you've gotten your meal, have a seat at one of the old wooden tables and enjoy the photos of famous patrons, from Bill Clinton and Tony Curtis to Dan Ackroyd and Bill Zane
EXTRAS/NOTES	Katz's deli has a wonderful history—it was established across Ludlow St. from its present location (it moved in the early 20th Century), and became a popular neighborhood hangout immediately—something that hasn't changed in over 100 years. Back in WWII, Katz's set up a sausage-mailing service for the boys overseas. Service is fast, but Katz's can be absolutely packed on the weekends with tourists, New York old-timers, village types, and the occasional celeb. And yes, it's the site of the famous faked orgasm in *When Harry Met Sally*.

—*Brad Wood*

Mama's Food Shop

Home cooking without the family.
$$
200 E. Third St., Manhattan 10009
(between Aves. A and B)
Phone (212) 777-4425

CATEGORY	American Home Cooking
HOURS	Mon–Sat: 11 AM–10:30 PM
SUBWAY	F to Second Ave.
PAYMENT	Cash only
POPULAR FOOD	Everything is popular and served in huge can't-eat-it-all-in-two-days portions; six entrées: meatloaf, fried chicken, grilled chicken, grilled salmon, roasted chicken, veggie plate; all come with one side, and you can add an extra side for a buck
DRINKS	Homemade ginger mint iced tea and lemonade, Coke, Diet Coke, coffee
SEATING	Seats about 20; bad for large groups, cozy for couples
AMBIENCE	Punky, funky, downtown flea market; as the menu says, "Mama Doesn't Do Decaf!" and "Shut Up and Eat It!!!"—the staff has adopted mama's unique flair for customer service

EXTRAS/NOTES The food really does taste homemade by mama, and despite the dodgy service Mama's is one of the best places to eat in NYC. Heat up your own food in the microwave next to the cashier (this isn't as bad as it sounds—honest). Bus your own table and put your dishes in the proper wash bin opposite where you ordered your food.

—Michael Connor

Mandarin Grill and Coffee House

(see p. 122)
Filipino
199 First Ave., Manhattan 10002
Phone (212) 673-3656

Manila Gardens

(see p. 122)
Filipino
325 E. 14ᵗʰ St., Manhattan 10003
Phone (212) 777-6314

Moustache

Flavorful Middle Eastern food in a charming setting.
$$

265 E. 10ᵗʰ St., Manhattan 10009
(between First Ave. and Ave. A)
Phone (212) 228-2022

CATEGORY	Middle Eastern
HOURS	Daily: noon–midnight
SUBWAY	L to First Ave.
PAYMENT	Cash only
POPULAR FOOD	Traditional sandwiches like falafel, leg of lamb, or even the spicy lamb sausage *Merguez* sandwich; spinach and cheese pitza; hummus, *tabouli,* and *baba ganoush*
UNIQUE FOOD	Fresh baked puffed-up pita bread; special desserts, including walnut and raisin filo roll and *basboussa,* a Semolina cake of yogurt and honey
DRINKS	Wine, beer, Turkish coffee, mint tea, Middle Eastern citrus and yogurt drinks, fresh lemonade and orange juice, coffee, tea, mineral water, soft drinks
SEATING	Seats about 75, including those in the garden out back
AMBIENCE	Although the inexpensive prices and laid-back atmosphere would suggest otherwise, this is a very charming place to bring a date or eat out with friends
EXTRAS/NOTES	Front dining area consists of muted color tones and romantic candle lighting in the evening, and during the warm weather months, the back garden offers patrons a

world away from the busy streets of
Manhattan.

OTHER ONES • From Chelsea to West Houston:
90 Bedford St., Manhattan, 10014, (212)
229-2220 (no outdoor dining at this
location)

—Shannon Godwin

New Manila Foodmart

(see p. 122)
Filipino
353 E. 14th St., Manhattan 10003
Phone (212) 420-8182

Old Devil Moon

(see p. 45)
Brunch/Southern American
511 E. 12th St., Manhattan 10009
Phone (212) 475-4357

One and One

(see p. 46)
Irish
76 E. First St., Manhattan 10009
Phone (212) 260-9950

The Organic Grill

(see p. 100)
Vegetarian
123 First Ave., Manhattan 10003
Phone (212) 477-7171

Panna II Garden
Indian Restaurant

*Indian comfort food with an in-
your-face décor that rivals the lights of Times
Square.*
$$
93 First Ave., Manhattan 10003
(between E. Fifth and E. Sixth Sts.)
Phone (212) 598-4610

CATEGORY	Indian
HOURS	Daily: noon–midnight
SUBWAY	6 to Astor Pl.; F to Second Ave.
PAYMENT	Cash only
POPULAR FOOD	Chicken *korma* and lamb curry, or have the *shag;* don't forget an order of *naan* to round out the meal (which also comes with a variety of side dishes and a complimentary dish of mango ice cream with every meal—YUM)
UNIQUE FOOD	Banana fritters
DRINKS	Cola, tea, and coffee
SEATING	Seats about 50; tables seat two to four in very tight quarters

AMBIENCE	Customers range from local neighborhood patrons to the occasional fashion model or Hell's Angel; with walls covered in Christmas tinsel, Fourth of July decorations, wrapping paper and chili pepper lights, Panna II provides an entertaining, if not dizzying, place to eat out with friends
EXTRAS/NOTES	They don't serve alcoholic beverages here, but customers are encouraged to bring their own. So if you're up for drinking, be sure to stop by one of the local stores and pick up a six-pack on your way to the restaurant. As soon as you hit the steps, be ready to be accosted by the maîtres d' of both Panna II and the neighboring restaurants.

—Shannon Godwin

Pink Pony

Blue-collar French Cuisine: THE downtown hang-out for artists, writers, actors, intellectuals, and street fashion designers.
$$$$
176 Ludlow St., Manhattan 10002
(between Houston and Stanton Sts.)
Phone (212) 253-1922

CATEGORY	French Coffeeshop/Café Literaire
HOURS	Daily: 11 AM–4 AM
SUBWAY	F, V to Second Ave.
PAYMENT	Cash only
POPULAR FOOD	A continuous conveyor belt of tuna melts, and other assorted warm sandwiches served to the starving artist types to keep them looking fashionably waifish, but never starving
UNIQUE FOOD	A nightly fixed menu for 16 bucks; every night it is something different, and everybody eats the same—quaint, huh?
DRINKS	Fine wines by the glass, imported beers; highest quality Italian coffees at 99¢ a-cup!
SEATING	Plenty of seats in a spacious area with romantic banquettes
AMBIENCE	Warm and welcoming by day, warm, welcoming, and packed by night
EXTRAS/NOTES	The three-course prix fix meal is the economical way for an *artiste* to see and be seen, as well as chow down; the food preparation is overseen by Lucien (of the reputable First Ave. bistro of his namesake). Remember that "old Village" used bookshop Tompkins Square Books that saw its demise last year? Well it lives on in the vast bookshelves of the Pink Pony's library; feel free to worm your way into a book, or bring your laptop along to write your own; catch up with the

impromptu goings-on of their cinema club, and poetry readings, or look into one of the most eclectic jukeboxes in town.

—*Nemo Librizzi*

Pommes Frites

(see p. 22)
Frites Stand
123 Second Ave., Manhattan 10003
Phone (212) 674-1234

Rosario's Pizza

(see p. 17)
Pizzeria
**173 Orchard St., Manhattan
10002**
Phone (212) 777-9813

Saint's Alp
Tea House

(see p. 10)
Tea House
39 Third Ave., Manhattan 10003
Phone (212) 598-1890

The Sanctuary

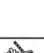

(see p. 100)
Vegetarian/Vegan
25 First Ave., Manhattan 10003
Phone (212) 780-9786

7A

(see p. 46)
Brunch
109 Ave. A, Manhattan 10009
Phone (212) 673-6583

Soba-ya

They say: "No Sushi, No Reservations." We say: Noodles worth the wait.
$$$
229 E. Ninth St., Manhattan 10003
(between Second and Third Aves.)
Phone (212) 533-6966

CATEGORY	Japanese Noodle Shop / Sushi Bar
HOURS	Daily: noon–4 PM, 5:30 PM–10:30 PM
SUBWAY	N, R to Eighth St.; 6 to Astor Pl.
PAYMENT	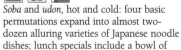
POPULAR FOOD	*Soba* and *udon,* hot and cold: four basic permutations expand into almost two-dozen alluring varieties of Japanese noodle dishes; lunch specials include a bowl of

the aforementioned noodles, along with a
generous assortment of appetizers and
extras—early birds can get to Soba-ya
before 6:30 PM and take advantage of the
dinner special, a similar combo

UNIQUE FOOD	The *kamonan* (noodles with slices of duck) makes the best dinner; it's also one of the most expensive items on the menu; the *shumai* (shrimp dumplings) are a treat
DRINKS	Sake, beer, tea, way-overpriced soda
SEATING	Thirty-five comfortably at tables
AMBIENCE	Simple, elegant, tasteful: wood and back-lit translucent wall paneling give the feel of a far-off place—an extraordinarily trendy hamlet in the Japanese countryside; cool bathrooms (a bidet for the ladies!); frequented by many native Japanese and not a few Village people.

—Joe Cleemann

Spice

(see p. 40)
Modern Thai
114 Second Ave., Manhattan 10003
Phone (212) 988-5348

Tiengarden Vegan and Natural Kitchen

*A place where even a meat-head can go and
leave feeling as though he'd actually eaten something.*
$$
170 Allen St., Manhattan 10002
(between Stanton and Rivington Sts.)
Phone (212) 388-1364

CATEGORY	Chinese Vegan
HOURS	Mon–Sat: noon–4 PM, 5 PM–10 PM
SUBWAY	F, V to Second Ave.
PAYMENT	Cash only
POPULAR FOOD	Everyone drools over the Buddha's Delight—*shiitake* mushroom and mixed vegetable in brown sauce; also recommend the *Seitan* Innovation (braised wheat gluten and veggies in ginger sauce), or the sweet and sour soy nuggets with pineapple and side of mixed rice (brown, red, and wild rice)—sublime
UNIQUE FOOD	What they call "Edible Sculptures" we might call *dim sum,* but after eating it we too will call it Edible Sculpture—the pan-fried seaweed-tofu rolls are most honorable (tofu rolled in *nori* seaweed and bean curd sheets, served with lemon)
DRINKS	Assortment of bottled, all-natural beverages, hot tea
SEATING	Sixteen seats at tables

AMBIENCE	A pristine white, meditative environment—no LSD inspired murals
EXTRAS/NOTES	This is the best vegetarian restaurant in the whole wide world.

—Nemo Librizzi

Veselka

Kielbasa anyone?
Since 1954
$$

144 Second Ave., Manhattan 10003
(corner of E. Ninth St.)
Phone (212) 228-9682

CATEGORY	Ukrainian Diner
HOURS	24/7
SUBWAY	N, R to Eighth St.; 6 to Astor Pl.
PAYMENT	VISA MasterCard AMERICAN
POPULAR FOOD	Amazing chocolate milkshakes, potato pancakes, cheese blintzes, borscht, three bean chili soup, and *pierogies*
UNIQUE FOOD	The vegetarian plate is a good choice if you're looking for something a little different; *kutya,* a traditional Ukrainian pudding made with wheat-berries, raisins, walnuts, poppyseeds, and honey and fresh challah bread, baked daily
DRINKS	Beer, soda, tea, and coffee
SEATING	About 100 people, and in warm weather, outdoor sidewalk seating is available
AMBIENCE	The service is friendly and the traditional, sparsely decorated diner is clean; atmosphere is laid back—perfect for drinking coffee, reading the paper, or meeting friends for brunch
EXTRAS/NOTES	Breakfast specials are served from 7 AM–noon on weekdays and to 4 PM on weekends. Expect an occasional wait for a table, especially for outdoor seating during the warm weather months, but the turnaround is quick and the food is well worth any waiting around you may have to endure. There is a table minimum of $3 a person.

—Shannon Godwin

Viva Herbal

The pizza Ray would make if he were a healthy hippie.
$$$

179 Second Ave., Manhattan 10003
(between E. 11ᵗʰ and E. 12ᵗʰ Sts.)
Phone (212) 420-8801
www.vivaherbalpizzeria.com

CATEGORY	Organic/Vegan/Kosher Dairy Pizzeria
HOURS	Sun–Thurs: 11 AM–11:30 PM Fri/Sat: 11 AM–1 AM

SUBWAY	L to 14th St.
PAYMENT	VISA · MasterCard · AMERICAN
POPULAR FOOD	A range of pizzas, salads, and pastas for any diet: kosher dairy, vegan, or organic; slightly more expensive than the average pizza joint, but you can eat well
UNIQUE FOOD	A wide variety of vegan pizzas on spelt (non-wheat) crusts, heaped high with miso-tofu, veggies, and other colorful, exotic toppings; recommended are Zen (with green tea tofu and pesto) and Ganja (with hempseeds, when available) pies
DRINKS	Natural sodas and juices, regular sodas, and an extensive tea bar with varieties of green and herbal teas
SEATING	Fifteen inside at small tables and a counter, 12 outside at small tables
AMBIENCE	The customers are more yuppie than hippie; the place has a warm, colorful, Californian feel; bright, fanciful, and occasionally psychedelic art by a local painter adorns the walls
EXTRAS/NOTES	Part of a New York backlash against Ray's-style pizza-as-usual places, Viva Herbal was created by owner Tony Iracani to give vegans a pizza place to call their own. If you crave tofu, soy sausage, and macrobiotic *nomato* sauce, this is the place to eat. And even if you're not a vegan, you may be pleasantly surprised by the variety and taste of these creative pizzas. Free delivery.

—*Peter Davis*

Yonah Schimmel Knishery

(see p. 16)

Knishes

137 E. Houston St., Manhattan 10002

Phone (212) 477-2858

> "A Hamburger is warm and
> fragrant and juicy.
> A hamburger is soft and non-threatening.
> It personifies the Great Mother herself who
> has nourished us from the beginning.
> A hamburger is an icon of layered circles,
> the circle being at once the most spiritual
> and the most sensual of shapes.
> A hamburger is companionable and faintly
> erotic. The nipple of the Goddess, the
> bountiful belly-ball of Eve.
> You are what you think you eat."
> —*Tom Robbins*

FLATIRON • GRAMERCY PARK • UNION SQUARE

Bachué
(see p. 98)
Vegetarian
36 W. 21ˢᵗ St., Manhattan 10010
Phone (212) 229-0870

Cosmic Cantina

Late-night, low-fat healthy burritos.
$$$
105 Third Ave., Manhattan 10003
(at 13ᵗʰ St.)
Phone (212) 420-0975

CATEGORY	Mexican Hole-in-the-Wall
HOURS	Daily: 11 AM–5 AM
SUBWAY	L to Third Ave.
PAYMENT	Cash only
POPULAR FOOD	Hearty Tex-Mex-with-a-twist: you can't go wrong with the burritos, particularly the Sarah Burrito with chicken, cheese, tomatoes, pinto beans, hot sauce, salsa, fat free sour cream, and the freshest lettuce in New York; the menu also includes *chimichangas,* chips and nachos, salads, *quesadillas,* and a number of specialty burritos
UNIQUE FOOD	All meals are free of sugar, lard, and chicken stock and are certified organic, making every dish somewhat unique; if you're looking for something even more unusual, try the Macro burrito with a little tofu sour cream
DRINKS	Juice, tea, lemonade, beer, sangria
SEATING	Tables are small with high, barstool-like seating for about 20
AMBIENCE	College students, late-night bar-goers, and locals out for a quick and inexpensive low-fat Tex-Mex fix; staff is laid back but efficient—orders are usually ready in minutes; stop by if you're in a hurry, not if you're looking for a place to sit back and relax
EXTRAS/NOTES	Dishes can be made with fat-free or dairy-free ingredients upon request, so if you're vegan or ultra-healthy, this could be a dining option. If you spend enough money and present a student ID, Cosmic Cantina has been known to offer a $2 discount.

—Shannon Godwin

Year-Round Fresh Goodness: Union Square Greenmarket

Greenmarket, a program of the Council on the Environment of New York City, has been around since 1976 and currently has 27 locations in the five boroughs. The program was started to benefit urban New Yorkers and surrounding farmers as well: We get fresh meat, cheese, and produce in the big city, and the growers have an opportunity to sell their wares and in the process, preserve farmland.

Greenmarket's largest location is Union Square, which is open Monday, Wednesday, Friday, and Saturday all year-round, rain or shine, between the hours of 8 AM and 6 PM. Of the 175 farmers and food producers involved in all of Greenmarket, a whopping 80 attend Union Square market at its summertime peak. Bringing fresh (and where appropriate organic and free-range) fruits, veggies, fish, lamb, beef, dairy products, eggs, honey, maple syrup, baked goods, plants, and even wool products in wintertime, the Union Square Greenmarket is frequented by some of the finest chefs in New York.

Walk through the marketplace on an autumn morning, and grab a hot cider and a fresh berry-filled muffin. When summer rolls around, pick up a cool organic lemonade and a petite basket of heavenly sweet grape tomatoes. Shuffle around during the lunch hour, buy some apples (which seem to be year-round here), some organic, rennet-free, Amish horseradish cheese (it's great even if you're not lacto vegan!), a loaf of fresh bread, and be lucky enough to score a table in the park. Stroll through during the market's last hour (don't cut it too close, though—these guys have long drives ahead of them and understandably, some sellers cut out early), and get discount flower bouquets, half-price muffins, and bags of marked down produce—what a deal, and it's all still fresh! Stop by Greenmarket's own table for recipes and listings of the other metro area markets.

Greenmarket at Union Square is what makes city living, especially New York City living, extra special—we get all the benefits of living in a pulsating metropolis and the best homegrown foods from farms in the surrounding region practically delivered to our doorsteps.

Here are only a small smattering of the growers who haunt Greenmarket at Union Square:

Prospect Hill Orchards sells seasonally cherries, peaches, pears, and apples at Union Square every Monday. They suggest you look for their green umbrellas!

Morehouse Merino, a wool seller, shows up from September through May at Union Square. They take off at 5 PM.

Beth's Farm Kitchen offers jams, chutneys, jellies, sugar-free spreads, and "old fashioned" goodies on Fridays at Union Square.

Beth's is right next to soft and salty **Martin's Pretzels**, which is at Union Square all days year-round.

Deep Mountain brings New Yorkers real Vermont maple syrup and maple candy to Union Square Market Friday and Saturdays from April–June and September–December.

Farmers and food producers change their schedules occasionally, so part of the beauty of this market, in my humble opinion, is the surprises you might find every time you attend. If you find a favorite seller, ask 'em when they'll be back. Greenmarket is a very friendly place.

Flatiron/Gramercy Park/Union Square: E. 17th St. and E. 14th St. (between Broadway and Park Ave.), Manhattan, (212)477-3220. Mon, Wed, Fri/Sat: 8 AM–6 PM. www.cenyc.org (check site for updates).

—*Lindy Settevendemie*

Eisenberg's Sandwich Shop

Depression-era lunch counter proves Old Deals make the Best Meals.
Since 1929
$$
174 Fifth Ave., Manhattan 10010
(at 22nd St.)
Phone (212) 675-5096

CATEGORY	Lunch Counter
HOURS	Mon–Fri: 6 AM–5 PM
	Sat: 7:30 AM–4:30 PM
SUBWAY	N, R to 23rd St.
PAYMENT	Cash only
POPULAR FOOD	Standard fare like burgers and club sandwiches, deli goods like liverwurst, hot pastrami, and turkey and chopped liver, but "if you don't see what you want on the menu, ask us if we can make it for you"
UNIQUE FOOD	You can eat here for under $5, especially if you come for breakfast: variously prepared eggs, bacon, French toast, home fries—nothing's expensive (least of all the coffee: 75¢ at press time)
DRINKS	Coffee, juice, soda (can or fountain), lime rickeys, lemonades, ice cream sodas, fresh milk shakes
SEATING	Seats around 35—most at the long counter, but a few at small tables along the wall

| AMBIENCE | Eisenberg's is an old restaurant in an old room where customers young and old cram in along an old lunch counter: sincere, simple, and, as expected, old-fashioned; can a place this small be a landmark? You wouldn't use it as a navigation aid, but it certainly has its spot marked as far as the neighborhood's history is concerned; old and well-loved, it's as close as any restaurant to the Flatiron Building—which is an undisputed landmark |

—Joe Cleemann

Ess-a-Bagel

(see p. 85)
Bagels
359 First Ave., Manhattan 10010
Phone: (212) 260-2252

Home's Kitchen

Why go to Chinatown when you can eat at Home's?
$$
22 E. 21ˢᵗ St., Manhattan 10010
(between Broadway and Park Ave.)
Phone (212) 475-5049 • Fax (212) 777-1819

CATEGORY	Chinese
HOURS	Mon–Fri: 11 AM–11 PM
	Sat/Sun: noon–11 PM
SUBWAY	N, R to 23ʳᵈ St.
PAYMENT	VISA MasterCard AMERICAN EXPRESS DISCOVER
POPULAR FOOD	Choose anything, especially the *General Tso* (batter-covered and perfectly fried tofu and chicken, drenched in a soy-based sticky spicy tangy sauce, and mixed with baby corn, green peppers, and the occasional carrot—during lunch, comes with bowl of white or brown rice, and choice of soup, soda, or egg roll)
UNIQUE FOOD	Try the wheat gluten sautéed in a ginger and scallion soy-based sauce, mixed with winter bamboo and black mushrooms, atop layers of veggie-ham
DRINKS	Home's Punch (a blend of pineapple juice, lemonade, and ginger ale), Home Made Ice Tea, Home Made Lemonade, virgin piña colada, soda, hot tea
SEATING	Tables for 40
AMBIENCE	Friendly, helpful, and efficient staff—especially during the lunchtime crunch, when the food comes within seconds of ordering

REMEMBER THE NEEDIEST!

EXTRAS/NOTES While the regular menu is decently priced and well within the *Hungry?* budget, flip the menu over and go for the incredible lunch and dinner specials that come with so many extra treats.

—*Marie Estrada*

Java 'n' Jazz

A place to grab a quick bite, meet a friend, or nurse a wonderfully complicated coffee.

$$

868 Broadway, Manhattan 10003
(between 17th and 18th Sts.)
Phone (212) 473-4200
www.java-n-jazz.com

CATEGORY	Coffee House/Sandwich and Salad Shop
HOURS	Mon–Thurs: 6:30 AM–10:30 PM Fri: 6:30 AM–midnight Sat: 7:30 AM–midnight Sun: 8 AM–10:30 PM
SUBWAY	L, N, R, Q, W, 4, 5, 6 to Union Sq.
PAYMENT	VISA MasterCard AMERICAN
POPULAR FOOD	Known for its pricey but terrific coffees and teas, Java 'n' Jazz has surprisingly affordable food, including a wide variety of sandwiches and huge, rich desserts—the banana cream pie is especially good, or go for a more austere but no less delicious peanut butter cookie with a rich, frothy hot chocolate
UNIQUE FOOD	Although choose-your-ingredients-and-we'll-mix-it salad bars have sprung up all over the city, this one's a stand-out: vegetables are fresh and delicious, selection is varied; after you choose a small or large bowl of *arugula,* spinach, romaine, or organic *mesclun,* grab a list of ingredients and circle as many as you want: fried onions, black beans, roasted sweet peppers and ripe grape tomatoes, soy bacon, *kalamata* olives, tofu, grilled chicken, fresh mozzarella, 19 different dressings, etc.
DRINKS	Dozens of teas and coffees available by the cup or by the pound; chai tea latte (hot or cold), terrific seasonal drinks, such as hot cider and eggnog latte for the fall
SEATING	Tables and chairs; comfy couches and rockers in the back
AMBIENCE	Restful, bright and airy, this is a nice, low-pressure place to start or wind up a date
EXTRAS/NOTES	The art on the walls ranges in quality from inspired to tragically misguided, but it's all for sale. Regular live jazz concerts are sometimes a little amateurish but always atmospheric and entertaining.

—*Joanna Jacobs*

Kabab King of New York

Inventive Mediterranean, Pakistani, and Indian cuisine under one roof? So many options, so little time.

$$

16 E. 23rd St., Manhattan 10010
(between Broadway and Park Ave.)
Phone (212) 475-7575/3005
www.kababking.com

CATEGORY	Mediterranean/Pakistani/Indian
HOURS	Mon–Sat: 7 AM–midnight Sun: 11 AM–midnight
SUBWAY	N, R, 6 to 23rd St.
PAYMENT	VISA [MasterCard] [cards]
POPULAR FOOD	Falafel sandwich with choice of fixings and sauces; *döner* kebab sandwich or platter; shepherd salad sandwich—diced tomatoes, cucumbers, parsley, red onions tossed with oil and vinegar; tandoori chicken
UNIQUE FOOD	Oven-baked on the premises "Turkish Pizza" such as *beyaz peynirli pide*—feta cheese, parsley, and tomatoes on a thin hand-braided crust; *mantarli peynirli pide*—crusty dough stuffed with mushroom, feta cheese, herbs, and spinach; and for lamb lovers, the *lahmacun,* flat bread topped with ground lamb and chopped garden vegetables
DRINKS	Sweet or salty *lassi*—cool Indian yogurt drink, Pakistani-style special tea, coffee, tea, and a self-serve icebox filled with soda
SEATING	About 25 at two-person tables
AMBIENCE	Informal, old-style pizza parlor meets Old World Mediterranean—the staff is very friendly, patient, and helpful even during lunch when Kabab King gets a bit crazy
EXTRAS/NOTES	Head straight to the baker's area in the back, where all of the freshly made Turkish pizzas are displayed on a low counter—two can easily share one. And when you ask for extra red sauce or *tahina*—"extra anything" you better mean it, 'cause these guys are generous!
OTHER ONES	• Ride the 7: 73-01 37 Rd., Queens, 11372, (718) 457-5857 • Ride the 7: 74-15 37 Rd., Queens, 11372, (718) 205-8800

—Marie Estrada

Dawg Fact:

Thirty-six million pounds of hot dogs are sold in New York supermarkets each year, second only to Los Angeles.

Moe's Falafel

Flatiron favorite for Falafel. White sauce?
Hot sauce? You bet.

$

SW corner of 21ˢᵗ St. and Fifth Ave.,
Manhattan 10010

CATEGORY	Falafel Cart
HOURS	Mon–Fri: 10 AM–3 PM (extended summer hours include weekends and evenings)
SUBWAY	N, R to 23ʳᵈ St.
PAYMENT	Cash only
POPULAR FOOD	Great falafel sandwich (on pita) for a song; during lunch rush, meat trays (including rice, lettuce, falafel, and sauce) sell like hotcakes would at some kind of kooky hotcake cart
UNIQUE FOOD	The combination platter gives you a lot of everything (chicken, falafel, and lamb) for about $4
DRINKS	Soda, Snapple, water
SEATING	No seats
AMBIENCE	Enjoy lunch on the streets of the world's greatest city; Moe's is a favorite among cabbies and office workers, and the latter form long lines around lunchtime (cabbies have their own arrangements—no one said life is fair)

—Joe Cleemann

Molly's Pub & Restaurant

Landmark

Sawdust on the floor, rebels on the
wall, Guinness on draught, and terrific pub
food on your plate.

Since 1960

$$$

287 Third Ave. Manhattan 10010
(at 23ʳᵈ St.)
Phone (212) 889-3361

CATEGORY	Irish Pub
HOURS	Daily: 11 AM–4 AM
SUBWAY	6 to 23ʳᵈ Street
PAYMENT	VISA
POPULAR FOOD	Big burgers for hungry workers, idlers, and drinkers; a huge plate of fish and chips may be too much food for the casual eater, but experts will make the extra effort and go home bloated—which isn't the worst thing that can happen
UNIQUE FOOD	The buffalo burger tastes as good as its bovine rival, and probably encourages renewal of America's tragically depleted bison (that's what nerds call buffalo) population—such are the sad ironies of capitalism that one might save an animal by eating it—*bon appétit*

DRINKS	Full bar, water, soda, etc.
SEATING	Seats 50 or so, at tables, in booths, and along the bar
AMBIENCE	Dark paneling; not much light; James Connelly and Co. get the place of honor on the wall—it could be a dump, but it's welcoming instead; draws an eclectic crowd

—Joe Cleemann

Old Town

A down-to-earth, old-fashioned pub, serving New Yorkers since the second Cleveland Administration.

Since 1892

$$$

45 E. 18th St., Manhattan 10010
(between Broadway and Park Ave.)
Phone (212) 529-6732

CATEGORY	Pub
HOURS	Mon–Sat: 11:30 AM–1 AM Sun: noon–11:30 PM
SUBWAY	L, N, R, Q, W, 4, 5, 6 to 14th St./Union Sq.
PAYMENT	VISA MasterCard AMERICAN EXPRESS
POPULAR FOOD	Nothing fancy, but great burgers and sandwiches (chicken caesar, BLT)
UNIQUE FOOD	The daily specials, such as Friday's fish 'n' chips, are basic and irresistible; while not unique, Old Town stands apart from the pack—it's an absolutely delicious grilled dog completely smothered by mounds of perfectly seasoned chili
DRINKS	All the basics plus a large selection of beer from the full bar downstairs
SEATING	Lots of worn, wooden booths and tables over two floors
AMBIENCE	An ancient, weathered pub: slightly crooked staircase leading to the upstairs restaurant, dented tin ceilings, patched-up cushions in the wooden booths; framed photos and signed book jackets on the walls suggest up-and-coming literati have eaten here
EXTRAS/NOTES	Old Town has a reputation for being a popular publishing hangout, among both editors and authors. It's also appeared in the movie *The Last Days of Disco,* and the downstairs bar used to appear in the opening credits to *Late Night with David Letterman.*

—Brad Wood

Dawg Fact:

Did you know that July is National Hot Dog Month?

Pick a Bagel on Third

(see p. 85)
Bagels
297 Third Ave., Manhattan 10010
Phone: (212) 686-1414

Rainbow Falafel

*Cheap, tasty Middle Eastern grub
vegetarians can eat and meat-eaters
can love.*
$
26 E. 17th St., Manhattan 10003
(at Union Sq. West)
Phone (212) 691-8684

CATEGORY	Middle Eastern
HOURS	Mon–Sat: 8 AM–7 PM
SUBWAY	L, N, R, Q, W, 4, 5, 6 to 14th St./ Union Sq.
PAYMENT	Cash only
POPULAR FOOD	There aren't too many items on the menu, but Rainbow is one of New York's favorite spots for falafel—as in falafel sandwich; also chicken *shawarma* sandwich and lentil soup
DRINKS	Soda (try the coconut), iced tea, coffee, tea, Turkish coffee
SEATING	No seating available
AMBIENCE	If you come anywhere near lunch time (noon–2 PM), be prepared to wait outside: the line runs down the block and other lunch spots in the area have started to give away free samples in the hopes of tempting the regulars away
EXTRAS/NOTES	If you are looking for a cheap place to eat (like on the day before payday when you have to scrape together change from the couch), this is the place to hit. The owner, Hamal, took over the space eight years ago from a friend who was running a candy store. He says that the reason Rainbow Falafel is so popular is the healthy vegetarian choices and his grandmother's unique recipe for falafel.

—*Larry Ogrodnek*

Republic (Union Square)

*Poor man's swanky
Pan-Asian: hip, loud, and always jumping.*
$$$
37 Union Sq. West, Manhattan 10003
(between 16th and 17th Sts.)
Phone (212) 627-7168

CATEGORY	Trendy Noodle Joint
HOURS	Sun–Wed: 11:30 AM–11 PM Thurs–Sat: 11:30 AM–midnight

SUBWAY	L, N, R, Q, W, 4, 5, 6 to 14th St./ Union Sq.
PAYMENT	
POPULAR FOOD	Most popular is #23 on the menu—glass noodles with chicken, vegetables, lime juice, and ginger dipping sauce; *pad* Thai, the ubiquitous pan-Asian restaurant offering, comes with a choice of either shrimp and squid or chicken and vegetables; appetizers are fantastic, particularly the grilled calamari, marinated in soy-glaze, scallions, and sesame seeds
UNIQUE FOOD	Chicken *udon* with coconut milk-spinach sauce is a shocking green and very tasty; seared marinated salmon with curried rice and vegetables was cooked perfectly— crisp on the outside, moist and juicy on the inside—its flavor balanced by the plump raisins in the rice and the *daikon* and carrots
DRINKS	Full bar, soda, bottled water, and more exotic choices: Thai iced coffee, green tea, and lemon grass-ginger iced tea, in addition to seasonal fresh juices (carrot, carrot apple, carrot orange, orange, carrot beet, lime lemonade, and watermelon juice)
SEATING	Bar seating for 30, outdoor seating on Union Square, a very limited smoking section, and large picnic-style tables in the back.
AMBIENCE	Style-wise, walks the fine line between trendy and yesterday's news: pale green walls, blond wood tables, black slate bar, simple white ceramic dishes, dim mood lighting, large black and white photos of people with noodles—the scene lets you feel ultra chic, just like the many ultra-hip twentysomethings, but less like the few blue-shirted bankers and older folk mixed in
EXTRAS/NOTES	The motto here is "think noodles," and it's good advice. Most of Republic's dishes are noodle based, mixed with unique and delectable combinations of very fresh ingredients. The food comes quickly, rushed from the kitchen to your table as soon as it's ready. Beside that, Republic sells a variety of merchandise imprinted with the signature logo of its name in an arc with a red star dotting the i. Long sleeve and short sleeve T-shirts, girl's tank tees, orange fishermen's caps, black baseball caps, etc. Republic offers catering and free delivery.

—Sarah Winkeller

Teriyaki Boy

(see p. 91)
Japanese Fast Food/Sushi
18 Lexington Ave., Fl. 1, Manhattan 10010
Phone (212) 260-4420

Uncle Moe's Burrito & Taco Shop

Strap on the feedbag: these burritos are huge.
$$
14 W. 19th St., Manhattan 10011
(at Fifth Ave.)
Phone (212) 727-9400

CATEGORY	Mexican Eat-in/Take-out/Delivery
HOURS	Mon–Fri: 11:30 AM–9:30 PM
	Sat: noon–7 PM
SUBWAY	N, R to 23rd St.; L, N, R, Q, W, 4, 5, 6 to 14th St./Union Sq.; F, V to 23rd St./14th St.
PAYMENT	Cash only
POPULAR FOOD	The Uncle Moe's burrito (meat or vegetable filling with cheese and *pico de gallo*) is a favorite; appetizers like the *quesadilla,* the super *quesadilla,* and the super nachos are meals unto themselves; platters give you rice, beans, *pico de gallo,* and whatever else you're willing to pay for
UNIQUE FOOD	Have some yarbles—if you got any yarbles, that is—dig deep, loosen your belt, and order the California Burrito (two fillings, guacamole, *pico de gallo,* cheese, lettuce, and sour cream or non-fat yogurt, the SUV of burritos); or opt for the Watsonville, "a smaller version of the California Burrito"
DRINKS	Lemonade, juice, soda; or bring your own bottle
SEATING	Seats around 50
AMBIENCE	As the hours tend to suggest, Uncle Moe is targeting (and nailing) office workers; but he's on the border of the Flatiron District and Chelsea, so this isn't the really stiff kind of office worker: it's the fun kind— the kind that sees the humor in Dilbert
EXTRAS/NOTES	The Park Slope digs are more laid back, cool. Whereas the Flatiron location is adorned with photos of southwestern taco joints, Brooklyn opens up space for psychedelic rock concert posters. And it has longer hours, especially on the weekends (Sun–Thurs noon–10 PM, Fri/Sat noon–11 PM). *And* it sells beer.
OTHER ONES	• Around Prospect Park: 341 Seventh Ave., Brooklyn, 11215, (718) 965-0006

—Joe Cleemann

Union Square Greenmarket

(see p. 70)
Market
E. 17th St. and E. 14th St., Manhattan 10031
Phone (212) 477-3220

Zen Palate

(see p. 102)
Pan-Asian/Vegetarian
34 Union Square East, Manhattan 10003
Phone (212) 614-9291

MIDTOWN WEST

B. Frites

(see p. 22)
Belgian Fries
1657 Broadway, Manhattan 10019
Phone (212) 767-0858

Baluchi's Indian Food

(see p. 176)
Northern Indian
240 W. 56th St., Manhattan 10019
Phone (212) 397-0707

Burritoville

(see p. 31)
Mexican
352 W. 39th St., Manhattan 10018
Phone (212) 563-9088
and
625 Ninth Ave., Manhattan 10036
Phone (212) 333-5352

Cho Dang Gol

*Tofu dishes that won't impugn
one's manhood.*
$$$$
55 W. 35th Street, Manhattan 10001
(at Sixth Ave.)
Phone (212) 695-8222

CATEGORY	Korean
HOURS	Daily: 11:30 AM–10:30 PM
SUBWAY	B, D, F, V, N, R, Q, W to 34th St./ Herald Sq.
PAYMENT	
POPULAR FOOD	Free appetizers (small bowls of fish, *kimchi*, etc.), all very good; the first ten items under "Main Dishes" stay just within budget range: these include heaping

flavorful Korean casseroles, some with meat, and nearly all of which incorporate Cho Dang Sol's signature ingredient, delicious hand rolled tofu; the "large" is large enough for two; come at lunchtime and find these same dishes at a discount

UNIQUE FOOD The aforementioned hand rolled tofu finds its way into many of the dishes and tastes good even for those who consider tofu subversive; if you have the financing, try one of the pan-fried specialties: they arrive on very hot stone plates, many accompanied by leafy vegetables and sauce (special, seasoned, etc.)—eat as you would *moo shu* pork at a Chinese restaurant

DRINKS Tea, soda, wine, beer (Korean and domestic), Korean liquor, sake, Korean rice wine

SEATING Seats about 60 at the *maru* and at conventional tables

AMBIENCE Fine woodworking buttresses the platform upon which the *maru*—a very low table (you can sit there if you're willing)—rests; clientele includes many Koreans and plenty of everyone else (Cho Dang Gol is a block from the Empire State Building)

—*Mayu Kanno*

Crêpe Café

(see p. 24)
Crêpe Cart
W. 53rd St. (between Fifth and Sixth Aves.),
Manhattan 10019

Dakshin

Flavorful Indian food, intimate atmosphere.
$$$
741 Ninth Ave., Manhattan 10028
(corner of W. 50th St.)
Phone (212) 757-4545
www.dakshin.info

CATEGORY Indian

HOURS Mon–Thurs: noon–3 PM, 5 PM–10:30 PM
Fri/Sat: noon–3 PM, 5 PM–11 PM
Sun: noon–3 PM, 5 PM–10 PM

SUBWAY C, E to 50th St.

PAYMENT

POPULAR FOOD Chicken *mangalorean* fry (a stir-fried chicken entrée with green peppers and chilies) is almost too flavorful for the faint of tongue—order it mild if you're worried; chicken *chettinad* (a more sedate semi-dry chicken served with crushed black pepper); basmati rice (served with fresh peas); *naan* is served warm and is firmly textured and sprinkled with parsley; the mango lassi is sweet, but is served in a size that disappears too quickly

UNIQUE FOOD   The Jhinga Jaltoori appetizer (sautéed shrimp and vegetables served with sliced *naan*) is a delicious beginning for two diners, though you might have trouble making out the shrimp amid the sauce; for the vegetarians, a good choice is the Hyderabadi Baghare (rich eggplant in mild coconut sauce)

DRINKS   Full bar, Indian beer, *lassi*

SEATING   Table seating for 50

AMBIENCE   The dining room is open yet intimate, too dim to read the menu (think candlelight without the candles); neighborhood residents—treating themselves and guests to a quality meal—make up the majority of patrons; they're joined by a fair number of Indians, which is a pretty fair testimonial

EXTRAS/NOTES   The lunch menu is discounted considerably (enough to put Dakshin in the $$ or $$$ range!), and an all-you-can-eat lunch buffet includes chicken and lamb. Take-out will save you a bundle on service and extras. Free delivery. Coupons sometimes available on Dakshin's comprehensive web site.

OTHER ONES   • Upper East Side: 1713 First Ave., Manhattan, 10128, (212) 421-1919

—Andrew Yang

Famous Famiglia

(see p. 109)
Pizzeria
686 Eighth Ave., Manhattan 10036
Phone (212) 382-3030
and
1630 Broadway, Manhattan 10019
Phone (212) 489-7584

Gourmet Wok

Very cheap Chinese—we're talking dinner for less than five bucks.
$
597 10th Ave., Manhattan 10036
(at W. 43rd St.)
Phone (212) 947-6808

CATEGORY   Chinese

HOURS   Mon–Thurs: 11 AM–11 PM
Fri/Sat: 11 AM–midnight
Sun: noon–11 PM

SUBWAY	A, C, E to 42nd St.
PAYMENT	Cash only
POPULAR FOOD	A pint of Hunan shrimp contains six (count 'em, six) fresh jumbo shrimp with broccoli, baby corn, peppers, watercress, carrots, and snow peas; expansive menu includes Cantonese-style noodles with shrimp in soup and chicken with *udon* (Japanese rice noodles) in curry sauce; chef's specials, served in quarts only, feature popular General Tso's, the Seafood Delight (lobster, scallops, and shrimps with mixed vegetables)
UNIQUE FOOD	Fried chicken wings (worth a little guilt; four at a time or individually), fried half chicken, French fries: the folks at the Gourmet Wok have a fryer, and they're not afraid to use it
DRINKS	Soda and Snapple
SEATING	Six tables for about 20, but most business is carry-out and delivery
AMBIENCE	Very brightly lit; the almost ubiquitous picture of a Chinese waterfall is so enormous that the image is noticeably warped in places; open view of the woks in action; clean, lavender interior helps, but no one is making the trip here to sit down; service known to perk up if you can speak Mandarin or Cantonese, even at a grade-school level
EXTRAS/NOTES	The Gourmet Wok is a Chinese take-out place, like many other run-of-the-mill renditions throughout New York (and elsewhere). But it's a good Chinese take-out place. And it actually prices pints and quarts, making a meal for one more economical than you'd have a right to expect. Food tastes exactly what you think it would taste like, coming from a good Chinese take-out joint, with a measure of freshness that keeps regulars returning. If you're feeling healthy, you can get most dishes steamed, with the sauce served on the side, for an extra 25¢. Stay away from the fried seafood though—it's all breading.

—*Andrew Yang*

H & H Bagels

(see p. 84)
639 W. 46th St., Manhattan 10036
Phone: (212) 595-8000

"Coffee and cigarettes, you know? That's, like, the breakfast of champions.

—*Jim Jarmusch*

How Bagels Made it to New York and How New York Makes Bagels

The bagel was born in the late 17th century in Vienna and given to the King of Poland as a thank you for saving the city from invaders. Sources differ on the origin of the bagel. The shape of the bagel (more oblong in its formative years) was to resemble a stirrup, or *bugel* in German, since horseback riding was the King's favorite hobby (*or* perhaps, because the freed Austrians grabbed hold of the king's stirrups as he galloped by). Sources note that eventually bagels became gifts for women in labor and later as teething rings for their babies—which is apparently still done today!

Whichever the origin, by the 1900s, bagels were in New York, and at first the only people who ate them were those who brought them to us— Eastern European Jews. And bagels were sold in Jewish bakeries to everyone, made of flour, water, yeast, and malt, and neighbors got curious.

Around that time, instead of Americanizing our meals as we were often encouraged to do, we began to venture out of bounds when it came to our taste buds. We tried new things! And as cities began to diversify ethnically, eventually, bagels became available everywhere. In due course, someone decided to slather cream cheese, butter, jelly, whitefish, chopped liver, and even eggs and bacon (!) on these "stirrups from the old country," and voila! You have the New York Bagel.

Note: The best bagels are hand rolled, boiled (which makes it soft and chewy), and then baked to create the semi-tough shell. Each step must be completed precisely to make the ultimate bagel. Ask anybody who makes 'em. They are very serious about the process.

H & H Bagels is arguably the most famous bagelry in New York. They opened in 1972 and were the first to ship bagels to Israel (they finally made it to their homeland!). These are do-it-yourself bagels, leaving you to put your toppings on elsewhere, and their freshness doesn't last more than a day. You can buy homemade Kosher toppings at the store and some drinks are available, but this is literally and simply a bagel store. H & H is very proud of its list of satisfied celebrity customers. To name a few: Bill Clinton, Kevin Bacon, Cher, Tom Hanks, Ann Landers, and Jerry Stiller. H & H ships fresh bagels all over the world, and you can order from their site www.hhbagels.com if you so desire. *Upper West Side: 2239 Broadway (at W. 80th St.), Manhattan,*

10024, (212) 595-8003; Midtown West: 639 W. 46th St. (at 12th Ave.),Manhattan, 10036, (212) 595-8000. H & H is open 24/7. That's right. This is New York.

Next up is **Murray's Bagels**—another NYC favorite. More like a little café, Murray's offers A-1 bagels and many, many terrific varieties of cream cheese (try the sun-dried tomato and roasted garlic). All the smoked fish you could hope for, and great deli sandwiches, served of course, on bagels. Four different soups daily, and famous Guss's Sour Pickles for 40 cents a pop. The bagels are done just right and if you can't get a table inside, there are benches outside (at the Sixth Ave. location). Free delivery for a minimum order of seven bucks. *From Chelsea to West Houston: 500 Sixth Ave. (between 12th and 13th Sts.), Manhattan, 10011, (212) 462-2830; From Chelsea to West Houston: 242 Eighth Ave. (between W. 22nd and W. 23rd Sts.), Manhattan, 10011, (646) 638-1335.*

Pick a Bagel on Third is a nice, big sit-down or take-out, diner-type bagel shop. They've got whatever you want: bagels, appetizers, baked goods, deli meats, salads, catering, espresso, juice and tossed salad bars, etc. The menu notes that bagels are hand-rolled—of course, the mark of a true bagelry. Try the walnut and raisin cream cheese or the chopped liver, just to be authentic. Tons of smoked fish to sample. Free delivery (minimum depends on distance and time of order). *Flatiron/ Gramercy Park/Union Square: 297 Third Ave. (between E. 22nd and E. 23rd Sts.), Manhattan, 10010, (212) 686-1414.*

Last but not least, in what could be an exhaustive listing of bagel places, is **Ess-a-Bagel.** Established in 1976, this fully Kosher shop is small and serves line-order style, and has a few slightly cramped tables. But wait! It's entirely worth the little bit of elbow room you get for their famous bagels. They've got all the fixin's and offer catering too. Go to Ess-a for a taste of authentic New York. (The original) *Flatiron: 359 First Ave. (at E. 21st St.), Manhattan, 10010, (212) 260-2252; Midtown East: 831 Third Ave. (between E. 50th and E. 51st Sts.), Manhattan, 10022, (212) 980-1010.*

These are just some of the stellar bagels in New York. There's not nearly enough space to describe them all. Don't be afraid to do a taste-test of your own—there are plenty of shops to choose from, and who knows, you might just come upon the best chopped liver you've ever tasted.

—*Lindy Settevendemie*

Hale and Hearty Soups

(see p. 125)

Soup Shop

462 Seventh Ave., Manhattan 10018

Phone (212) 971-0605

and

49 W. 42nd St., Manhattan 10036

Phone (212) 575-9090

and

55 W. 56th St., Manhattan 10019

Phone (212) 245-9200

Hallo Berlin

The best wurst for satisfying the worst hunger.

$$$

402 W. 51st St., Manhattan 10019

(at Ninth Ave.)

Phone (212) 541-6248

CATEGORY	German
HOURS	Mon–Sat: 11 AM–10 PM
	Sun: 4 PM–10 PM
SUBWAY	C, E to 50th St.
PAYMENT	VISA MasterCard AMERICAN
POPULAR FOOD	Hallo Berlin specializes in the kind of (admittedly heavy) foods you'd find at a pushcart or a roadside stand in Germany: standards like potato pancakes with applesauce, sauerkraut, cabbage, and potatoes; its fame rides on its sausage: bratwurst, boiled *weinerwurst, currywurst,* and *bockwurst*
UNIQUE FOOD	Sauerbraten is more expensive but comes highly recommended
DRINKS	Beer—German beer, naturally—gets top billing, but wine and soda are also available
SEATING	Tables for 24
AMBIENCE	Loyal customers brave the cramps and the crowds for the food and the drink in Hallo Berlin's popular—and authentically no-frills—dining area
EXTRAS/NOTES	Some gripe that the 51st St. location is cramped. Those wanting to stretch out should consider the more spacious Hallo Berlin Wine and Beer Garden at 626 10th Ave., where an outdoor beer garden beckons during the warmer months. Or, if no walls can confine your restless spirit, get wurst on the go: the Hallo Berlin pushcart (which, by some accounts, started it all) is at the intersection of Fifth Ave. and 54th St.
OTHER ONES	• Midtown West: Hallo Berlin Wine and Beer Hall, 626 10th Ave., Manhattan, 10036, (212) 977-1944

- Midtown West: Hallo Berlin Cart, corner
of 54th St. and Fifth Ave., Manhattan
—*Joe Cleemann*

Island Burgers and Shakes

*Great burgers (and chicken sandwiches), but
it shows in the tab.*

$$$

766 Ninth Ave., Manhattan 10001

(Between W. 51st and W. 52nd Sts.)

Phone (212) 307-7934

CATEGORY	Burger Joint
HOURS	Daily: noon–10:30 PM
SUBWAY	C, E to 50th St.
PAYMENT	Cash only
POPULAR FOOD	Sixty-three types of burgers (and as many *churascos*—grilled chicken sandwiches—in the same varieties), including: the Tijuana (with bacon, jack, guacamole, and onion), Cowboy (barbecue sauce, onion, bacon, cheddar, ranch, sourdough), Slick Willie's (ham, relish, American, bacon, sour cream, barbecue sauce, onion)
UNIQUE FOOD	*Tabouli* salad and Capo San Lucas salad (chips, cheddar, jack, salsa, guacamole, jalapeño, onion, peppers, and tomato), Genoa sandwich (pesto, roasted peppers, mozzarella, tomatoes, onions, *ciabatta*); Island doesn't serve fries—there's no room for a fryer in the facility—instead, there are big baked potatoes, "naked" and with bacon, butter, sour cream, cheddar, and chives
DRINKS	Soda and shakes (malteds, floats, milkshakes)—the Black and White (vanilla milk shake with chocolate sauce) is the most popular; BYOB from the convenience store across the street
SEATING	Seating for about 28 at round tables
AMBIENCE	Colored spheres illuminate primary-colored tables; the dining room is oddly dim given all of the bright red and yellow; paintings and mirrors shaped like surfboards adorn the walls, with some aged, fading advertisements completing the '60s diner mood; young regulars bring guests—every other table seems to have someone telling a newcomer about how great the food is
EXTRAS/NOTES	Portions are very healthy, with the burgers consisting of thick, almost spherical slabs of ground beef, and the *churascos* far heftier than the portion you might think of with the phrase grilled chicken breast—they found some big chickens. Throw in a baked potato and one of the milk shakes, and this place starts to add up. Don't

order takeout: the main appeal to Island is the fresh slab of meat with the ingredients virtually melting into it. The effect is lost unless you get it immediately, made to order and steaming hot.

—Andrew Yang

La Paloma Burritos

Outstanding value Mexican— tasty, cheap, even guilt-free.

$$

359 W. 45th St., Manhattan 10036
(at Ninth Ave.)
Phone (212) 581-3844

CATEGORY	Burrito Joint/Mexican
HOURS	Daily: 11 AM–11 PM (delivery 11:30 AM–10 PM)
SUBWAY	A, C, E to 42nd St.
PAYMENT	VISA MasterCard AMERICAN DISCOVER
POPULAR FOOD	Regulars come for the house special *asada* burrito (flour tortilla filled with charcoal broiled beef or chicken, rice, red or black beans, cheese, sour cream, and guacamole with a side of mild *pico de gallo*); veterans offer rapid-fire specifications that are followed reliably (e.g. chicken *asada* burrito, black beans, no dairy)
UNIQUE FOOD	The Maria Burrito—all of the ingredients of the *asada,* but with steamed chicken as the main ingredient; the loss in flavor hurts, but anyone ordering the Maria Burrito isn't using flavor as their main criterion
DRINKS	Sodas and Snapple, with a few Mexican sodas thrown in
SEATING	Three tables seat about 10
AMBIENCE	Not unpleasant: a bright, clean, modest dining room adorned with Mexican pictures and knickknacks; the staff is quick and efficient—frequented almost exclusively by Hell's Kitchen natives, who are there simply to keep their heads down, eat, and enjoy
EXTRAS/NOTES	An *asada* burrito is nearly excessive for one diner, large enough to satisfy two dainty patrons—not that there are many of those visiting La Paloma. Becomes quite busy during peak take-out times, with the occasional 10 minute wait. Call your order in.

—Andrew Yang

Lakruwana

(see p. 223)
Sri Lankan
358 W. 44th St., Manhattan 10036
Phone (212) 957-4480

Mandoo Bar

Thriving Pan-Asian dumpling house in the heart of K-Town.

$$

2 W. 32nd St., Manhattan 10001
(between Fifth and Sixth Aves.)
Phone (212) 279-3075• Fax (212) 279-3073

CATEGORY	Pan-Asian Dumpling House
HOURS	Daily: 11 AM–11 PM
SUBWAY	B, D, F, V, N, R, Q, W to 34th St./ Herald Sq.
PAYMENT	Cash only
POPULAR FOOD	*Mandoo* (dumplings) come ten per serving, boiled or fried; try the vegetable *mool mandoo* (boiled vegetable dumplings made with bright green spinach dough) or seafood *mandoo* (pumpkin-colored dough filled with shrimp and scallops, and a mix of shallots, and scallions)
UNIQUE FOOD	The steamed *kimchi mandoo* would satisfy any *kimchi* lover's cravings—filled with spicy spicy *kimchi* mixed with a tiny bit of tofu, pork, and vegetables
DRINKS	Korean import beer, Chung-Ha, red house wine, American beer, soda, mineral water
SEATING	Twelve cafeteria-style tables with benches (and individual butt pads) seat 20 comfortably
AMBIENCE	Think Japanese fused with Dutch industrial—long narrow space, warm yellowish tones (plateware and all), polished light wood tables on silver castors, black and white framed photos, and shadow box lighting
EXTRAS/NOTES	From the street, you can watch the dumpling chef create the dumplings. Mandoo receives many thanks from those of us who've just about had it with overly doughy from the freezer Chinese takeout dumplings. And even if you've never thought much of tofu, try the fried tofu with special house sauce—you'll be pleasantly rewarded.

—*Marie Estrada*

Market Café

(see p. 45)
Brunch
496 Ninth Ave., Manhattan 10018
Phone (212) 564-7350

Meskerem

(see p. 51)
Ethiopian
468 W. 47th St., Manhattan 10036
Phone (212) 664-0520

Papaya King

(see p. 111)
Hot Dogs
255 W. 43rd St., Manhattan 10036
Phone (212) 944-4590

Prêt a Manger

(see p. 104)
Sandwich Shop
530 Seventh Ave., Manhattan 10018
Phone (646) 728-0750
and
1350 Sixth Ave., Manhattan 10019
Phone (212) 307-6100

Soup and Smoothie Heaven

Soup too good to be healthy for you.
$
316 Fifth Ave., Manhattan 10001
(between 31st and 32nd Sts.)
Phone (212) 279-5444

CATEGORY	Soup Shop
HOURS	Mon-Fri: 7:30 AM–7 PM
SUBWAY	B, D, F, V, N, R, Q, W to 34th St./ Herald Sq.
PAYMENT	Cash only
POPULAR FOOD	Butternut squash and apple soup (with chunks of vegetables); lobster and crab bisque (with generous morsels of seafood), and cream of broccoli with monterey jack cheese (the cheese will throw you over the edge!)
UNIQUE FOOD	Chicken pot pie stew—just what it sounds like—chicken pot pie made into a stew
DRINKS	Fruit shakes, fruity power smoothies, and fresh squeezed vegetable and fruit juices
SEATING	None
AMBIENCE	Open your closet, hang some fruit and vegetables and there you have it— S&S Heaven
EXTRAS/NOTES	Soup options change every day and come in three sizes—and you get a free banana and a sesame roll with every medium or large order!

—*Marie Estrada*

"New York impressed me tremendously because,
more than any other city in the world,
it is the fullest expression of our modern age."
—*Leon Trotsky*

Teriyaki Boy

You either love or hate this place—
we love it.

$$

106 W. 43rd Street, Manhattan 10036

(at Sixth Ave.)

Phone (212) 764-0200

CATEGORY	Japanese Fast Food/Sushi
HOURS	Mon–Fri: 11 AM–9 PM
	Sat/Sun: 11:30 AM–6 PM
SUBWAY	B, D, F, V to 42nd St.
PAYMENT	Cash only
POPULAR FOOD	Utilitarian sushi joint serves good, simple raw fish and assorted Japanese favorites to the masses: *sashimi* (just the fish), sushi (fish with rice), and the usual lineup of rolls, along with various combinations of meat and rice—pick and choose a suitable combination from the Big Boy-style service island
DRINKS	Tea, soda, assorted Japanese concoctions
SEATING	Seating for about five
AMBIENCE	Simple—what you'd expect for a world-wide fast food chain
EXTRAS/NOTES	There are a handful of locations in Manhattan, and some thrive while others die. Moreover, hours of operation vary with location. So call before you go.
OTHER ONES	• Financial District: 22 Maiden Ln., Manhattan, 10038, (212) 385-8585
	• Flatiron/Gramercy/Union Square: 18 Lexington Ave., Fl. 1, Manhattan, 10010, (212) 260-4420
	• Midtown West: 885 Ninth Ave., Manhattan, 10019, (212) 307-7202
	• Midtown East: 150 E. 46th St., Manhattan, 10017, (212) 867-5771
	• Upper East Side: 1380 First Ave., Manhattan, 10021, (212) 717-0760
	• Upper East Side: 1640 Third Ave., Fl 1, Manhattan, 10128, (212) 987-7150

—*Marie Estrada & Joe Cleemann*

Woorijip

Fresh, home-cooked food and
friendly atmosphere justify the
name woorijip, *which means "our house."*

$$

12 W. 32nd St., Manhattan 10001

(at Fifth Ave.)

Phone (212) 244-1115

CATEGORY	Korean
HOURS	24/7
SUBWAY	B, D, F, V, N, R, Q, W to 34th St./Herald Sq.

PAYMENT	
POPULAR FOOD	If you're looking to sample a variety of Korean dishes, or are just indecisive, the 16-item buffet (pay by the pound) is the ideal starting place: it changes daily, with *kimchi* pancakes, seasoned spinach, and *bul go gi* (marinated beef) among the staples
UNIQUE FOOD	Many varieties of *djuk,* a sweet rice cake treat; fresh *kimchi* is available in several sizes; amazing *miso* soup, packed with tofu and seaweed
DRINKS	Tea, coffee, beer, soda, and imported Korean beverages such *Haitai* (crushed fruit drink)
SEATING	Seats 60–70 at the counter up front and at tables of varying sizes throughout
AMBIENCE	Bright, casual, and lively; cheesy Asian pop music often blares over the speakers
EXTRAS/NOTES	Here's a tip for the buffet: don't weigh your plate down with rice; it's more economical to get a $1 order on the side. In addition to the buffet, there's a noodle bar and a large selection of prepared *ban chan* (side dishes) and *do si lak* (complete meals). Imported packaged snacks, such as crisps and candy, are found up front. So many choices make eating at Woorijip a bit overwhelming, so you'll definitely want to return. If you live or work in the neighborhood, you could easily eat there daily without getting tired of it.

—*Bob Gourley*

MIDTOWN EAST

Better Burger

(see p. 112)
Burgers/Hot Dogs
565 Third Ave., Manhattan 10016
Phone (212) 949-7528

Burritoville

(see p. 31)
Mexican
866 Third Ave., Manhattan 10022
Phone (212) 980-4111

The Comfort Diner

(see p. 44)
Comfort Food
214 E. 45th St., Manhattan 10017
Phone (212) 867-4555

Koreatown:
A Little Bit of Seoul in NYC

The first time you find yourself on 32ⁿᵈ St. between Fifth Ave. and Broadway in the wee hours of the early morning, you'll have happened upon one of New York City's treasures—the heart of Koreatown and its incredible eateries, many of which are open 24 hours every day of the week.

K-Town, as Koreatown is affectionately called by folks who work in and visit this largely commercial neighborhood, is bordered by 31ˢᵗ and 36ᵗʰ Sts. and Fifth Ave. and Broadway, near destinations such as the Empire State Building and Macy's Department Store.

In the 1960s and 1970s, K-Town's 32ⁿᵈ St. consisted of a few wholesale shops and a handful of restaurants. The city never drew up a formal plan or agreement to create a Korean commercial district in Manhattan; most Koreans settled in Queens. But rents were low and foot traffic high because of the nearby office buildings and its proximity to the garment, flower, and gift shop districts. As the shops and restaurants succeeded, more Korean businesses settled in the area. Then the 1965 Immigration Act abolished discriminatory immigration quotas based on national origin, increasing immigration from Korea and soon non-food related Korean businesses opened—such as karaoke places and bars—and by the mid-1980's K-Town was in full swing.

Today, K-Town is a bustling area that boasts travel agencies, accounting offices, law firms, bookstores, video shops, cosmetic and perfume shops, electronic boutiques, bars, karaoke lounges and cafes, and, of course, many, many wonderful restaurants.

With the exception of a few special spots, K-Town dining can strain the wallet, and should be reserved for those naughty but oh-so-necessary nights of splurging. However, on weekdays (and sometimes on Saturday), these same restaurants offer amazing LUNCH SPECIALS, which include many of the same entrees that are served for dinner.

Abb Goo Jung Korean Restaurant is your stop for delicious treats such as *bul go gi* (slices of marinated beef, grilled or barbecued) over rice in a clay pot, broiled eel over rice, "mixed mountain" vegetables with rice, spicy whiting fish casserole, and much more! *Koreatown: 10 W. 32ⁿᵈ St., Manhattan, 10001, (212) 594-4963. Open 24/7. Visa Amex Discover.*

Dae Dong offers diners the choice of prime rib, *bul go gi*, chicken teriyaki, deep fried pork loins, salmon, or shrimp tempura, in a box served with white rice, salad, California rolls, fried dumplings, pan fried noodles, and soup. Lunch specials: Mon–Fri: 11 AM–3 PM. *Koreatown: 17 W. 32nd St., Manhattan, 10001, (212) 967-1900. Mon–Sat: 11 AM–midnight. Visa MC Amex.*

Hahn Ah Reum is a wonderful supermarket that carries Korean and Japanese delicacies alongside seafood and produce. *Koreatown: 25 W. 32nd St. Manhattan, 10001, (212) 695-3283. Daily: 9 AM–midnight. Visa MC Amex Discover.*

Kang Suh Korean/Japanese Restaurant is one of our favorites for big group barbecue dining with 29 options on its lunch special menu, a number of which are vegetarian. Lunch special: Mon–Fri: 11 AM–2:30 PM. *Koreatown: 1250 Broadway, Manhattan, 10001, (212) 564-6845/6846. Open 24/7. Visa MC Amex Discover.*

Kum Gang San is the little sister of the Flushing Queens restaurant, serving both Korean and Japanese dishes. It has been called Western-friendly, and is also one of the top spots for late night eating. Lunch special: Mon–Fri: noon–3 PM. *Koreatown: 49 W. 32nd St., Manhattan, 10001, (212) 967-0909. Open 24/7. Visa MC Amex.*

Mandoo Bar serves freshly made-on-the premises Vietnamese-Korean dumplings. See review p. 89. *Koreatown: 2 W. 32nd St., Manhattan, 10001, (212) 279-3075. Daily: 11 AM–11 PM. Visa MC Amex.*

New York Kom Tang Soot Bul Kal Bi is home of the Gold Box Special Lunch Box. Sushi, tempura, and California rolls are served alongside well-known Korean entrees in the Japanese style bento box. Entrées such as *gal bi gui* (boneless beef), *bul go gi*, and chicken or salmon teriyaki come with salad, deep fried vegetables (onions, squash, potato, and green pepper), and fried rice. Lunch special: Mon–Sat: 11 AM–3 PM. *Koreatown: 32 W. 32nd St., Manhattan, 10001, (212) 947-8482. Open 24/7. Visa MC Amex Discover.*

If you can't decide whether you want to go Korean or Chinese, look no further than **Sang Choon Chinese Restaurant**—famous for it's Korean-style Chinese food. Lunch special: Mon–Fri: 11:30 AM–3 PM. *Koreatown: 30 W. 32nd St., Manhattan, 10001, (212) 629-6450. Daily: 10 AM–10 PM. Cash only.*

Won Jo Korean Restaurant has something for everyone, with over 30 soup, stew, rice, noodle, and sautée dishes, and Korean and Japanese lunch boxes that include California roll, salad, *japchae*, and pan fried dumpling. Lunch special: Mon–Fri: 11:30 AM–3 PM. *Koreatown: 23 W. 32nd St., Manhattan, 10001, (212) 695-5815. Open 24/7. Visa MC Amex.*

If you're looking to sample a variety of Korean dishes, or are just indecisive, the 16-item buffet ($4.99 a pound) at **Woorijip** is the ideal starting place. Woorijip doesn't need to offer lunchtime specials—they're a bargain ALWAYS! See review p. 91. *Koreatown: 12 W. 32ⁿᵈ Street, New York, 10001, (212) 244-1115. Open 24/7. Visa MC Amex Discover.*

Pssst: Ever wonder what all those little side dishes before the meal are called? *Bansan* is the word for side dishes.

So… *Matshikgay moni desey yo!* (Enjoy and eat plenty!)

—*Marie Estrada*

Ess-a-Bagel
(see p. 85)
Bagels
831 Third Ave., Manhattan 10022
Phone: (212) 980-1010

Hale and Hearty Soups
(see p. 125)
Soup Shop
22 E. 47ᵗʰ St., Manhattan 10017
Phone (212) 557-1900

Jaiya
Artful Thai sizzles on Third.
$$$
396 Third Ave., Manhattan 10016
(at E. 28ᵗʰ St.)
Phone (212) 889-1330
www.jaiya.com

CATEGORY	Thai
HOURS	Mon–Fri: 11:30 AM–midnight Sat: noon–midnight Sun: 5 PM–midnight
SUBWAY	6 to 28ᵗʰ St.; N, R to 28ᵗʰ St.
PAYMENT	VISA MasterCard AMERICAN
POPULAR FOOD	Hot basil, fresh chili, Indian, and "jungle" curry—people come here for the nuanced and powerful spices; the Thai-style chicken soup will clear your sinuses, but a tamer palate can enjoy less fiery dishes like the beef with mushrooms and bamboo shoots
UNIQUE FOOD	The menu is vast; some unique features are the Dancing Shrimp (a kind of Thai ceviche) and two variants of frog legs
DRINKS	Full bar
SEATING	Seats 60 at comfortable tables
AMBIENCE	Perfect for late dinners with friends, Jaiya is always crowded with casual diners and busy types angling for take-out

EXTRAS/NOTES	Owners Pok and Wanne started their first Jaiya in Elmhurst in 1978 and didn't stop at opening the Manhattan location. Most recently they started the Jaiya Beauty Salon, a few doors down from the original restaurant, allowing you to get a manicure and *pad* Thai from the same purveyors in a single afternoon.
OTHER ONES	• Ride the 7: 81-11 Broadway, Queens, 11373, (718) 651-1330

—Esti Iturralde

Kalustyan's

*International foods and a
Mediterranean vacation for your
palate.*

Since 1944

$$

123 Lexington Ave., Manhattan 10016

(at E. 29ᵗʰ St.)

Phone (212) 685-3451

www.kalustyans.com

CATEGORY	Mediterranean
HOURS	Mon–Sat: 10 AM–8 PM Sun: 11 AM–7 PM
SUBWAY	6 to 28ᵗʰ St.
PAYMENT	VISA MasterCard
POPULAR FOOD	Falafel, *kibbi* sandwiches, *basturma,* and vegetarian platters
UNIQUE FOOD	According to my veggie friends, this is the best vegetarian soup in the city (it's great if you're a carnivore, too)
DRINKS	Lots of unique sodas from Greece and even the Czech Republic in every flavor from mango to ginger and even milk
SEATING	Four small tables in the front window and one next to the counter
AMBIENCE	Bright and spotless; the take-away counter is upstairs on the second floor: it gets crowds at lunch but they move fast—know what you want or the counter guy will skip you over, moving on to one of the many moms with strollers who frequent the place
EXTRAS/NOTES	Kalustyan's is a gourmet food shop that sells everything Indian and Mediterranean from tea sets to fresh dates, and the lunch counter is part—but not all—of its charm. Take a look at the produce while you're there for a bite, or do so on-line on the web site.

—Michael Connor

REMEMBER THE NEEDIEST!

L'Annam

Quality Vietnamese—without having to fly to Saigon!

$$

393 Third Ave., Manhattan 10016
(corner of E. 28th St.)
Phone (212) 686-5168 • Fax: (212) 686-6552

CATEGORY	Vietnamese
HOURS	Sun–Thurs: 11:30 AM–11:30 PM
	Fri/Sat: 11:30 AM–12:30 AM
SUBWAY	6 to 28th St.
PAYMENT	VISA MasterCard American Express
POPULAR FOOD	Sliced fillet of beef with peanut sauce served with pineapple, cucumber, bean sprouts, tomato, herbs, and roasted peanut with choice of brown, fried, or white rice (take advantage of the lunch special); hot and sour soup with chunks of pineapple, straw mushrooms, celery, green paper, tomato, bean sprouts, roasted peanut, and fresh herbs—choice of fish and shrimp, chicken, shrimp wonton, or vegetables
UNIQUE FOOD	Sugar cane shrimp (shrimp wrapped in sugar cane, served with lettuce, fresh herbs, cucumber, and light sauce); shredded bean curd salad with *nuoc cham* sauce; home-made spicy pickle salad (mustard greens, carrot, cabbage, sesame seed, and plum sauce); sticky rice with coconut and yellow bean
DRINKS	Full bar including imported beer, coconut juice, Vietnamese espresso filter coffee (hot and iced), ginger iced tea, soda, fresh lemonade soda
SEATING	Seats 85–90
AMBIENCE	Everyone comes here—old, young, alone, big groups—and everyone feels comfortable
EXTRAS/NOTES	Unless you go for seafood, you can leave this fabulous joint with a big, satisfied gut for under eight bucks. The sticky rice is a must have—it's got little yellow lentils to give it a wonderful texture (perfect complex proteins, too). The place is pleasant during the weekend, when you may be in the company of the staff, using empty tables to chop mounds of vegetables.

—Marie Estrada

Les Halles

(see p. 23)
Bistro/*Frites*
411 Park Ave., Manhattan 10022
Phone (212) 679-4111

Eating Carni-free in NYC has Never Been so Delightfully Easy...

Most, if not all, restaurants in NYC serve vegetarian dishes alongside meat dishes. But why compromise? Here's a list of terrific completely vegetarian and vegan spots in New York City.

Angelica Kitchen is an entirely vegan and mostly organic restaurant that serves delightful dishes destined to stimulate your tired palate. *East Village: 300 E. 12th St. (between First and Second Aves.), Manhattan, 10003, (212) 228-2909. Daily: 11:30 AM–10:30pm. Cash only.*

Seven days a week the North Indian-inspired **Ayurveda Café** offers lunch and dinner specials featuring a complete meal of appetizers, entrees, and all the fixings including dessert and tea or coffee—lunch is $6.95 and dinner is $10.95. *Upper West Side: 706 Amsterdam Ave. (at W. 94th St.), Manhattan, 10025, (212) 932-2400. Daily 11 AM– 11 PM. Visa MC Amex Discover.*

Bachué serves wondrous dishes—most notably the Sensational Seitan. Everyday specials and special lunch prices. *Flatiron/Gramercy Park/ Union Square: 36 W. 21st St. (between Fifth and Sixth Aves.), Manhattan, 10010, (212) 229-0870. Mon–Fri: 8 AM–9:30PM, Sat: 10 AM–9:30 PM, Sun: 11 AM–6 PM. Visa MC Amex Discover.*

Ahh. . . **Bliss.** With a cheerful glance onto Bedford Ave, you'll know immediately that Bliss doen't just refer to the food. The strip is seasoned with the local warmth of Bedford, as are the strips of tofu, *seitan,* and *tempeh. Williamsburg: 191 Bedford Ave, (between N. Sixth and N. Seventh Sts.), Brooklyn, 11211, (718) 599-2547. Daily: 9 AM–11 PM. Cash only.*

If the vegetarian Italian eatery **Café Viva** were running for president, it would be the Green candidate. See review p. 107. *Upper West Side: 2578 Broadway, (at W. Ninth St.), Manhattan, 10025, (212) 663-VIVA (8482). Daily: 11 AM–11:30 PM. Cash only.*

Candle Café's motto is "Food from farm to table." Try the robust *seitan a la mojo de ajo* (grilled *seitan* in garlic sauce served with yellow rice, daily beans, guacamole, and cilantro tofu sour cream) or the Paradise Casserole (layers of sweet potato, black beans, and millet, surrounded by steamed greens, served with mushroom gravy). See review p. 119. *Upper East Side: 1307 Third Ave., (corner of E. 75th St.), Manhattan, 10021, (212) 472-0970. Mon–Sat: 11:30 AM–10:30 PM, Sun: 11:30 AM– 9:30 PM. Visa MC Amex.*

Expect a warm, pleasant experience at **The Greens,** a Chinese vegan restaurant that serves an amazing Peking-style cutlet made of crispy tofu and served with brown rice and thin pancakes. *Downtown Brooklyn West: 128 Montague St., (near Borough Hall Station), Brooklyn, 11201, (718) 246-1288. Mon–Thurs: 11 AM–10:30 PM, Fri/Sat: 11 AM–11 PM, Sun: 1 PM–10:30 PM. Visa MC.*

House of Vegetarian is one of the oldest Chinese vegan restaurants in New York City. Many dishes to choose from on the interesting menu. *Crossing Delancey/Chinatown: 68 Mott St., (off Canal St.), Manhattan, 10013, (212) 226-6572. Daily: 11 AM–10:30 PM. Cash only.*

A neighborhood hangout with a bar and jukebox, **Kate's Joint** features traditional vegan and vegetarian versions of comfort food. Dig into any one of Kate's hearty soups, or the Southern Fried UnChicken Cutlets, shepherd's pie, or Unturkey Club. *East Village: 58 Ave. B, (between E. Fourth and E. Fifth Sts.), Manhattan, 10009, (212) 777-7059. Sun–Thurs: 9 AM–midnight, Fri/Sat: 9 AM–1 AM. Visa MC Amex.*

Located in Kew Gardens, **Linda's Natural Kitchen** is a largely take-out deli and health food store (with counter seating for five). You'll find wonderful vegan and organic raw foods, casseroles, soups, smoothies, and desserts. *Central Queens: 81-22 Lefferts Blvd., (between 83rd Dr. and Austin St.), Queens, 11415, (718) 847-2233. Mon–Tues: 10 AM–7 PM, Wed: 10 AM–8 PM, Thurs/Fri: 10 AM–7 PM, Sat: 10 AM–6 PM, Sun: 11AM–5 PM. Visa MC Amex Discover.*

Lucky's Juice Joint lives up to its name with lots of different juice and shakes from which to choose. This deli/take-out/juice bar also offers specially prepared mostly vegan sandwiches, salads, soups, and even vegan jumbo hotdogs! Hours extended during summer and spring. *Downtown Fancy: 75 W. Houston St., (off W. Broadway), 10012, (212) 388-0300. Mon–Sat: 9 AM–6:30 PM, Sun: 10 AM–6:30 PM. Cash only.*

We love **Madras Mahal** and you will too after experiencing the all-you-can-eat lunch buffet for just $6.95! *Midtown East: 104 Lexington Ave., (between E. 27th and E. 28th Sts.), Manhattan, 10016, (212) 684-4010. Mon–Fri: 11:30 AM–3 PM, 5 PM–10 PM; Sat/Sun: noon–10 PM. Visa MC Amex Discover.*

Mavalli Palace features southern Indian cuisine—many items can be made vegan. The friendly and accomodating staff will abstain from using *ghee* or yogurt upon your request. *Midtown East: 46 E. 29th St., (between Park and Madison Aves.), Manhattan, 10016, (212) 679-5535. Tues–Sun: noon–3 PM, 5 PM–10 PM. Visa MC Amex.*

Mei-Ju Vege Gourmet is a $3.50 per pound Chinese buffet. Need we say more? See review p. 13. *Crossing Delancey (Chinatown):* 154 Mott St., *(between Broome and Grand Sts.), Manhattan, 10013,* (646) 613-0643. *Daily: 8 AM–8 PM. Cash only.*

Lunch is the meal of the day at **The Organic Grill,** a relaxing vegan-friendly vegetarian restaurant with tasty offering such as barbecue *seitan,* tofu *masala,* and grilled tofu sandwiches. *East Village:* 123 First Ave., *(at St. Mark's Pl.), Manhattan, 10003,* (212) 477-7171. *Mon–Thurs: 11 AM–10 PM, Fri: 11 AM–11 PM, Sat: 10 AM–11 PM, Sun: 10 AM–10 PM. Visa MC Amex Discover.*

Sacred Chow is a mostly organic café/bakery that serves some of the best vegan delicacies in town—but watch out for honey (always ask the counter person). Among the best choices are the truffles and pizza. *Around Washington Square Park:* 522 Hudson St., *(between Charles St. and W. Tenth St.), Manhattan, 10014,* (212) 337-0863. *Mon–Fri: 7:30 AM–9:30 PM, Sat/Sun: 8:30 AM–9:30 PM. Cash only.*

The Sanctuary is a vegan heaven indeed. Indulge in the mix of ethnic fare from soups, fake meat, salads, and more—try the *aloo gobi* and tofu vegan cheesecake. *East Village:* 25 First Ave., *(between E. First and E. Second Sts.), Manhattan, 10003,* (212) 780-9786. *Tue/Wed: 11:30 AM–9 PM, Thurs–Sat: 11:30 AM–10 PM, Sun: 11:30 AM–8:45 PM. Visa MC Amex Discover.*

Caribbean Vegetarian with vegan options is the rule at **Strictly Roots.** "We serve nothing that crawls, swims, walks, or flies." See review p. 140. *The Harlems:* 2058 Adam Clayton Blvd., *(between W. 122nd and W. 123rd Sts.), Manhattan, 10027,* (212) 864-8699. *Daily: noon–9 PM. Cash only.*

Tiengarden is a Chinese vegan eatery where even a meat-head can go and leave feeling as though he'd actually eaten something. See review p. 66. *East Village:* 170 Allen St., *(between Stanton and Rivington Sts.), Manhattan, 10002,* (212) 388-1364. *Mon–Sat: noon–4 PM, 5 PM–10 PM. Cash only.*

Uptown Juice Bar serves truly inventive vegetarian fare that'll convert even the staunchest carnivore. See review p. 142. *The Harlems:* 54 W. 125th St., *(between Fifth and Lenox Aves.), Manhattan, 10027,* (212) 987-2660/9501. *Daily: 8 AM–10 PM. Cash only.*

Veg-City Diner serves up "meat" and potatoes—and vegetarians don't have to hold the meat. See review p. 41. *From Chelsea to West Houston:* 55 W. 14th St., *(between Fifth and Sixth Aves.), Manhattan, 10027,* (212) 490-6266. *Daily: 10 AM–4 AM. Visa MC Amex Discover.*

Vegecyber is a wonderful vegetarian Chinese health food and frozen gourmet store that has a few cooked items. Have a $3.50 lunch box that comes with a vegetable protein like *seitan* or wheat gluten and a side vegetable—all over rice. Or for dinner, buy a frozen vegetarian salmon or chicken drumstick for about three bucks. Tiny section for reading and eating. *Crossing Delancey/Chinatown: 210 Center St., (between Canal and Grand Sts.), Manhattan, 10013, (212) 625-3980. Daily: 9:30 AM– 7 PM. Visa MC Amex Discover.*

Owned by the folks of House of Vegetarian, **Vegetarian Dim Sum House** specializes in vegetarian/vegan versions of traditional Chinese *dim sum*. The menu consists of pages and pages of dishes ranging between one to five dollars. *Crossing Delancey/Chinatown: 24 Pell St., (between Bowery and Mott St.), Manhattan, 10013, (212) 577-7176. Daily: 10:30 AM–10:30 PM. Cash only.*

Go for lunch or brunch at **Vegetarian Paradise 2 (VP2)**, a Chinese vegan restaurant— so many choices, so little time! *Around Washington Square Park: 144 W. Fourth St., (at Sixth Ave.), Manhattan, 10012, (212) 260-7130. Daily: noon– 10:15 PM (take-out until 10:45 PM). Visa MC Amex Discover.*

Just next door, try the Chinese vegan take-out version of VP2. **Vegetarian Paradise 2 GO (VP2 GO).** *Around Washington Square Park: 140 W. Fourth St., (at Sixth Ave.), Manhattan, 10012. (212) 260-7049. Daily: noon–11 PM (take-out until 10:30 PM). Visa MC Amex Discover.*

The third installment of these Chinese vegan eateries, **Vegetarian Paradise 3 (VP3)**, almost feels and tastes like a different restaurant from its predecessors. Don't expect the same menu, either. The Golden Buddha is recommended. *Crossing Delancey/Chinatown: 33 Mott St., (at Pell St.), Manhattan, 10013, (212) 406-6988. Mon–Thurs: 11 AM–10 PM, Fri–Sun: 11 AM–11 PM. Visa MC.*

Veggie Castle is a true Brooklyn gem. Operating out of a converted White Castle, this Jamaican restaurant offers a rich menu of healthy, creative, colorful vegan meals and baked goods such as "Home of the Veggie Castle Burger." See review p. 213. *Around Prospect Park: 2242 Church Ave., (between Flatbush and Bedford Aves.), Brooklyn, 11226, (718) 703-1275. Daily: 8 AM–11 PM. Cash only.*

Eat well and live well at **Viva Herbal**, a pizzeria with choices for any diet: vegan, kosher dairy, or organic. Don't miss the Zen pizza with green tea tofu and pesto. See review p. 67. *East Village: 179 Second Ave., Manhattan, 10003, (212) 420-8801. Sun–Thurs: 11 AM–11:30 PM, Fri/Sat: 11 AM–1 AM. Visa, MC, Amex.*

Savor Pan-Asian, mostly Chinese and Japanese flavors at **Zen Palate.** If you like faux meat, try the basil vegetarian ham (soy-based vegetarian ham, low-cal Conjex, fresh soy bean, and black mushrooms in a basil sauce, with brown rice and a fried taro spring roll). *Union Square: 34 Union Square East, (corner of 16th St.), Manhattan, 10003, (212) 614-9291. Mon–Sat: 11:30 AM–3 PM, 5:30 PM–10:45 PM; Sun: 5:30 PM–10:45 PM. Visa MC Amex.*

Other Ones:

- *Midtown West: 663 Ninth Ave., (at 46th St.), Manhattan, 10036, (212) 582-1669.*
- *Upper West Side: 2170 Broadway, (between W. 76th and 77th Sts.), Manhattan, 10024, (212) 501-7768.*

—*Rebecca Wendler & Marie Estrada*

Madras Mahal

(see p. 99)
Vegetarian
104 Lexington Ave., Manhattan 10016
Phone (212) 684-4010

Manapaty Milant Corp.

Tiny shop brimming with delicious gourmet fare.
$$
158 E. 39th St., Manhattan 10017
(between Lexington and Third Aves.)
Phone (212) 682-0111 • Fax (212) 697-2276

CATEGORY	Gourmet Take-out/Specialty Foods
HOURS	Mon–Fri: 7 AM–9 PM
	Sat/Sun: 10 AM–9 PM
SUBWAY	4, 5, 6, 7, S to 42nd St./Grand Central
PAYMENT	
POPULAR FOOD	Try the "special" (available every day): heaping servings of any three of their gourmet salads, a "free" cup of soup, and a piece of bread—it's enough food to last you for two meals; *basmati* rice and chicken, smoked tuna with pasta, and bean salad; homemade chicken vegetable soup is tasty and not too salty, or try the soup of the day
UNIQUE FOOD	Gourmet salads, *bococcini* (baby mozzarella) in olive oil with parsley and hot peppers, vegetarian *naan,* crab meat cakes (with onion and fresh herbs), veggie burgers, mini spinach pies (with feta cheese), hummus, *baba ganoush,* half a

lemon roasted chicken and two salads with a cup of soup (offered every night); gourmet sandwiches; *baba ganoush* or hummus with mixed greens and fresh tomato in pita bread; crabmeat cake with fresh tomato, lettuce, and mayonnaise on French bread

DRINKS	Brewed Colombian coffee, herbal and regular tea, juice, and soda
SEATING	Strictly take-out: find a park
AMBIENCE	Staff is friendly, and incredibly efficient: you barely have to nod in the direction of a salad before it's in a container, wrapped, and ready to go, while the guy at the cash register looks at your wallet expectantly
EXTRAS/NOTES	Milant's menu claims it has the lowest prices in New York on cheese, coffee beans, olive oils, and smoked salmon, as well as the best prices on baguettes, French, semolina, or whole wheat. The sheer quantity and variety of options is overwhelming. You won't be able to linger too long over making up your mind if you come here when it's crowded—Milant has standing room for at most five people, and you'll get to know them all extremely well by the time you're done ordering.

—Sarah Winkeller

Mavalli Palace

(see p. 99)
Vegetarian
46 E. 29th St., Manhattan 10016
Phone (212) 679-5535

Mishima

The red lantern marks the spot of this Japanese standout.
$$$
164 Lexington Ave., Manhattan 10016
(at E. 30th St.)
Phone (212) 532-9596 • Fax (212) 448-0171

CATEGORY	Japanese/Sushi
HOURS	Mon–Thurs: noon–2:45 PM, 5:30 PM–10:45 PM Fri: noon–2:45 PM, 5:30 PM–11pm Sat: 5 PM–11 PM Sun: 5 PM–10:30 PM
SUBWAY	6 to 28th St.; N, R to 28th St.
PAYMENT	
POPULAR FOOD	Individual rolls start at hard-to-beat prices (just over $2) and are known for their remarkable freshness
UNIQUE FOOD	Regulars rave about the soft-shell crab roll
DRINKS	Beer, wine, and sake
SEATING	Seats 60 at tables and bar, mostly upstairs
AMBIENCE	This high-value sushi joint has finally added a second floor, making the most of

the crowds it usually draws; the expansion
brought in glossy new tables and décor,
an improvement on the formerly cramped
and somewhat drab restaurant

—*Esti Iturralde*

Prêt a Manger

*Marge Simpson once said "Honey, we can't
afford to shop at any store that has its own
philosophy." The sandwich bargains at this New Age
British Import prove her wrong.*

$$

287 Madison Ave., Manhattan 10017
(between E. 40th and E. 41st Sts.)
Phone (212) 867-0400
www.pretamanger.com

CATEGORY	Sandwich Shop
HOURS	Mon–Fri: 7 AM–5 PM
SUBWAY	S, 4, 5, 6, 7 to 42nd St./Grand Central
PAYMENT	Cash only
POPULAR FOOD	Brie, basil, and fresh tomato on a baguette, super slub, Big BLT, roasted peppers and parmesan cheese wrap, lemon cake
UNIQUE FOOD	Double cheddar sandwich sauced with fruit and onion chutney (made with balsamic—not the cheap stuff—vinegar and stewed for hours); Thai chicken miracle mayo sandwich made with coconut and shrimp
DRINKS	100% natural fresh squeezed vegetable and fruit juices, yogurt drinks and fruit "blends" or smoothies, cappuccino, latte, mocha
SEATING	Upwards of a 100
AMBIENCE	Starbucks meets Ikea meets the new breed of spa-like trendy *au natural* sandwich shop you'll find downtown; Midtown's lunch gang shows up in force to take advantage of tasty, interesting, and surprisingly affordable handmade sandwiches, wraps, sushi, and baked goods made ready quickly
EXTRAS/NOTES	If you're a *Babe* fan, or a concerned meat eater, know that Prêt ham comes from pigs that have been reared outdoors on a vegetarian diet and that Prêt uses only fresh, high quality ingredients.
OTHER ONES	• Financial District: 60 Broad St., Manhattan, 10004, (212) 825-8825
	• Midtown West: 530 Seventh Ave., Manhattan, 10018, (646) 728-0750
	• Midtown West: 1350 Sixth Ave., Manhattan, 10019, (212) 307-6100
	• Midtown East:6 E. 46th St., Manhattan, 10017, (212) 661-9414

—*Joe Cleemann & Marie Estrada*

Pretzel, Hot Dog, and Sausage Cart

Pretzel or hot dog on the go?
Mohamed's your man.

$

Northeast corner of 41ˢᵗ St. and Third Ave.,
Manhattan 10017

CATEGORY	Cart
HOURS	Mon–Fri: 11/11:30 AM–6 PM (summer) Mon–Fri: 11/11:30 AM–4:30 PM (winter)
SUBWAY	4, 5, 6, 7, S to 42ⁿᵈ St./Grand Central
PAYMENT	Cash only
POPULAR FOOD	There are three items on the menu, and you could buy all three (plus a drink or two) for less than $10: the extra-large pretzels are crispy and golden brown on the outside, soft, warm, and doughy on the inside, and have the perfect amount of salt; you can also get a good, solid hot dog, or a nice thick Golden-D sausage
DRINKS	Soda (Pepsi, Diet Pepsi, Coke, Diet Coke, Lipton Iced Tea), Snapple
AMBIENCE	Two red and yellow umbrellas, a stack of large, plump pretzels, and a menu written in six-inch high mustard yellow letters are enough to get any hungry passerby to whip out his wallet. . .and many business people do, eating for $3 or $4
EXTRAS/NOTES	Vendor Mohamed has been working this corner for four and half years. Before that, he was at 34ᵗʰ and 5ᵗʰ for seven years. No one can say the food's unique, but who goes to a hot dog and pretzel cart looking for innovation? Besides, there's nothing quite like holding a warm New York pretzel in your mittened hand on a nippy fall afternoon.

—Sarah Winkeller

Soup & Smoothie Heaven

(see p. 90)
Sandwiches
316 Fifth Ave., Manhattan 10001
Phone (212) 279-5444

Teriyaki Boy

(see p. 91)
Japanese Fast Food/Sushi
150 E. 46ᵗʰ St., Manhattan 10017
Phone (212) 867-5771

"Sharing food with another human being is an
intimate act that should not be indulged in lightly."
--M.F.K. Fisher

UPPER WEST SIDE

Ayurveda Café

(see p. 98)
Vegetarian/Indian
706 Amsterdam Ave., Manhattan 10025
Phone (212) 932-2400

Awash Ethiopian Restaurant

*Refined East African so good you
have to remind yourself to breath and chew.*
$$$
947 Amsterdam Ave., Manhattan 10025
(at W. 107th St.)
Phone (212) 961-1416

CATEGORY	Ethiopian
HOURS	Mon–Fri: 1 PM–midnight
	Sat/Sun: noon–midnight
SUBWAY	1 to 103rd or 110th St.; 2, 3 to 96th St.
PAYMENT	VISA MasterCard AMERICAN
POPULAR FOOD	Both veg and non-veg folks swear by the vegetarian combo which includes all vegetable dishes and salad: *key sir alicha* (red beets, carrots, and potato in a sweet sauce), string beans and carrots in spicy garlic sauce, *gomen* (collard greens, onions, garlic, green peppers), *yemsir kik wat* (split red lentils in *berbere*—hot red pepper—sauce), *shiro* (ground chick peas, chopped onion, tomato), *yater kik alicha* (split peas, onions, green peppers, herbs); also popular is the Awash Special, which includes Awash *Tibs* (spiced beef, charcoal broiled), *kitfo* (steak tartar, chopped and seasoned with *kibbe*—herbed butter) and *mitmita* (very hot pepper), and choice of three vegetable dishes
UNIQUE FOOD	*Gored gored* (raw beef cubes in *berbere* sauce with butter)
DRINKS	Full bar stocked with *Tej* (honey wine), domestic, imported, and African beer such as St. George, Morechamp, and Addis; spiced hot tea, iced tea, coffee, espresso, and cappuccino (hot or iced)
SEATING	Sixty at tables, three at bar counter
AMBIENCE	Ethiopians, locals, and academics happily feasting in an open yet cozy and elegant setting that's as perfect for a romantic date as for large groups; graceful owner Boge commissioned a famous Ethiopian artist to paint all of the oil paintings on the walls, including one of the Four Lost Kings of Ethiopia

EXTRAS/NOTES   *Injera* (soured spongy flatbread) serves as food, plate, and utensil. Unless a ridiculously big eater is among your party, most entrées and combinations can easily feed two.

—Marie Estrada

Baluchi's Indian Food

(see p. 176)
Northern Indian
283 Columbus Ave., Manhattan 10023
Phone (212) 579-3900

Burritoville

(see p. 31)
Mexican
166 W. 72ⁿᵈ St., Manhattan 10023
Phone (212) 580-7700
and
451 Amsterdam Ave., Manhattan 10024
Phone (212) 787-8181

Café Viva

If Café Viva was running for president, it would be the Green candidate.

$$
2578 Broadway, Manhattan 10025
(at W. Ninth St.)
Phone (212) 663-VIVA

CATEGORY	Pizzeria
HOURS	Daily: 11 AM–11:30 PM
SUBWAY	1, 2, 3 to 96ᵗʰ St.
PAYMENT	Cash only
POPULAR FOOD	Regular slice and Sicilian
UNIQUE FOOD	Whole wheat dairy-free lasagna (with soy cheese and organic tomato sauce)
DRINKS	Soda (including china cola and ginger brew), juices, teas, no alcohol
SEATING	Six tables of four; outdoor seating for 32 in the summer
AMBIENCE	Casual, families, neighborhood atmosphere—great for a quick bite before heading to Symphony Space
EXTRAS/NOTES	The menu of this friendly and delicious Upper West Side take-out and dine-in Italian eatery proudly proclaims KOSHER DAIRY and below this, NATURALLY ITALIAN. Not only can every pizza be ordered with either regular, wheat, corn meal, or spelt crust, but Café Viva also offers healthy dishes like artichoke lasagna and organic tofu spinach ravioli. However, even though this may sound like a bad

outtake from Woody Allen's send-up of California cuisine in *Annie Hall*, everything at Café Viva is as tasty as it is good for you, not to mention cheap. Macro health and flavor for micro budgets; wide menu for vegetarians, including unbleached flour and no preservatives. Be sure to try the amazingly tasty garlic bread, or have a salad served with knotty, homemade croutons.

—*Jeff Gomez*

EJ's Luncheonette

(see p. 124)
Diner
447 Amsterdam Ave., Manhattan 10024
Phone (212) 873-3444

El Malecón

(see p. 146)
Dominican
464 Amsterdam Ave., Manhattan 10024
Phone (212) 864-5648

El Rey de la Caridad Restaurant

Beans and rice with a twist of bachata, merengue, salsa, boleros, and Marc Anthony.
$$
973 Amsterdam Ave., Manhattan 10025
(at W. 108th St.)
Phone (212) 222-7383/2107 • Fax (646) 698-6560

CATEGORY	Dominican
HOURS	Daily: 8 AM–11 PM
SUBWAY	1 to 103rd or 110th St.
PAYMENT	VISA [cards]
POPULAR FOOD	Yellow rice flecked with onion and green pepper with a bowl of red beans—*arroz y habichuelas rojas; carne guisada* (beef stew), *carne asada* (roasted beef), and *maduros* (sweet plantains fried in butter)
UNIQUE FOOD	Traditional soups include cow feet, hen, pig ears, tripe, soupy squid with rice; octopus salad, octopus stew, octopus in garlic sauce, goat stew, *mofongo* (mashed fried green plantain with pork)
DRINKS	*Café con leche,* beer, soda, juices (orange; carrot; orange and milk; orange, carrot, and milk; oats), lemonade, soda, malts, and shakes (papaya, *mamey,* pineapple, banana, oats and milk, wheat, passion fruit)
SEATING	Plenty of tables for about 20, and seven at the counter
AMBIENCE	Casual and homey atmosphere of families, cabbies, neighborhoodies, and the occasional Columbia student

EXTRAS/NOTES　Communicating your order can be a bit tricky as a majority of the staff speaks only a little English. Another hint: It'll be tough, but try not to stuff yourself silly with the toasted buttered bread that comes before every meal as the portions here are huge—expect to leave with a doggie bag, distended gut, and the satisfied glow that comes with good food at good prices. Lunch special served every day of the week until 4 PM. Free delivery with no minimum.

—Marie Estrada

Empire Szechuan

(see p. 151)
Chinese/Pan-Asian
2574 Broadway, Manhattan 10025
Phone (212) 663-6006

Fairway Market and Café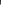

(see p. 131)
Market/Café
2127 Broadway, Manhattan 10023
Phone (212) 595-1888

Famous Famiglia

Comfortable and tasty New York semi-chain pizza joint.

$

734 Amsterdam Ave., Manhattan 10025
(at W. 96th St.)
Phone (212) 864-7193
www.famousfamiglia.com

CATEGORY	Pizzeria
HOURS	Daily: 10 AM–1 AM
SUBWAY	1, 2, 3 to 96th St.
PAYMENT	Cash only
POPULAR FOOD	Cheese and Sicilian slices
UNIQUE FOOD	Garlic knots
DRINKS	Sodas and some juices, teas
SEATING	Seats about 30 in six booths where four people can sit, four booths for two
AMBIENCE	Casual, neighborhood atmosphere draws families alongside the usual pizza-nos
EXTRAS/NOTES	Even though the city is overrun with hundreds of pizza joints, including more than a few with the word "Famous" as part of their title (including a branch of the Ray's pizza dynasty which are known variously as Ray's Famous, Ray's Original, and Ray's Famous Original), the small Famous Famiglia chain manages to live up to the name by offering some of the best slices and whole pies anywhere. Each location is clean and staffed by friendly red-shirted guys with Italian accents who

routinely call customers "Boss" or "Chief" and have been reputed to knock a nickel or dime off the price, rounding down to the nearest dollar. Customers dine in on pasta just as often as they get a slice to go on a paper plate (eating half of it before they're out the door). In the summer they have an Italian ice cart outside, and throughout the week men and women stop in late at night for a snack on their way home from dates or a night out. Always bustling, Famous Famiglia is a neighborhood—and New York— institution. Other Famous Famiglias at Newark Airport, Terminals A and C, and, mysteriously, in Ann Arbor, MI.

OTHERONES
- From Chelsea to West Houston: 61 Chelsea Piers, Manhattan, 10011, (212) 803-5552
- Midtown West: 686 Eighth Ave., Manhattan, 10036, (212) 382-3030
- Midtown West: 1630 Broadway, Manhattan, 10019, (212) 489-7584
- Upper West Side: 734 Amsterdam Ave., Manhattan, 10025, (212) 749-1111
- Upper West Side: 2859 Broadway, Manhattan, 10025, (212) 865-1234
- Upper East Side: 1284 First Ave., Manhattan, 10021, (212) 288-1616
- Upper East Side: 1398 Madison Ave., Manhattan, 10029, (212) 996-9797
- Way Uptown: 4007 Broadway, Manhattan, 10032, (212) 927-3333

—*Jeff Gomez*

Gray's Papaya

(see p. 111)
Hot Dogs
2090 Broadway, Fl. 1, Manhattan 10023
Phone (212) 799-0243
and
402 W. Eighth St., Manhattan 10001
Phone (212) 260-3532

Harry's Burritos
(see p. 48)
Mexican Cantina
241 Columbus Ave., Manhattan 10023
Phone (212) 580-9494

H & H Bagels

(see p. 84)
Bagels
2239 Broadway, Manhattan 10024
Phone: (212) 595-8003

Are You Ready for a Hot Beef Injection?

The frank truth about New Yorkers and their beloved hot dogs…

Everyone wants a piece of hot dog fame. The *dachshund* sausage (German for "little dog") was invented in Frankfurt, Germany in 1484. Both Vienna, Austria and Coburg, Germany have laid counterclaims to the hot dog's antecedents. Whichever dog whelped it, the sausage was first served on a roll in the 1860s, and sold from a German immigrant's cart in Manhattan's Bowery— making it a New York specialty.

The origin of the name "hot dog" is still debated. Some claim that Yale students coined it to describe the sausages sold off of wagons by their dorms. Others say the name first appeared when used by an entrepreneurial vendor during one cold April baseball game at the Polo Grounds in 1901. Sports cartoonist Tad Dorgan supposedly portrayed the catchy name in his next illustration, after which the tasty (and cheap) snack reached instant and permanent fame. However, a copy of the fateful cartoon has yet to be found.

In New York, you usually can't go wrong with a dog from a street cart. It's the perfect filling snack for anyone on the run to her next appointment, or chronically strapped for cash. Stands serving **Sarbrett** and **Hebrew National** dogs usually charge between $1 and $2 (mustard and relish optional) and they're everywhere. But a number of permanent joints (even restaurants) serve both the classic dog and interesting variations of it.

Several bear a strange affiliation to fruit—the papaya. But why a papaya? The answer dates back to 1923, when a 16-year-old Greek immigrant named Gus Poulos arrived at Ellis Island. Finding fame and fortune in his new home, he amassed enough money to buy a deli, then took a vacation to Florida. There, he was enamored by the great variety of tropical fruits, and decided to bring a little of the tropics back to Manhattan with him. After a while, his papaya and banana juice concoctions caught on, so he opened up a few juice stores in the area. His German wife introduced the frankfurter into the picture, and the rest is history. In the 1960s his restaurants officially became known as **Papaya King**, and are now probably best known for their grilled dogs. In the same vein is **Gray's Papaya**, which serves the amazing Recession Special (two dogs and a fruit drink for $2.45). Finally, there's **Seventh Avenue Papaya**, which adds burgers and fries into the mix, at unbeatable prices.

On a traditional front, you can't beat **Katz's Delicatessen**, which has been around since 1888, in no small part due to delicious hot dogs. They're a little more expensive, but definitely worth it—again, these are served in their casings and cooked on a grill, with all the basic condiments. Similarly, **Old Town** serves a chili dog that's not to be missed—again with the casing, and this time sliced carefully and smothered in mounds of delicious, not-too-spicy chili. See review p. 76.

For a unique hotdog experience, don't miss **F&B**. It abandons tradition and makes hotdogs into hip, exciting dining (for a little more money). Here you'll find the Danish-style hotdog—the *pølser*—served in its casing (which adds flavor and is none too common nowadays) and garnished with fried onions. See review p.36.

Finally, it's a little out of the way and a little too familiar, but if you happen to be in Coney Island, don't forget to check out the original **Nathan's Famous**. The huge stand is located right on the main strip when you get off the subway, and serves all that Nathan's has to offer, from fish sandwiches to burgers. But it would be wrong to ignore the dogs, served here since 1916. They're what Coney Island is all about.

(Source: web site of the National Hot Dog & Sausage Council, a project of the American Meat Institute—www.hot-dog.org)

—Brad Wood

Just a few places to go for dogs in Manhattan:

- **Better Burger** (for the health-conscious): *Midtown East: 565 Third Ave., Manhattan, 10016, (212) 949-7528. Daily: 11:30 AM–9:30 PM.*

- **Dawgs on Park:** *East Village: 178 E. Seventh St., Manhattan, 10009, (212) 598–0667. Mon–Thurs: 7 AM–11 PM, Fri/Sat: 7 AM–3 AM.*

- **F&B:** *From Chelsea to West Houston: 269 W. 23rd St., Manhattan, 10011, (646) 486-4441. Daily: 11 AM–11 PM.*

- **Gray's Papaya:** *Upper West Side: 2090 Broadway, Fl. 1, Manhattan, 10023, (212) 799-0243. Open 24/7; Upper West Side: 402 W. Eighth St., Manhattan, 10001, (212) 260-3532. Open 24/7.*

- **Hallo Berlin Cart** (see review p. 112)

- **Katz's Delicatessen:** *East Village: 205 E. Houston St., Manhattan, 10013, (212) 254-2246. Sun–Thurs: 8 AM–10 PM, Fri/Sat: 8 AM–3 AM.*

- **Old Town:** *Flatiron/Gramercy/Union Square: 45 E. 18th St., Manhattan, 10003, (212) 529-6732. Daily: 11:30 AM–midnight.*

- **Papaya King:** *Midtown West: 255 W. 43rd St., Manhattan, 10036, (212) 944-4590. Sun–Thurs: 8 AM–1 AM, Fri/Sat: 8 AM–3 AM.;*

> *Upper East Side: 179 E. 86ᵗʰ St., Manhattan,*
> *10028, (212) 396-0648. Sun–Thurs: 8 AM–1 AM,*
> *Fri/Sat: 8 AM–3 AM. ; Upper East Side:*
> *121 W. 125ᵗʰ St., Manhattan, 10027,*
> *(212) 665-5732. Sun–Thurs: 8 AM–1 AM, Fri/Sat:*
> *8 AM–3 AM.*
>
> • **Seventh Avenue Papaya:** *Upper East Side:*
> *225 Seventh Ave., Manhattan, 10011,*
> *(212) 352-9060.*

Jerusalem Restaurant

Middle Eastern good enough to gladden the heart of the most unabashed pitaphile.

$$

2715 Broadway, Manhattan 10025
(between W. 103ʳᵈ and W. 104ᵗʰ Sts.)
Phone (212) 865-2295

CATEGORY	Syrian/Middle Eastern
HOURS	Daily: 10 AM–4 AM
SUBWAY	1 to 103ʳᵈ St.; 2, 3 to 96ᵗʰ St.
PAYMENT	Cash only
POPULAR FOOD	Falafel combination sandwiches, lamb *shawarma* gyro (with choice of lettuce, tomato, onion, *tahina*, pickled radishes, and lemon juice in an oven-warmed pita)
UNIQUE FOOD	Everything is exceptional here, so design your own sandwich or platter using any one or all of the following: falafel, hummus, *baba ganoush,* feta, *tabouli* spinach, grape leaves, fava beans, *shawarma,* shish kebab, chicken, grilled onions, olives, hot peppers, pickled radishes
DRINKS	Turkish coffee, Jerusalem tea, and fully stocked icebox filled with Snapple, soda, and bottled water
SEATING	Tables for five inside, five at the counter; storefront seating, low table with four chairs surrounded by potted plants
AMBIENCE	Feels like you've stepped into your uncle's kitchen right in the middle of him telling a story about the good old days in Syria— small, everyone knows and everyone loves the charming manager, Ali
EXTRAS/NOTES	Platters also come with pita. On the counter is red sauce in a metal bowl called *shtta* in Arabic and *harif* in Hebrew—take it easy with this stuff or you'll be hurtin' in the mornin'. Seat yourself at the counter, and as you decide on what to order, Ali (sometimes accompanied by his lovely

wife Fatma) will surely hand you a piece
of fresh pita with oh-so-smooth hummus
or *baba ganoush*—to titillate your taste
buds. While you wait, order a Turkish
coffee and you'll see it done the right
way—in an old steel canister on
the stove.

—*Marie Estrada*

Koronet's Pizza

(see p. 226)
Pizzeria
2848 Broadway, Manhattan 10025
Phone (212) 222-1566

La Embajada

*Super-cheap breakfast combinations
and lunch specials served super-fast.*
$$
953 Amsterdam Ave., Manhattan, 10025
(between W. 106th and W. 107th Sts.)
Phone (212) 663-7225/3441/0137

CATEGORY	Dominican
HOURS	Daily: 9 AM–9 PM
SUBWAY	1 to 103rd or 110th St.; 2, 3 to 96th St.
PAYMENT	Cash only
POPULAR FOOD	Extensive menu *del día* including *pollo al carbon* (rotisserie chicken), *pollo al horno* (baked chicken), rotisserie chicken, *filete de pollo al limon* (chicken filet with garlic lemon sauce), *chicharron de pollo* (fried chicken chunks), *bistec en salsa* (steak stew), *pargo frito* (fried king fish), *moro* (rice with beans); all plates served with *arroz y habichuelas* (choice of *rojas, negras, blancas* [red, black, or white beans]) or *tostones* (fried green plantains), *maduros* (sweet plantains fried with butter), or french fries
UNIQUE FOOD	Green plantains *mangu* (mashed) or *guineo* (boiled), *yuca* (cassava), *longaniza* (Spanish sausage—available for breakfast only); fish in coconut sauce, tripe soup, corn custard
DRINKS	*Café con leche,* hot chocolate, hot oat (in the morning), hot tea, espresso, guava and pear juices, *jugo los tres golpes* (carrot and orange juice with milk), carrot with orange juice, and a variety of *batidos* (fruit and milk shakes)
SEATING	Thirty at tables, 10 at the counter
AMBIENCE	The staff of pretty Dominican ladies and handsome gents is always patient and more than willing to listen to a fumbled effort at placing an order in *español;* seat yourself at the counter—that's where all the action is

EXTRAS/NOTES	Cabbies pit stop at La Embajada on weekdays so you know it's good. Homemade cornbread. The awning reads: The Embassy.

—Marie Estrada

Lenny's Bagels

Skip anything for an Everything Bagel from Lenny's.

$

2601 Broadway, Manhattan 10025
(at W. 98th St.)
Phone (212) 222-0410

CATEGORY	Bagel Shop
HOURS	Mon–Sat: 6 AM–8 PM Sun: 6 AM–7 PM
SUBWAY	1, 2, 3 to 96th St.
PAYMENT	Cash only
POPULAR FOOD	Over a dozen varieties of bagels but the most loved are the everything, pumpernickel, onion, sesame, and cinnamon raisin
UNIQUE FOOD	Not unique to New York but Lenny's Everything Bagel (generous coating on both sides; most everything bagels in the city are coated only on the top), sports big chunks of roasted garlic and onion, large grains of kosher salt, as well as poppy and sesame seeds
DRINKS	Soda, bottled juices, fresh teas, and coffee
SEATING	Counter seats three, as well as a handful of tables where approximately 12 people can sit
AMBIENCE	Mostly take-out, but some neighborhood people eat here
EXTRAS/NOTES	With a cameo on *Seinfeld* among its numerous credits, H&H Bagels may be the city's most famous bagel, but it's certainly not the most tasty. Lenny's Bagels offers one of the widest selections of freshly baked bagels anywhere (and that's saying a lot for a city that's so closely associated with the tasty boiled bread). And even though Lenny's charges an extra nickel for their wares, it's still much cheaper than H&H's, and don't forget that they taste much better. Also offered is a wide selection of cream cheeses and sandwich fixings.

—Jeff Gomez

"I will not eat oysters. I want my food dead.
Not sick, not wounded, dead."

—Woody Allen

Saigon Grill

You don't want to Miss Saigon Grill.

$$

2381 Broadway, Manhattan 10024
(corner of W. 87th St.)
Phone (212) 875-9072/9073

CATEGORY	Vietnamese
HOURS	Daily: 11 AM–midnight
SUBWAY	1, 2, 3 to 86th St.
PAYMENT	VISA
POPULAR FOOD	Go for the *cha gio* (spring roll) appetizer and try the curry *bo*—an especially tasty concoction of beef and assorted veggies simmering in a sauce made from curry and coconut milk, served with pancakes
UNIQUE FOOD	If pad Thai's your thing, check out Vietnam's favored challenger: *bun xao,* served (like so many other dishes) with incomparable *nuoc cham* sauce
DRINKS	Domestic and imported beer, fresh lemon iced tea, ginger iced tea, lemon soda
SEATING	Seats about 50, almost always crowded, usually a short wait for one of the cramped tables—worth it
AMBIENCE	Seating and décor are Spartan in the way that most people would use the term—though not, perhaps, in the manner of that infamous city-state's historically well-documented eating arrangements; vibrant, busy, and bustling like an Athenian agora in the time of Themosticles
EXTRAS/NOTES	The many, many newspaper and magazine raves hanging in the front window of Saigon Grill seem evenly split between those simply praising the restaurant's spectacular, low-priced cuisine, and those shrewdly observing that the restaurant's spectacular, low-priced cuisine belies its modest eating environment. Adding new levels of analysis to the discourse, *Hungry?* observes that effusive, voluminous praise from New York City's best-regarded reviewers belies a restaurant's modest eating environment. But it's all well deserved!
OTHER ONES	• Upper East Side: 1700 Second Ave., Manhattan, 10128, (212) 996-4600

—Joe Cleeman

Sarabeth's West

(see p. 46)
Brunch
423 Amsterdam Ave., Manhattan 10024
Phone (212) 496-6280

Tom's Restaurant

Sing it Suzanne Vega: Doo, doo, doo doo, Doo, doo, doo doo.

$$

2880 Broadway, Manhattan 10027
(corner of W. 112th St.)
Phone (212) 864-6137

CATEGORY	Diner
HOURS	Sun–Wed: 6 AM–1:30 AM Thurs–Sat: noon–midnight
SUBWAY	1 to 110th or 116th Sts.
PAYMENT	Cash only
POPULAR FOOD	Grilled cheese with tomato on rye, side of fries, and a Broadway milkshake—coffee ice cream with chocolate syrup
UNIQUE FOOD	Steak-cut French fries covered with American cheese
DRINKS	Milkshakes, egg creams, juices, fountain soda, coffee, tea
SEATING	Booths and a counter for about 40
AMBIENCE	No-frills diner, always packed—expect to wait before and after eight
EXTRAS/NOTES	This is the meeting place for the Real Cosmo Kramer of Seinfeld fame—so expect tourists with flashing cameras—ALL THE TIME. And yes, this is THE Tom's Diner associated with Suzanne Vega. If you don't believe me, check out the web site devoted to Suzanne Vega: www.vega.net or is this just part of the urban legend?

—*Marie Estrada*

Zhong Hua Restaurant

General Tso's tofu so good you'll want to know: Who is General Tso?

$$

844 Amsterdam Ave, Manhattan 10025
(between W. 101st and W. 102nd Sts.)
Phone (212) 864-7997
www.atastychinese.com

CATEGORY	Chinese Take-out
HOURS	Mon–Thurs: 11 AM–11:30 PM Fri/Sat: 11 AM–midnight Sun: noon–11:30 PM
SUBWAY	1, 2, 3 to 96th St. or 103rd St.
PAYMENT	Cash only
POPULAR FOOD	General Tso's tofu served over clumpy white rice (half-inch cubes of crispy stick-to-the-teeth battered tofu, a few bright green broccoli florets—all sautéed in a tangy sweet-and-spicy soy-based sauce, infused with chunks of whole chili)

UNIQUE FOOD	Jalapeños with choice of beef, shrimp, squid, pork, or chicken served with very spicy special sauce over white rice; fresh squid with green pepper, baby shrimp with peanuts and hot pepper sauce
DRINKS	Refrigerator stocked with sodas and canned iced teas
SEATING	Two tables for two
AMBIENCE	Teeny-tiny
EXTRAS/NOTES	Take the tofu to go, walk across the street, and watch a couple rounds of hoops or a game of concrete softball at the nearby park—or catch a flick a few blocks away on Broadway. Zhong Hua has a sister restaurant in Brooklyn, Wan You. It's a Mexican Chinese restaurant that serves—you guessed it, Mexican staples alongside Chinese food. Plus, all prices include tax!
OTHER ONES	• Brooklyn: 274 Troutman St., 11237, (718) 386-8787/7979

—Marie Estrada

UPPER EAST SIDE

Baluchi's Indian Food

(see p. 176)

Northern Indian

1431 First Ave., Manhattan 10021

and

1565 Second Ave., Manhattan 10028

Phone (212) 288-4810

and

1724 Second Ave., Manhattan 10128

Phone (212) 996-2600

and

1149 First Ave., Manhattan 10021

Phone (212) 371-3535

Burritoville

(see p. 31)

Mexican

1606 Third Ave., Manhattan 10128

Phone (212) 410-2255

and

1489 First Ave., Manhattan 10021

Phone (212) 472-8800

Didjaknow?

Edgar Allen Poe, former resident of the Bronx, was so incredibly poor and starving that he would send his mother-in-law out to scour nearby fields for edible roots.

Candle Café

"Food from farm to table."

$$$$

1307 Third Ave., Manhattan 10021
(corner of E. 75ᵗʰ St.)
Phone (212) 472-0970 • Fax (212) 472-7169
www.candlecafe.com

CATEGORY	Vegetarian/Vegan
HOURS	Mon–Sat: 11:30 AM–10:30 PM
	Sun: 11:30 AM–9:30 PM
SUBWAY	6 to 77ᵗʰ St.
PAYMENT	VISA [MasterCard] [AMERICAN]
POPULAR FOOD	Try the robust *seitan a la mojo de ajo* (grilled *seitan* in garlic sauce served with yellow rice, daily beans, guacamole, and cilantro tofu sour cream), or the Paradise Casserole (layers of sweet potato, black beans, and millet, surrounded by steamed greens, served with mushroom gravy)
UNIQUE FOOD	*Seitan chimichurri* (South American marinated *seitan* skewers served with creamy citrus herb dressing); or choose any three sides of the 15 options offered in the Good Food Side Dishes (including *hijiki,* blue corn-quinoa corn bread, grilled *tempeh,* steamed or grilled tofu, baked sweet potato, yellow *basmati* rice, caramelized onions, baked beets); choice of balsamic vinaigrette, carrot ginger, ginger soy, lemon tahini, sherry wine vinaigrette, mushroom gravy, plum tomato, or spicy peanut sauce
DRINKS	Juice bar with fresh juice concoctions under descriptive and fitting titles: Very Veggie Juices, Fruition Nutrition, Farmacy (Flu and Cold Fighter); all kinds of organic beverages such as beer, wine, soy milk cappuccino, and mulled apple cider
SEATING	Around 50 at tables, including five at juice/wine bar
AMBIENCE	Delightful, vibrant, and friendly atmosphere—plenty of warm tones
EXTRAS/NOTES	While a hungry mouth and wallet can eat well at Candle Café and feel like she's had a choice in the matter, it wouldn't be tough to break the *Hungry?* bank—and why the hell not? The food is absolutely worth every penny—organic, fresh, and extremely good for your body and the environment.

—*Marie Estrada*

The Comfort Diner

(see p. 44)
Comfort Food
142 E. 86ᵗʰ St., Manhattan 10028
Phone (212) 426-8600

Too Brown? Or Too Off-White?

What accounts for the sad dearth of Filipino restaurants in food-crazy Manhattan?

For one thing, this often hearty, very earthy fare gets a bad rap for being a cholesterol-watcher's nightmare, a perception that's not totally off-the-mark. Many traditional Filipino dishes—such as *adobo* (meat simmered in garlic and vinegar), *lechon* (roast pig), and *kare-kare* (oxtail peanut stew)—are meat-based. Little bits of meat will even pop up in ostensible vegetable dishes. The smoke from innumerable barbecue stands at the annual Philippine Independence Day fair along Fifth Avenue in June is enough to create an atomic mushroom cloud visible for miles. Perhaps the most notorious Philippine food, *balut,* is a duck embryo you crack out of its shell and slurp down—feathers, tiny bones and all. This carnivorousness, odd in an island-nation not lacking for seafood, is largely due to the strong Iberian influence on the cuisine, but even Chinese-influenced dishes such as *pancit* (the generic Filipino term for noodles) tend to have some meat in them for flavoring. Off the bat, then, this is a bit of a turn-off to fans of Asian cuisine looking for something more typically Asian, i.e., lighter and healthier.

This is a pity, because Filipino food is so much more varied than *adobo* would have you believe. *Sinigang,* a soup often made with *bangus* (milkfish, a rather bland, firm-fleshed saltwater cousin to catfish) and soured with radishes or tamarind, is very similar to Thai *tom yum gung.* *Bangus* is the staple seafood of the cuisine, delicious in all its guises—fried, grilled, baked and stuffed, or boiled. Many other regional dishes share more of an affinity with Asia than with Europe in their use of seafood, chilies, coconut milk, fish paste and fish sauce, and tamarind. Granted, Filipino cooking does not have the inventive spicing or the broader range of ingredients that characterize the rest of Southeast Asia. But what it lacks in sophistication, it more than makes up for in sheer flavorfulness and straightforwardness.

However, many traditional Filipino dishes are a challenge to present appealingly. "Everything's brown," notes one native chef. Or off-white. But this is nothing a little inventiveness can't fix. One visit to **Cendrillon**, the chic Tribeca restaurant that has made Filipino food the inspiration for its Pan-Asian menu, proves that even brown food can look world-class pretty. *Adobo* is presented in a small clay pot. The fresh *lumpia* (a spring roll made with hearts of palm and lettuce) comes in a crêpe wrapper that turns a beautiful shade of light purple from chef Romy Dorotan's addition of yam. And it tastes pretty good, too. Cendrillon is perhaps the only upscale Filipino restaurant in the city and has a larger ratio of Western to Filipino customers than the rest. Beautifully decorated, with ivory-inlaid tables, original artwork on the walls and an open kitchen, Cendrillon has acquired a following of chic neighborhood types as well as city Pinoys wanting to give their non-Filipino friends a rather more special introduction to the cuisine. Though the food is a bit gussied up to qualify as authentic Filipino, it's still delicious, if a bit pricey. Cendrillon does offer *merienda* items (think midday *tapas*) between noon and dinner that are easier on the budget, such as *halo-halo*, various types of *pancit*, and spring rolls. Their takes on Filipino desserts are not to be missed, particularly the *buko* (young coconut) and *ube* (purple yam) pies. **Cendrillon:** *Downtown Fancy: 45 Mercer St., Manhattan, 10013, (212) 343-9012. Tues–Sun: 11 AM–11 PM.*

Another reason Filipino restaurants are scarce in Manhattan is that many Filipinos who emigrate here tend to be highly-skilled professionals— nurses, doctors, or white-collar workers, rather than entrepreneurs. Those immigrants who *do* go into the restaurant business tend to do so where there are higher concentrations of Filipinos, which is why there are so many more Filipino restaurants in New Jersey and in Woodside, Queens. Rents in Manhattan are also so astronomical as to make profitability a constant challenge for any restaurant.

Also, with the exception of Cendrillon, Filipino restaurants in the city tend to be mom-and-pop operations catering to a native crowd rather than designed to please the wider Western market. Often, little thought is given to presentation—the décor tends to be time-warped '60s Formica or simply utilitarian—and service is on the leisurely side. These are not exactly places you go to impress a date, though you will both eat well.

The handful of Pinoy restaurants that *have* sprung up in Manhattan tend to be clustered around Stuyvesant Town on the Lower East Side, in the square mile bordered by First and Second Aves. and by E. 12th to E. 14th Sts. This is no accident. This now-gentrified area had been, from the '70s to the early '90s, a somewhat seedy strip, enlivened in the main by a cluster of hospitals, which meant a lot of Filipino nurses around, which meant either plenty of potential customers or amenable landlords. (Filipino nurses are rumored to have bought up quite a bit of real estate in the neighborhood before it went semi-yuppie and real estate prices shot through the roof.) This also accounts for the unusual number of Filipino groceries (two) that sprang up in the area.

The best-known mid-market Filipino restaurant in Manhattan, **Elvie's Turo-Turo**, has been around since 1993, catering not just to the hospital crowd now but also to a growing and loyal tribe of East Village residents, NYU students, and the occasional tourist. The proprietress, Elvira Cinco, used to work in advertising for the Yellow Pages. After getting laid off, she decided to turn her side business catering at street fairs into a full-time occupation, and the Yellow Pages' loss became Manhattan's gain. Elvie's popularity owes a bit to the cheery and welcoming, if rather generic, décor—terra cotta painted walls, baskets, wooden tables and chairs. It almost looks like a *taqueria*. It doesn't hurt that you can pig out deliciously for about $10, dessert included, and get your food in minutes. I once spotted a couple bravely trying to use chopsticks here. They must have brought their own. A friendly tip: Filipino food is eaten with proper cutlery or, on occasion, with your fingers, unless stabbing a chicken leg or a chunk of meat with a stick is your idea of fun. **Elvie's Turo-Turo:** *East Village: 214 First Ave., Manhattan, 10009, (212) 473-7785. Mon–Sat: 11 AM–9 PM, Sun: 11 AM–8 PM.*

A block down on the same side, there's **Mandarin Grill and Coffee House,** and along E. 14th St. between First and Second Aves. is **Manila Gardens Restaurant.** The two joints are somewhat less homey, and in fact do become nightclub/karaoke joints after dark, though the food is stellar. **New Manila Foodmart,** a grocery on the northwest corner of E. 14th St. and First Ave., also has a tiny lunch counter in back that serves Filipino favorites daily. Everything from the *adobo* to the *dinuguan* (pig's blood stew) and *pinakbet* (vegetables sautéed with fish paste) is well worth a try. There is a good choice of *merienda* items such as *turon* (caramelized bananas fried in a spring-roll wrapper), *bibingka* (glutinous rice cake), and *guinataan* (a thick, sweet "soup" made with coconut milk, tapioca and fruit). **Mandarin Grill:** *East Village: 188 First Ave., Manhattan, 10009, (212) 673-3656. Daily: 11 AM–10 PM.* **Manila Gardens:** *East Village: 325 E. 14th St., Manhattan, 10003, (212) 777-6314. Daily: 11 AM–11 PM.* **New Manila Foodmart:** *East Village: 353 E. 14th St., Manhattan, 10003, (212) 420-8182. Daily: 9 AM–9 PM.*

Roosevelt Avenue in Woodside, Queens, which has a huge Filipino population, has become a Filipino restaurant row. **Ihawan** morphs into a karaoke/nightclub joint at night, and is perhaps the best-known, but there are many more holes-in-the-wall and barbecue joints that fill up on weekends. **Barrio Fiesta,** a dim, unpretentious joint, serves perhaps the best and most authentic *kare-kare* anywhere in New York, with a rich, thick sauce that tastes as if your grandmother had roasted and ground the peanuts up herself with a mortar and pestle. And don't miss **Krystal's Café and Pastry Shop,** recently visited by President of the

Philippines Gloria Macapagal-Arroyo, for fabulous Filipino deserts (some Italian pastries, as well). You can also shop for virtually anything Pinoy along this strip, including crates of the distinctively silky, sweet Philippine mango in the summer and, if you're brave, the notorious *balut*. **Ihawan:** *Ride the 7: 40-06 70th St., Queens, 11377, (718) 205-1480. Mon–Sat: 11 AM–9 PM, Sun 11 AM–8 PM.* **Barrio Fiesta:** *Ride the 7: 65-14 Roosevelt Ave., Queens, 11377, (718) 429-4878.* **Krystal's Café and Pastry Shop:** *Ride the 7: 69-02 Roosevelt Ave., Queens, 11377, (718) 898-1900. Mon–Thurs, Sun: 8 AM–midnight, Fri/Sat: 8 AM–3 AM.*

MABUHAY SA INYONG LAHAT!!!!

—*Melissa Contreras*

Dakshin

(see p. 81)
Indian
1713 First Ave., Manhattan 10128
Phone (212) 421-1919

Doc Watson's Restaurant and Pub

Elementary meals at elementary prices.
$$
1150 Lexington Ave., Manhattan 10021
(between E. 79th and E. 80th Sts.)
Phone (212) 737-0095
www.docwatsons.com

CATEGORY	Bar and Grill
HOURS	Daily: 11 AM–4 AM
SUBWAY	6 to 77th St.
PAYMENT	Cash only
POPULAR FOOD	Perfect with a beer, Doc's Nachos (generous mound of chilli, cheddar cheese, fresh chopped tomato, raw onion, topped with sour cream, salsa, and guacamole), or Doc Watson's house sandwich (toasted white bread, Irish bacon, and a fried egg, served with french fries); plenty of burger options including veggie and turkey burgers
UNIQUE FOOD	Try the beans on toast sandwich—Heinz baked beans on Texas toast; or Doc's Fish Burger
DRINKS	Full bar
SEATING	Twenty at tables indoors and 10 in the backyard garden area
AMBIENCE	Country

123

EXTRAS/NOTES　Follow a festive Friday night with a
brunch at Doc Watson's—from
11:30 AM–4 PM and it comes with a choice
of TWO alcoholic drinks—Mimosa,
Champagne cocktail, Bloodymary,
Screwdriver, or beer. Doc's presents
traditional live Irish music every Sunday
night from 8:30 PM–11:30 PM with the
band "Aonach."

　　　　　　　　　　　　　　　　—*Marie Estrada*

EJ's Luncheonette

*If the gods ate middle-American diner fare
(and lived in the '40s), they'd eat here.*
$$$
1271 Third Ave., Manhattan 10021
(corner of E. 73rd St.)
Phone (212) 472-0600

CATEGORY　Diner/American

HOURS　Mon–Sat: 8 AM–11 PM
Sun: 8 AM–10:30 PM

SUBWAY　6 to 77th St.

PAYMENT　Cash only

POPULAR FOOD　Simple, hearty, HUGE portions of
breakfast fare: buttermilk pancakes,
Frontier Multigrain Flapjackes, EJ's low fat
cinnamon honey granola made with EJ's
signature blend of oats, nuts, dried fruit,
and served with whole or skim milk, or
yogurt

UNIQUE FOOD　EJ's crunch French toast (thick-cut and
coated with almonds and corn flakes); The
Minute Man (two poached or soft-boiled
eggs served with lettuce and tomato and
toasted challah bread)

DRINKS　Fountain drinks (shakes, egg cream
sodas), juice bar, wine, beer, Stewart's
Root Beer, Dr. Brown's soda

SEATING　Plenty of seats at booths and tables

AMBIENCE　Retro-'40s look with soda fountain, blue
vinyl booths, and Formica tables

EXTRAS/NOTES　During breakfast, HUGE portions here
folks. During lunch, portions are much
more reasonable—try EJ's weekday blue
plate specials. T-shirts, baseball shirts,
hats, coffee mugs, and low fat cinnamon
honey granola for sale. Gift certificates
also available.

OTHERONES　• Upper West Side: 447 Amsterdam Ave.,
Manhattan, 10024 (212) 873-3444
• From Chelsea to West Houston:
432 Sixth Ave., Manhattan, 10011
(212) 473-5555

　　　　　　　　　　　　　　　　—*Marie Estrada*

Famous Famiglia

(see p. 109)
Pizzeria
1284 First Ave., Manhattan 10021
Phone (212) 288-1616
and
1398 Madison Ave., Manhattan 10029
Phone (212) 996-9797

Hale and Hearty Soups

All hale to the guardians of good and hearty soups.
$
849 Lexington Ave., Manhattan 10021
(between E. 64th and E. 65th Sts.)
Phone (212) 517-7600 • Fax (212) 517-7699

CATEGORY	Soup Shop
HOURS	Mon–Fri: 9:30 AM–8 PM
	Sat: 10:30 AM–6 PM
	Sun: 11 AM–5 PM
SUBWAY	6 to 68th St.
PAYMENT	Cash only
POPULAR FOOD	Soup! Try: tomato and basil with rice, mushroom artichoke, turkey chili, sloppy Joe (served over rice), ginger carrot artichoke, and crab bisque; all soups come with choice of seven grain, sourdough, or signature oyster crackers (baked in-house)
UNIQUE FOOD	Try the Senegalese chicken soup—made with peanut butter and topped with fresh peanuts; chilled peach, chilled spiced apple (perfectly cooling during humid summer months)
DRINKS	Fresh brewed iced tea, fresh squeezed lemonade, Perrier, Fresh Samantha, coffee, and tea
SEATING	Around 20 snuggly at tables
AMBIENCE	Clean, simple, urban modern with friendly and efficient service; expect a crowd and a wait during lunch hours
EXTRAS/NOTES	Hale's proudly boasts over 40 varieties of soup, many of which are dairy free and vegetarian—call ahead to hear the daily specials, and if you place your order over the phone, you'll avoid the lines and lunch crowd. Sizes come in small cup, large cup, bowl, bread bowl, and soup and sandwich combo; sandwiches served on Tuscan flat bread. Tossed-to-order salads also available. Free delivery.
OTHER ONES	• From Chelsea to West Houston: 75 Ninth Ave., Manhattan, 10011, (212) 255-2400
	• Midtown West: 462 Seventh Ave., Manhattan, 10018, (212) 971-0605

- Midtown West: 49 W. 42nd St., Manhattan, 10036, (212) 575-9090
- Midtown West: 55 W. 56th St., Manhattan, 10019, (212) 245-9200
- Midtown East: 22 E. 47th St., Manhattan, 10017, (212) 557-1900
- Downtown Brooklyn West: 32 Court St, Brooklyn, 11201, (718) 596-5600
- Fond Farewell: 4 World Trade Center

—*Marie Estrada*

Lexington Candy Shop

If it weren't for the veggie burger on the menu, you'd swear you were in a time warp.

Since 1925

$$

1226 Lexington Ave., Manhattan 10028
(corner of E. 83rd St.)
Phone Butterfield 8-0057. . .(or for you moderns, (212) 288-0057)

CATEGORY	Historic Diner
HOURS	Mon–Sat: 7 AM–7 PM
	Sun: 9 AM–6 PM
SUBWAY	4, 5, 6 to 86th St.
PAYMENT	VISA [cards] (min. $10)
POPULAR FOOD	No frills diner food all done right—try the buttery grilled cheese
UNIQUE FOOD	Buffalo burger
DRINKS	Egg creams, milkshakes, fountain sodas, made-to-order lemonade
SEATING	Seats 30 in booths and long counter
AMBIENCE	Think Mayberry circa 1925—green booths, a long counter with vinyl stools, pink and fuschia tiles, vertical striped wallpaper—with Mrs. Robinson playing in the background
EXTRAS/NOTES	"Don't be surprised if you see a celebrity or two also enjoying a step back in time." Bathroom hidden in the back—keeps the UES riff raff out.

—*Marie Estrada*

Luke's Bar and Grill

The Upper East Side isn't just dogs and pizza, it's also got Luke's juicy burgers and beer.

$$$$

1394 Third Ave., Manhattan 10021
(between E. 79th and E. 80th Sts.)
Phone (212) 249-7070

CATEGORY	Bar and Grill
HOURS	Mon–Sat: 11:30 AM–2 AM
	Sun: 11:30 AM–midnight
SUBWAY	6 to 77th St.
PAYMENT	Cash only

POPULAR FOOD	Very well-made American pub staples—customers swear by the juicy hamburgers; also try the chicken salad, buffalo wings, and chewy mozzarella sticks; spinach salad, roasted chicken
UNIQUE FOOD	Mussels in white wine sauce
DRINKS	Full bar
SEATING	About 33 tables
AMBIENCE	Dark, wood-paneled, comfortable neighborhood spot with bustling wait staff in a saloon-like setting, weekend brunches attract families, night owls in the evening
EXTRAS/NOTES	Wheelchair friendly.

—Marie Estrada

Papaya King

(see p. 111)
Hot Dogs
179 E. 86ᵗʰ St., Manhattan 10028
Phone (212) 396-0648

Saigon Grill

(see p. 116)
Vietnamese
1700 Second Ave., Manhattan 10128
Phone (212) 996-4600

Sarabeth's At The Whitney

(see p. 46)
Brunch
945 Madison Ave., Manhattan 10021
Phone (212) 570-3670

Sarabeth's East

(see p. 46)
Brunch
1295 Madison Ave., Manhattan 10128
Phone (212) 410-7335

Soup Burg

*Great griddle food in a
no-frills setting.*
$
1150 Lexington Ave., Manhattan 10021
(between E. 79ᵗʰ and E. 80ᵗʰ Sts.)
Phone (212) 737-0095

CATEGORY	Dinerette
HOURS	Mon–Sat: 6 AM–8 PM
	Sun: 8 AM–3 PM
SUBWAY	6 to 77ᵗʰ St.
PAYMENT	Cash only
POPULAR FOOD	On the grill: omelettes, two-egg and American cheese on a roll, buttery just

how we like it tuna melt on toast, chili cheeseburger, Texas cheeseburger, special triple decker #1 tuna with sliced egg, L and T; *chili con carne* (chili with meat)

UNIQUE FOOD Sardine sandwich served on white

DRINKS Vanilla or chocolate egg creams, milk shakes, soda, variety of bottled and canned juices in tomato, pineapple, grape, cranberry, and grapefruit, coffee, hot chocolate, assorted herbal teas

SEATING Three stools at counter

AMBIENCE Hole-in-the wall with two guys working the grill two feet away from you and the counter

EXTRAS/NOTES Take the food to go or take advantage of the free and fast delivery. Expect to smell fried if you decide to stay and eat.

—*Marie Estrada*

Teriyaki Boy

(see p. 91)
Japanese Fast Food/Sushi
1380 First Ave., Manhattan 10021
Phone (212) 717-0760
and
1640 Third Ave., Fl. 1, Manhattan 10128
Phone (212) 987-7150

Vermicelli

I've got champagne taste and beer money. Elegant.
$$$$
1492 Second Ave., Manhattan 10021
(between E. 77th and E. 78th Sts.)
Phone (212) 288-8868

CATEGORY Vietnamese

HOURS Daily: 11:30 AM–11 PM

SUBWAY 6 to E. 77th St.

PAYMENT VISA [cards]

POPULAR FOOD Try the *bun cari cai* (warm vermicelli noodles served beneath vegetables, lettuce, and peanuts in a curry sauce); *bun ga nuong* (spicy barbecued chicken cooked with lemon grass, bell pepper, onion, and roasted peanuts over warm vermicelli); *bo luc lac* (marinated steak served cubed with cucumbers and lettuce leaves)

UNIQUE FOOD *Suon nuong* (charcoal grilled pork chops marinated in lemon grass, honey, and garlic); *com chen* (house fried rice mixed with shrimp, pineapple, green peas, bean sprouts, egg, and fresh chilis)

DRINKS Full bar which includes Miss Saigon and 33 (Vietnamese beer)

SEATING Tables for over 40

AMBIENCE   Open space, sparkling clean, high ceilings, and polished wood; charming, helpful, and attentive staff

EXTRAS/NOTES   Pricey for dinner unless you go vegetarian, but the under six dollar lunch menu (Daily: 11:30 AM–4 PM) is incredibly good and varied with over 20 different bento box specials and various soup and vermicelli noodle dishes to choose from— many of which are offered at twice the price during dinnertime.

—*Marie Estrada*

Totonno Pizzeria Napolitano

(see p. 227)
Pizzeria
1544 Second Ave., Manhattan 10028
Phone (212) 327-2800

THE HARLEMS

AM PM Fried Fish, Chicken & Donuts

Fried food good.
$
330 W. 125ᵗʰ St., Manhattan 10027
(at St. Nicholas Ave.)
(212) 678-0139

CATEGORY   Fried Fish and Donut Joint

HOURS   Mon–Fri: 8 AM–8 PM
Sat: 9 AM–8 PM
Sun: 11 AM–6 PM

SUBWAY   A, B, C, D to 125ᵗʰ St.

PAYMENT   Cash only

POPULAR FOOD   Seven piece jumbo shrimp with chips, french fries with cheese, three chicken wings with chips, chicken nuggets—no extra charge to substitute chips for fried rice; donuts, bagels, muffins, and danishes available all day long

DRINKS   Coffee, hot chocolate, tea, soda

SEATING   Three chairs and a standing bar

AMBIENCE   Not much to look at inside, but there's always something interesting happening outside on 125ᵗʰ St.

EXTRAS/NOTES   If you're pressed for time or simply must have the greasy goodness NOW, the standing counter or one of the three waiting chairs along the wall was made for you. Others can carry the food to nearby Morningside Park—and if so, don't forget to stop at St. Nicholas Deli across the street and pick up a roll for the pigeons.

Owner Johnny Koo is not much of a
talker but he fries up a mean flounder and
whiting which, made on the spot, always
arrives hot, fresh—and with a sweet smile.

—*Marie Estrada*

D.M.E.'s Southern Style Food

*Southern American take-out serving it
up fast, cheap, and all night long.*

$$

100 W. 124ᵗʰ St., Manhattan 10027

(corner of Lenox Ave., a.k.a. Malcolm X Blvd.)

Phone (212) 316-9181

CATEGORY	Southern American
HOURS	24/7
SUBWAY	2, 3 to 125ᵗʰ St.
PAYMENT	[VISA] [MasterCard] [AMERICAN EXPRESS] (min. $20 purchase)
POPULAR FOOD	Carni-lovers meat loaf, whiting fish, chopped pork, or chicken barbecue—all meals include two sides and cornbread; peach cobbler
UNIQUE FOOD	Pig's feet (available Sat and Sun only)
DRINKS	Fruit-flavored sodas, coffee, tea, hot chocolate
SEATING	One table seats two
AMBIENCE	Basic hole in the wall frequented by neighborhood folk and late night Lenox loungers
EXTRAS/NOTES	D.M.E. owners recently opened a promising restaurant next door called Mom's Place, which seats about 50 in a chic minimalist setting; serves breakfast, lunch, dinner, and has brunch specials that fit the *Hungry?* bill on the weekend; same phone number as D.M.E.

—*Marie Estrada*

Fairway Market

(see p. 134)

Market

2350 12ᵗʰ Ave., Manhattan 10027

Phone (212) 234-3883

Flavored with One Love Caribbean Restaurant & Catering

*West Indian so good it makes you want to be corny and
sing: One love, one heart, come to Flavored and feel
alright.*

$$

1941 Madison Ave., Manhattan 10035

(between E. 124ᵗʰ and E. 125ᵗʰ Sts.)

Phone (212) 426-4446

CATEGORY	West Indian/Guyanese Buffet
HOURS	Mon–Fri: 8 AM–9 PM
	Sat: 9 AM–9 PM

SUBWAY	4, 5, 6 to 125th St.
PAYMENT	Cash only
POPULAR FOOD	*Roti* with curry chicken, curry goat, or vegetables
UNIQUE FOOD	Codfish cakes, *roti* skins, *polliry,* cow foot soup
DRINKS	Sweet West Indian beverages—*sorrel* (brewed from hibiscus flowers), *mauby* (from tree bark), bottled and can soda, juices, beer, wine, coffee, peppermint tea
SEATING	Tables for 20
AMBIENCE	Polished cherry stained tables, sparkling clean; buffet-style—choice of small (healthy) and large (hefty) portions from ten main selections that include *roti,* curried meats, fish, stew, and seafood
EXTRAS/NOTES	A healthy portion of any main dish, choice of side, and a mound of rice is just right. Or invent a meal from soup and any of the wonderful sides: cabbage, *callaloo,* chickpeas, green salad, fried plantains, macaroni and cheese, okra, spinach, or sweet yams for just about five and change—leave room for carrot cake or sweet bread—decadent but oh-so-worth it. Established in 1996 by a mother and her two daughters, this place has made good by its motto: "Meals bursting with flavor, served in a warm and delightful atmosphere." People get ready!

—*Marie Estrada*

Keriann's Nice & Spicey Restaurant

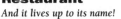

And it lives up to its name!

$$

62 E. 125th St., Manhattan 10035
(between Madison and Park Aves.)
Phone (212) 828-3862

CATEGORY	West Indian
HOURS	Daily: 8 AM–midnight
SUBWAY	4, 5, 6 to 125th St.
PAYMENT	Cash only
POPULAR FOOD	Give your 'buds a treat and have the oxtail stew, jerk chicken, or *escoveitched* fish (whole fish fried with onions, carrots, and hot pepper), served with rice and choice of vegetables; saltfish and *ackee* (breakfast), variety of *rotis*—vegetable, goat, beef, chicken, oxtail
UNIQUE FOOD	Goat head or cow cod soup
DRINKS	Variety of root drinks, carrot juice, and the Jamaican Squeez'r Soda
SEATING	Four tables seat eight comfortably
AMBIENCE	Robust home cooking in a narrow railroad style setting; expect neighborhood B-boys and Jamaican patrons mixing casually

with gracious owners; red tables, fresh flowers, a Bob Marley clock, and hand-painted waterscape mural with pink flamingos

EXTRAS/NOTES Keriann's is not light cooking. There is a lot of goat and beef, curried and stewed. And the fish dish is fried—but everything is fresh, perfectly spiced, and oh-so tasty.

—Marie Estrada

Manna's Soul Food & Salad Bar Restaurant

Southern food that'll make you yell: "Heck! I wish I'd mastered that two-fisted shovel."

$$

2331-2333 Eighth Ave. (a.k.a. Frederick Douglass Blvd.), Manhattan 10027
(between W. 125th and W. 126th Sts.)
Phone (212) 749-9084

CATEGORY	Southern Buffet
HOURS	Mon–Sat: 7:30 AM–8 PM
	Sun: 10 AM–7 PM
SUBWAY	A, B, C, D to 125th St.
PAYMENT	Cash only
POPULAR FOOD	Macaroni and cheese that's buttery, creamy, slightly sharp, and baked until the top layer of cheese is browned to a crisp; feast like a fat queen for $3.99 per pound on 30 absolutely fresh cold choices—don't miss the banana pudding; $4.99 per pound on 30 hot choices including curry chicken, cornish hen, spaghetti with meat, smothered pork chops, stewed porgy fish, collard greens, stewed cabbage, barbecue honey wings, crab cakes, honey barbecue pork rib tips, mouth watering tender oxtails, Manna's special fried chicken
UNIQUE FOOD	Savanna's Best Hog Chitt'lings prepared with red wine and garlic sauce
DRINKS	Homemade lemonade and iced tea, Jamaican soda, ginseng soda, Snapple, OJ and apple juice, coffee, tea (black, herbal, ginseng)—available with honey
SEATING	Upstairs seating for 50 with the best unobstructed view of historic 125th St. Harlem
AMBIENCE	Near-bare white walls, polished wooden tables, track lighting, and ceiling fans give the room a clean, crisp feeling; expect all kinds of wonderful tunes including Jill Scott, Luther Vandross, James Brown, Ella, Billie, and, of course, Bob Marley
EXTRAS/NOTES	Still got room? The peach cobbler is simply wonderful. Hint for the meat-loving crew—add a side of vegetables to your ribs and chicken and you'll pay

$3.99 per pound. So eat your vegetables! Specials include jerk chicken (Thurs and Sat), pig's feet and turkey wings (Sat), and salmon (Fri).

OTHER ONES
- The Harlems: 486 Lenox Ave., Manhattan, 10037, (212) 234-4488
- The Harlems: 51 E. 125th St., Manhattan, 10035, (212) 360-4975

—*Marie Estrada*

Massawa Restaurant

A slice of East Africa in Morningside Heights.

$$

1239 Amsterdam Ave., Manhattan 10027
(corner of W. 121st St.)
Phone (212) 663-0505/0545 • Fax (212) 663-1800

CATEGORY	Eritrean and Ethiopian
HOURS	Daily: 11:30 AM–midnight
SUBWAY	1 to 116th St.
PAYMENT	VISA MasterCard AMERICAN DISCOVER
POPULAR FOOD	*Timtimo* (red lentils, yellow split peas, chopped red onions, and garlic cooked in berbere sauce), special *tebsie* (cubes of tenderloin tips sautéed with green peppers, onions, tomatoes, and a hot spice)
UNIQUE FOOD	*Fitfit* (spicy and addictive salad of fresh green hot peppers tossed with chopped *injera*, tomato, onion, and olive oil)
DRINKS	Have the hot spiced tea with cardamom, cinnamon, cloves, and other spices; coffee, espresso, cappuccino, iced tea, Perrier, variety of juices and soda, domestic and foreign beer
SEATING	Tables for 20
AMBIENCE	Refined décor, with tables set near enough to achieve intimacy—far enough apart so that the convivial hum of voices never disturbs conversation
EXTRAS/NOTES	Super deal during-the-week Luncheon Buffet until 2 PM and Massawa Lunch Specials until 4 PM. During dinner hours, expect to pay more and there's lag time between food ordering and food arriving—but the glorious food is well worth the wait.

—*Marie Estrada*

"Yes, that was and still is the best bread. It came from the kitchen of a very simple woman, who knew instinctively that she could solace her loneliness through the ritual of honest cooking. It taught me, although I did not understand it then, a prime lesson in survival. I must eat well."

—*M.F.K. Fisher, Last House*

Fairway Market

There's nothing really secret about Fairway. Everybody knows about it and nearly everyone's shopped there. But knowing about it—and talking about it—still lends the knower, the shopper, or the talker some measure of *in-ness* with the infuriating in-crowd.

It's a supermarket—really, a pair of supermarkets—that offers enormous selections of food, from the mundane to the gourmet, in a warehouse setting, and at warehouse prices. The two Manhattan locations (it's been suggested that another will open in Redhook, Brooklyn) offer fresh fruit and vegetables, exotic cheeses and spreads, foreign and domestic varieties of most consumables—commodity and specialty. Wide selections abound for the vegetarian and the health-conscious, and impressive (in some cases awe-inspiring) choices for the carnivorous and the indulgent.

Fairway's *not* for the timid. Especially on the weekends you may be in for long waits and big crowds at the various counters (the take-a-number machines mitigate what would otherwise be a dog-eat-dog melee, but memorize your number and be quick on the draw or you'll be out in the cold). And the check-out lines can easily back up all the way down the aisles, something that many a first time visitor will fail to notice since the floor managers keep the space behind the registers clear. But these managers (who police the lines and keep them moving with relentless speed and efficiency) will send the unwitting cutter to the back before those waiting have worked themselves into a lynch mob furor, i.e. in seconds.

The **Harlem** location was established first and is bigger and more remote, but includes parking. For those without cars, or who'd rather not wander through a few blocks of West Harlem's eerily deserted industrial waterfront to and from the subway, there's a Fairway shuttle. Gather ten or more people who share a building, a street, a neighborhood, etc.—it doesn't matter so long as everyone shows up at the appointed pick-up at the appointed time. Negotiate the schedule with your confederates (say, every second Sunday from 2 to 5). Fairway will provide the transportation. **Dial (212) 939-0300 for details.**

Harlem's Fairway carries a full array of almost everything. Most impressive is its refrigerated section: a giant, walk-in room that houses seafood, meat, deli goods, and several aisles' worth of foods frozen, cold, and chilled. A wall-full of loaner coats greets guests to this terrific arctic market, which alone occupies more square footage than many of the city's lesser supermarkets. *The Harlems: 2350 12th Ave. (at W. 133rd St.), Manhattan, 10027 (212) 234-3883. Daily: 8 AM–11 PM.*

The **Upper West Side** location is noticeably more cramped. Look for the endless procession of taxi cabs, the big blue awning, and the heaps of apples, oranges, bananas, pears, etc. that lay in bins beneath it. You enter near the produce (as is the supermarket custom): fruits and vegetables piled up over your head. The cheeses, representing the world's great cheese-producing regions, are straight ahead, along with dips and spreads. To the left you find the bakery, the deli, and some of the more exotic dressings, oils, and pre-made snacks. To the right—in the next room—are the aisles of more-standard supermarket fare through which the aforementioned lines weave. Behind them, back-to-back counters: meat and fish, wide varieties, all looking substantially fresher than what you'd find at almost any other supermarket in the city. Upstairs: a café and a sizeable natural foods section. *Upper West Side: 2127 Broadway (at W. 74th St.), Manhattan, 10023, (212) 595-1794. Daily: 6 AM–1 AM.*

Whichever location you choose, Fairway provides excellent foods at very good prices. Grab a fresh baguette and some turkey, a bagel, some hummus or tabouli, a pack of Euro-cookies, and eat on the go, at work, in the park, for a snack, etc. Or take home a few shopping bags worth of fresh tomatoes, live mussels, hot sausage, and cook it yourself.

Whatever you do, carry your Fairway bag proudly, and remember that those aren't *real* Rolexes, and that—no matter how convincing or charming someone is—the Brooklyn Bridge can only be purchased one way: by sending a check or money order for the rock-bottom amount of $10,000 to Joseph Cleemann c/o *Hungry?*

—*Joe Cleemann*

Mity Fine Restaurant

Soul-full southern food "where kindness is mixed into every dish."

$

24 W. 125th St., Manhattan 10027
(between Lenox and Fifth Aves.)
Phone (212) 348-4848

CATEGORY	Southern Cafeteria
HOURS	Mon–Sat: 7:30 AM–7:30 PM
SUBWAY	2, 3 to 125th St.
PAYMENT	Cash only
POPULAR FOOD	Daily specials served by the pound with free bread and drink over seven dollars—Monday's barbecue ribs and roast chicken, Tuesday's smothered turkey wings and meat loaf, oxtail on Wednesday, pepper steak and smothered pork chops on

Thursday, fresh fish on Friday, beef stew on Saturday, and Sunday roast and fried chicken—15 daily sides to complement such choices as mashed potatoes, black eyed peas, mac and cheese, okra and tomatoes, yams, collard greens, and peas and rice

UNIQUE FOOD	Lettuce and tomato sandwich for a buck!
DRINKS	Assorted herb tea, coffee, hot chocolate
SEATING	Booths and tables inside for approximately 40
AMBIENCE	Mity Fine wears its age mighty well—much more busy during the weekend
EXTRAS/NOTES	Try to save room for dessert—the homemade cobbler, homemade bread pudding, and Mityfine banana pudding are simply divine.

—Marie Estrada

Papaya King

(see p. 111)
Hot Dogs
121 W. 125ᵗʰ St., Manhattan 10027
Phone (212) 665-5732

Royal Caribbean Restaurant

Caribbean done right and done in a jiffy.
$
2167 Adam Clayton Powell Blvd., Manhattan 10035
(between E. 128ᵗʰ and E. 129ᵗʰ Sts.)
Phone (212) 665-0685

CATEGORY	Caribbean/Jamaican
HOURS	Mon–Sat: 10 AM–10 PM
SUBWAY	2, 3 to 125ᵗʰ St.
PAYMENT	Cash only
POPULAR FOOD	Oxtail stew, jerk chicken, fried whiting fish, chicken wings, macaroni and cheese, plantains, candied yams, collard greens, vegetable patties
UNIQUE FOOD	Brown stew chicken, cow foot soup
DRINKS	Bottled Jamaican cream and juice-flavored sodas, carrot juice, Irish Moss, *sorrel,* V8 Splash
SEATING	Carry out
AMBIENCE	Not a looker this here hole in the wall, but you came for the fantastic food and speedy service, yes?
EXTRAS/NOTES	Hungry hippo sized portions, and all main dishes come with choice of—whoa—not two, but a whoppin' THREE sides!

—Marie Estrada

REMEMBER THE NEEDIEST!

Rusty's Happy Choice

Almost always open Jamaican fast-food joint— ya gotta sleep sometime!

$$

445 W. 125ᵗʰ St., Manhattan 10027

(between Amsterdam and Morningside Aves.)

Phone (212) 666-7755

CATEGORY	West Indian/American
HOURS	Mon–Sat: 8 AM–11 AM
SUBWAY	1 to 125ᵗʰ St.
PAYMENT	Cash only
POPULAR FOOD	Specialty here is stews: try the oxtail with a side of yellow rice and candied yams; lots of Jamaican breakfast combinations: choose from saltfish and *ackee,* liver and banana, mackerel and banana, *callaloo* and banana, cornmeal porridge, and saltfish and boiled dumplings
DRINKS	Jamaican sodas in a variety of fruit and cream flavors, ginger beer, "Sexual Treatment" drinks: Irish Moss, Tiger Bone, *sorrel,* fresh squeezed carrot juice, Roots Man Tonic, coffee, hot chocolate, *serosi* tea (Jamaican bitter tasting cleansing tea)
SEATING	Counter with four stools
AMBIENCE	Relaxed hole-in-the wall frequented by neighborhood folk at all hours of the day and night with interesting eye-candy— deer-head, Bob Marley poster, and a framed baj-relief white long-haired cat clock next to a painting of the Ethiopian ruler of the 1940s known as (chant it with me) *The King of Kings, The Lord of Lords, Conquering Lion of the Tribe of Judah, Elector of Jah*
EXTRAS/NOTES	Rusty's is largely a take-out operation, but stay and chat with Hopeton the friendly manager and cook. He's a wealth of information about Jamaica. Chinese *lo mein* and sweet and sour chicken are also available.

—*Marie Estrada*

Sisters Caribbean Cuisine

Utterly divine eclectic Caribbean and Southern, prepared with a sophistication seldom seen at prices this reasonable.

$$

1931 Madison Ave., Manhattan 10035

(enter at E. 124ᵗʰ St.)

Phone (212) 410-3000

CATEGORY	Caribbean/Trinidadian/Guyanese/Southern
HOURS	Daily: 9 AM–9 PM
SUBWAY	4, 5, 6 to 125ᵗʰ St.

PAYMENT	
POPULAR FOOD	Choice of 12 main dishes; the must have favorites for lunch or dinner are the stewed chicken from Trinidad (savory and robust but not spicy) and the delightful and smoky jerk chicken—served with rice and vegetables; and there is a truly enlightened vegetable plate that doesn't make vegetarians feel like second class citizens—sneak in the pineapple tart (it's homemade)
UNIQUE FOOD	Guyanese/Trinidadian *callaloo* prepared with okra, crushed garlic, and, alas, secret spices
DRINKS	Canned and bottled soda, health drinks, *sorrel,* homemade lemonade, coffee, tea, and hot chocolate
SEATING	Seats 12 at tables
AMBIENCE	Intimate, friendly, and relaxed—tastefully framed family photos, and fresh flowers everyday at the counter; Sisters makes the urban asphalt and grime seem very, very far away
EXTRAS/NOTES	There's something reminiscent of a country home about Sisters, established in 1995 by two sisters from Guyana. During the morning hours of the workweek, service is thankfully swift and you can be in and out with your sautéed codfish or eggs with grits and bacon in no time. But the food—breakfast, lunch, or dinner—is truly worth lingering over.

—*Marie Estrada*

Slice of Harlem II

Deep dish pizza slice or pie that'll make you wanna puta your fingers to your lips and kissa the world!

$$

308 Lenox Ave., Manhattan 10027
(between W. 125th and W. 126th Sts.)
Phone (212) 426-7400

CATEGORY	Pizzeria
HOURS	Mon–Thurs: 6:30 AM–10 PM Fri/Sat: 6:30 AM–midnight Sun: noon–10 PM
SUBWAY	A, B, C, D to 135th St.
PAYMENT	
POPULAR FOOD	Full-meal deep dish pepperoni slice, the lasagna pie made with ground beef and ricotta cheese, the Hawaii pie made with Canadian bacon, pineapple, scallions, and Gruyère cheese, and the Sweet Garden no sauce pie made with grilled asparagus, zucchini, broccoli rabe, peas, and Fontina cheese
UNIQUE FOOD	Harlem Bayou covered with generous amounts of shrimp, clams, and mussels

138

DRINKS	Stewart's soda, Nantucket Nectars, Snapple, two-liter soda, coffee, tea, hot chocolate
SEATING	Two levels of seating: big groups, package-toting shoppers, baby carriages—this large, bright, and friendly place can surely accommodate
AMBIENCE	Much respect to the fine slice and pies put out by the Original Slice of Harlem, but this baby sister to the Lenox Ave. location most definitely gives big sis' some competition as "Harlem's finest brick oven pizzeria."
OTHER ONES	• The Harlems: 2527 Eighth Ave., Manhattan, 10030, (212) 862-4089

—Marie Estrada

Solar Gardens Health Foods

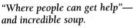

"Where people can get help"—
and incredible soup.

$

18 E. 125ᵗʰ St., Manhattan 10035

(between Fifth and Madison Aves.)

Phone (212) 427-1644

CATEGORY	Health Food and Herb Shop
HOURS	Mon–Sat: noon–7 PM
SUBWAY	2, 3, 4, 5, 6 to 125ᵗʰ St.
PAYMENT	Cash only
POPULAR FOOD	Daily soups: seaweed, yellow or green split pea, lentil, navy bean, and vegetable (depends on what owners Marylee and Paakobena feel like cookin' up—Paakobena's only soup cooking day is Thursday), sandwiches, granola, and *wasabi* chips
UNIQUE FOOD	Peanut butter soup—yum
DRINKS	Water (only water)
SEATING	Carry out or standing room only
AMBIENCE	Narrow—think cozy alchemist's shop
EXTRAS/NOTES	Husband and wife team Marylee and Paakobena opened Solar Gardens in 1982. While it's primarily a wonderful herbal shop where one can find the highest quality chaparral leaves, frankincense, *Gotu kola,* echinacea, saw palmetto berries, and ginger (hand peeled and cut, pill-sized ginger root in a dime bag), there's no soup like Solar's soup, which comes in two sizes—medium or large. Eat in the shop so you can chat with Paakobena, who is a wealth of knowledge about the mind, body, and spirit—and he can teach you more than a thing or two about Ghana and West Africa's system of naming.

—Nemo Librizzi & Marie Estrada

Strictly Roots

"We serve nothing that crawls, swims, walks, or flies."
$$

2058 Adam Clayton Blvd., Manhattan 10027
(between W. 122nd and W. 123rd Sts.)
Phone (212) 864-8699

CATEGORY	Caribbean/Vegetarian/Vegan
HOURS	Mon–Sat: 11 AM–10 PM Sun: noon–6 PM
SUBWAY	2, 3 to 125th St.
PAYMENT	Cash only
POPULAR FOOD	All kinds of vegetarian and vegan delights—get a more than generous scoop of tofu tempura, curry bean curd, or veggie chicken with collard greens, steamed cauliflower and carrots, brown rice, and a side of navy beans—a different bean dish is offered every night; finish with the famous sinus clearing (sometimes tear-inducing) ginger bread pudding or orange ginger cake and a shot of "Bad Man"—a stamina brew including, among other ingredients, cashew, sea moss, and soy milk—and you'll be better than good to go
DRINKS	Icebox filled with vitamin waters, ginger beer, and fresh juices; root tonics, carrot juice, *sorrel* (hibiscus) brewed in house
SEATING	Tables for 22
AMBIENCE	Informal—take your plate to a table and relax alone, chat with a friend, or watch the chess match in the corner—it's all good
EXTRAS/NOTES	Walk away feeling like you've done good for your body, your pocketbook, and the world. Over 70 percent of the ingredients used are organic. Every item on the rotating menu costs between one and three dollars. Also available are veggie burgers, tofu sandwiches, and tacos.

—*Marie Estrada*

Sylvia's

(see p. 47)
Southern American/Brunch
328 Malcolm X Blvd., Manhattan 10027
Phone (212) 996-0660

"If toast always lands butter-side down,
and cats always land on their feet,
what happens if you strap toast on the back of a cat
and drop it?"

—*Steven Wright*

Tang S Restaurant

Hole-in-the-wall gem for stupendous soups that put the ssss behind Tang.

$

306 St. Nicholas Ave., Manhattan 10027
(between W. 125th and W. 126th Sts.)
Phone (212) 864-5179 or (212) 865-5745

CATEGORY	Chinese/Take-out
HOURS	Mon–Thurs: 10:30 AM–11:30 PM
	Fri/Sat: 10:30 AM–12:30 AM
	Sun: noon–midnight
SUBWAY	A, B, C, D to 125th St.
PAYMENT	Cash only
POPULAR FOOD	Fried chicken wings and pork fried rice without doubt
UNIQUE FOOD	Hot and sour soup—tangy and spicy, filled with tofu, snow peas, mushrooms, carrots, and whatever other vegetables the cook feels like throwin' in—comes with two bags of freshly deep-fried wontons
DRINKS	Home made ice tea, canned soda
SEATING	One table, one chair for one person
AMBIENCE	Patrons are most definitely not at Tang S for the ambience—always cramped and filled with people waiting for their orders—must be the liquid grub that keeps us all coming

—*Marie Estrada*

Tremes Jamaican Restaurant and Bakery

Neighborhood Jamaican joint you wish were in your neighborhood.

$$

2086 Seventh Ave. (a.k.a. Adam Clayton Blvd.), Manhattan 10027
(between W. 124th and W. 125th Sts.)
Phone (212) 678-9881

CATEGORY	Jamaican
HOURS	Mon–Thurs: 7 AM–10 PM
	Fri/Sat: 7 AM–midnight
	Sun: 8 AM–9 PM
SUBWAY	2, 3 to 125th St.
PAYMENT	Cash only
POPULAR FOOD	A wide selection of standard Jamaican fare, including patties, *roti,* fried dumplings, sweet fruit cakes, and spice buns; be sure to check out the daily lunch specials, which consist of GENEROUS portions of curry chicken/goat, barbecue chicken (Tuesday), barbecue ribs (Thursday), oxtail, and jerk chicken— lunch specials are served with

combinations of rice and beans, plantains, cabbage, collard greens, yams, and macaroni and cheese

UNIQUE FOOD Authentic Jamaican favorites like saltfish and *ackee,* codfish, and *escovietch*

DRINKS Wide assortment of Jamaican Roots Drink, locally made juices, sea moss, ginger beer, coffee, tea, and soda

SEATING Tables inside for 15 and a cozy counter for two

AMBIENCE Filled with neighborhood folk—good place to eat (or study) alone

EXTRAS/NOTES The food at Tremes is no secret in Harlem. If you want the barbecue chicken or ribs experience of a lifetime, better show up before noon on Tuesday/Thursday, respectively and get in line.

—Scott Gross

Uptown Juice Bar

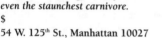

Truly inventive vegetarian fare that'll convert even the staunchest carnivore.

$

54 W. 125th St., Manhattan 10027
(between Fifth and Lenox Aves.)
Phone (212) 987-2660/9501
www.uptownjuicebar.com

CATEGORY Vegetarian/Juice Bar

HOURS Daily: 8 AM–10 PM

SUBWAY 2, 3, 4, 5 to 125th St.

PAYMENT Cash only

POPULAR FOOD Do yourself a favor and try the barbecue soy chunks; also recommend the eggplant fillet, delicious honey barbecue tofu, shepherd's pie, Ital Stew, and veggie steak—these come with four delicious sides—choose from cabbage, brown rice, okra, macaroni and cheese, and couscous

UNIQUE FOOD 100% veggie meat sandwiches: turkey, chicken, beef, fish, and veggie burgers, burger burgers, veggie patties, and veggie dogs; vegan pizzas with soy cheese; an incredible assortment of non-dairy pastries and muffins

SEATING Largely takeout, but seats about 10; bench out front

DRINKS Juice to suit any physical or mental ailment, deficiency, or abundance under creative title headings such as Juice to the Rescue, A Proper Way to Start Your Day, and Love Your Body

AMBIENCE Uptown Juice Bar, open just six years on 125th St., couched between a small fried fish joint and a mobile phone store, is already a Harlem institution

EXTRAS/NOTES Everyone stops at this juice bar and restaurant from sunrise to sunset, every day of the week for seriously savory homecooking, the freshest tastiest blended juices, and just about the friendliest staff—now that's rare. And the owners just opened a wonderful café in the rear!

OTHER ONES • Downtown Fancy: 116 Chambers St., Manhattan, 10007, (212) 964-4316

—Marie Estrada

West Africa Restaurant

Sit back, relax, and have some tasty African stew.

$$

2077 Seventh Ave., Manhattan 10027
(between W. 123rd and W. 124th Sts.)
Phone (212) 865-4250

CATEGORY	West African
HOURS	24/7
SUBWAY	2, 3 to 125th St.
PAYMENT	Cash only
POPULAR FOOD	A variety of tasty stews served over rice, including: beef and tomato (Ivory Coast), peanut (Guinea), okra, or *soupou kandja* (Mali); cassava leaves and stewed beef over white rice; grilled steak with marinated onion, house salad, and fried plantains
UNIQUE FOOD	*Thiebou dien* (Senegal): fish and tomato stew with cassava leaves, carrot, eggplant, served over rice; *thiebou yapp* (Senegal): lamb and mixed vegetables served over *jollof* rice
DRINKS	There's a cooler in the back stocked with bottled water, Snapple, Coca-Cola, and Vimto (a fruity British soda popular in Africa and the Arab world)
SEATING	Tables inside for approximately 30
AMBIENCE	A casual, friendly restaurant catering to the patchwork of African immigrants (from Guinea, Ivory Coast, Mali, Senegal, and Zaire) in the Harlem community; on an average night you'll hear conversations in English, French, and Fulani, the BBC or Charlie Rose on the tube, the muted prayers of Muslim men kneeling on rugs in the front, and the stereo humming with the soft rhythms of Sal Keta, Baba Mar, Ali Farka Toure, and Youssou N'Dour
EXTRAS/NOTES	Owner Mamadou Fatima Jartou and the entire staff at West Africa Restaurant wish to welcome everyone in NYC to their restaurant for "Good African Food and Culture." Friday nights, especially during Ramadan, are particularly festive, with patrons donning the tunics and gowns of their homelands before sitting down to enjoy their evening meals.

—Scott Gross

WAY UPTOWN

Capo Verde
(see p. 149)
589 Fort Washington Ave., Manhattan 10033
Phone (212) 543-9888

Carrot Top
A simple café—and a carrot cake empire.
$$
3931 Broadway, Manhattan 10032
(between 164th St. and 165th St.)
Phone (212) 927-4800

CATEGORY	Café/Bakery
HOURS	Mon–Sat: 6 AM–9 PM Sun: 7 AM–4 PM
SUBWAY	A, C, 1 to 168th St.; C to 163rd St.
PAYMENT	VISA MasterCard AMERICAN EXPRESS DISCOVER
POPULAR FOOD	Carrot Top justifiably prides itself on its carrot cake, carrot muffins, and now carrot cookies, but it's a full service café as well, and breakfast pastries go fast; another favorite: two eggs and cheese on a roll—get it on a French croissant
UNIQUE FOOD	I like the sandwiches, particularly the chicken Caesar sandwich on a hero; the cheesesteak sub is also good (especially if you don't insist on comparing it to the Philadelphia version of the same)
DRINKS	Coffee, tea, soda, juice (*amontillado* stashed away in side seating area: take a look)
SEATING	Seats about 35
AMBIENCE	Drawing hospital workers, construction workers, and a reasonable cross-section of Washington Heights, Carrot Top is nothing fancy, but it's comfortable enough
EXTRAS/NOTES	What began as a humble cake-baking business became a city-wide carrot cake empire. Even if you've never made it up to Washington Heights, you may have unsuspectingly tasted Carrot Top's specialties before. If you can, buy cakes here for special occasions.
OTHER ONES	• Way Uptown: 5025 Broadway, Manhattan, 10034, (212) 569-1532

—Joe Cleemann

Coda Café
What is this place doing here?
$$
1030 St. Nicholas Ave., Manhattan 10032
(at 162nd St.)
Phone (212) 568-5405

CATEGORY	Café
HOURS	Mon–Thurs: 10 AM–10 PM

	Fri/Sat: 10 AM–when they feel like closing
	Sun: 10 AM–8 PM
SUBWAY	C to 163rd St.
PAYMENT	Cash only
POPULAR FOOD	Everything is cooked on the premises; the menu's still expanding, but the pastries get high marks; peach mango crumb cake and chocolate mouse brownies and muffins come highly recommended; if you're after something warm, try the homemade soup (changes daily, but varieties include Moroccan vegetable, tomato basil bisque, green tea, sweet potato, and corn chowder)
DRINKS	Coffee, tea, hot cocoa
SEATING	Seats 15
AMBIENCE	Looks like a gutted bodega, probably is a gutted bodega; the owners have taken a small slab of real estate in a not particularly glamorous corner of Washington Heights (and Washington Heights is not glamorous to begin with) and transformed it into something you might find much further downtown (it's decorated with a rotating selection of original artwork, too); draws locals, and not just the yuppies and hipsters now infiltrating the neighborhood
EXTRAS/NOTES	You have to give the owners, Shae Russell and Jeanne Lee, a ton of credit for starting the kind of café they've started in the neighborhood where they've started it. Hopefully their commitment to the community will pay off. They're optimistic: when they opened W. 181st, a procession of longtime neighborhood residents welcomed them with housewarming gifts.

—*Joe Cleemann*

Coogan's
A Washington Heights Institution.
$$

4015 Broadway, Manhattan
10032
(at 169th St.)
Phone (212) 928-1234
www.coogans.com

CATEGORY	Bar and Grill
HOURS	Daily: 11 AM–midnight
SUBWAY	A, C, 1 to 168th St.
PAYMENT	VISA MasterCard AMERICAN EXPRESS
POPULAR FOOD	Coogan's isn't shy about trying new things and some of its eclectic entrees (like the shell steak and filet of salmon) run pretty expensive, but Italian and Mexican options are cheaper and more than serviceable; a good, filling burger platter will keep you within the budget range

UNIQUE FOOD Content, size, and preparation of the house specials change frequently; the crab cakes—in whatever form they come—are always good

DRINKS Full bar

SEATING Plenty of seating in the dining area, and more space around the bar

AMBIENCE "A moose with sunglasses?"—not quite, but you'll see plenty of odd knickknacks, autographed photos, etc.; while the chain bars buy this crap from wholesalers and franchise outlets, Coogan's earns it: it's a sometime hangout for local politicians and celebrities; Pulitzer Prize winning *Daily News* columnist Jim Dwyer called it the most integrated bar in the world

EXTRAS/NOTES Coogan's gets high marks—and not just from us—for integration. The increasingly diverse colors and cultures of Washington Heights are on display, and you can see them all without a trip to the dish room or the kitchen. This New Jerusalem of neighborhood bars drives the point home with the annual Coogan's Salsa, Blues, and Shamrocks 5K Race around St. Patrick's Day. Check the web site for details.

—Joe Cleemann

El Malecón

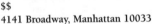

"El Rey del Pollo" reigns supreme.

$$

4141 Broadway, Manhattan 10033
(at 178th St.)
Phone (212) 927-3812 • Fax (212) 927-4913

CATEGORY Dominican

HOURS 24/7

SUBWAY A to 175th St. or 181st St.; 1 to 181st St.

PAYMENT VISA MasterCard American Express Discover

POPULAR FOOD Chicken Malecón-style: request an extra serving of the garlicky green *mojito* dip that accompanies it; feast cheap on hardy rice and beans; indulge your predilection for assorted plantains (the *maduros*—yellow plantains—are my favorite), or grab a simple but sublime *cubano* sandwich on the go

DRINKS Beer and wine

SEATING Almost never a problem: lots of tables and more space at the counter

AMBIENCE Pretty luxurious for its location, informal (but sparkling) wood paneling offset by big storefront windows and colorful tropical murals; most impressive: a wall of roasting, rotating chickens visible from street and wafting its irresistible aroma across the sidewalk

EXTRAS/NOTES And you thought the DR was a republic? Maybe, but you'll taste the benefits of enlightened monarchy as you gobble down some of the best and best-priced food in New York, courtesy of the self-proclaimed "King of Roast Chicken" (the comprehensive bilingual menu suggests an even broader authority in the Spanish-speaking world, where El Malecón is *"El Rey del Pollo"*).

OTHER ONES
- Upper West Side: 464 Amsterdam Ave., Manhattan, 10024, (212) 864-5648
- The Bronx: 5592 Broadway, 10463, (718) 432-5155

—*Mayu Kanno*

Emilou's Café

High-ceilinged café serving good meals for all appetites and one budget: small.

$

827 W. 181ˢᵗ St., Manhattan 10033
(at Pinehurst Ave.)
Phone (212) 795-9312 • Fax (212) 795-9314

CATEGORY	Café/Moroccan
HOURS	Daily: 9 AM–10 PM
SUBWAY	A to 181ˢᵗ St.
PAYMENT	Cash only
POPULAR FOOD	Specializes in quick, carefully prepared meals: an assortment of sandwiches and wraps (including hot chicken *parmigiana* sandwich on baguette with cheese and marinara sauce and the grilled chicken wrap) remains safely in the $5 range; salads incorporate Middle Eastern ingredients like hummus and *tabouli,* and come with a side of pita bread; plenty of fine breakfast options in the $1–$2 range
UNIQUE FOOD	The Hot Specials' Moroccan flavorings put this family-owned and operated establishment over the top: lemon chicken is cooked with ginger, garlic, and (of course) lemon, and is served with rice and salad; another favorite is the Mediterranean stew; great baklava
DRINKS	Variety of coffees and teas, fresh-squeezed juices are not cheap (orange juice, carrot juice, great lemonade) but they are, as the description implies, fresh squeezed; hot apple cider makes a nice drink on a cold day; BYOB for dinner
SEATING	Seats 20
AMBIENCE	Small and friendly, this colorful, high-ceilinged café is brightened further by sparse Moroccan décor; there used to be two Berber muskets hanging behind the counter, but they've come down
EXTRAS/NOTES	The same family owns Jesse's Place, a bar across the street that features live jazz three nights a week.

—*Mayu Kanno*

Picnicking in New York

Gotham may (now and forever!) boast the world's most awe-inspiring skyline. Manhattan's streets *may*, if you wish to stress what is by now a very, very tired analogy, be compared to canyons. Steel and concrete *are* commonly used construction materials (that's why the buildings are taller than four stories). And its 304 square miles *are* crisscrossed by 6,400 miles of road and 230 miles of subway lines, while some 60+ bridges and tunnels effectively nullify the natural impediments to travel. But those 304 square miles border on nearly 600 miles of waterfront, not all of it dingy, and nearly 15 of which are sandy beaches (that's the distance, as the bird flies, from the Empire State Building to Jacob Riis Park, on the Rockaway Peninsula in Queens). And they're served by 15,000+ parks and playgrounds, comprising over 26,000 acres. That's 85 acres for every square mile. So there are plenty of places to head for a picnic.

You probably know—or can guess—some of the best spots. **Central Park** is convenient to hundreds of delis and markets. If you're coming from the Upper West Side, **Fairway** is a great option for just about anything edible (see p. 134). Both Fairway locations are also close to **Riverside Park,** which is one of the best places to lounge on the Hudson. Like Central Park, popular **Prospect Park,** in Brooklyn, bears the stamp of Frederick Law Olmstead, the great 19th century Landscape Designer. Plenty of take-out places join the normal assortment of bodegas and supermarkets in nearby Park Slope, but if you're looking for something fresh and cheap, a decent **Green Market** operates outside its north entrance (at Grand Army Plaza) on the weekends. And **Battery Park,** serving the financial district's, tourists, gawkers, hawkers, and con-men, makes a good lunch spot and is within a stone's throw of most of the downtown locations listed on p. 2.

What about the less visited parks? One of the best parks in the city, by far, **Fort Tryon Park** is known for the museum located on its grounds, the Cloisters, which house the Met's medieval exhibits. Not quite the highest land in Manhattan (the highest natural point in the borough is four blocks down Fort Washington Avenue at **Bennet Park**), it occupies the highlands that dominate Manhattan's northern panhandle, commanding a breathtaking view of the Hudson Valley and the George Washington Bridge. But look no further than Fort Tryon's Heather Garden for flora and fauna, including the rare hummingbird. The nearby strip of parkland along the river is called **Fort Washington Park** on the map, and it's best accessed by heading west on 181st Street, taking a quick right, and crossing the Henry Hudson

Parkway on the pedestrian overpass. The path winds down to the riverbank, eventually affording a great view of New Jersey, Lower Manhattan, and Yonkers. The fabled **Little Red Lighthouse** rests just under the Great Gray Bridge, but it's been more or less inaccessible since September 2001, when the police department began sending patrol cars to secure the supports for the **George Washington Bridge.**

The best places to grab a lunch for either park lie on 181st Street and on Fort Washington and 187th. In addition to **Emilou's Café** (see review p. 147), 181st Street is home to the **Ft. Washington Deli Bakery** and its assortment of fresh deli goods and tempting pastries *(Way Uptown: 808 W. 181st St. at Ft. Washington, Manhattan, (212) 795-1891)*, to a wide selection of greasy spoon favorites (including pizza, burgers, fried chicken, and gyros) at **Exclusive Pizza** *(Way Uptown: 810 W. 181st St., Manhattan, (212) 795-0550)*. At 187th, **Capo Verde** specializes in gourmet burritos *(Way Uptown: 589 Fort Washington, Manhattan, (212) 543-9888)* and offers an outdoor dining area for those unwilling to trudge up to (or down to) one of the parks.

Another excellent little park, **Astoria Park** in Queens, offers great sunsets and a surreal view of the midtown skyline and the often-angry waters of the **Hell Gate.** Not just a cute name, the Hell Gate witnesses the union of Long Island Sound and the East River (itself a tidal straight connecting to New York Harbor). The battling tides of these bodies tug at the narrow Hell Gate from both sides, creating a treacherous, churning seaway marked by sporadic whirlpools, cross currents, and tidal falls (and, according to lore, not a few submerged wrecks). Also the quickest navigable route from Lower Manhattan to the Sound, it's easy to see how the mariners of bygone centuries came up with the strait's straightforward descriptive. Now you can watch huge steamers and barges effortlessly plow their ways up and down, to and from the wharves and powers stations in the Bronx and northern Queens. More entertaining—if more stomach turning—are the reckless pleasure boaters who challenge its waters for fun and profit.

If this sounds like an afternoon's viewing enjoyment to you, stock up on picnic food at the nearby Astoria Locations: **Sal, Kris & Charlie Deli** (see p. 168) and the **unnamed kabob cart** (see p. 168) provide great grab-and-go options. In the summer, nothing's more romantic than a few ice cream cones and a well-placed wager on the fate of a Boston Whaler. Get the ice cream at **La Guli Pastry Shop:** *(Astoria and Long Island City: 29-15 Ditmars Blvd., Queens, (718) 728-5612)* where an old-fashioned soda fountain dispenses homemade flavors.

The beaches along Staten Island may have packed in well-heeled tourists before (as usual) air travel, Interstate, and Robert Moses opened up more enticing frontiers, but even now a day at the beach can be just that. Sure, the surf is weak and the cloistered, bungalow-dominated neighborhood is reminiscent of *Copland*, but **South Beach Park** offers sun, sand, a boardwalk, and a great view of the Verrazano Narrows Bridge—and it's all easily accessible by bus. The #51 leaves from the Staten Island Ferry terminal and can get you to the park—marked by a sculptured school of dolphins—in 20 minutes to half an hour. Down a little further, along Midland Avenue, you'll find some descent options for grabbing lunch. The **Shop Smart** *(590 Midland Ave., Staten Island, (718) 987-4940)* offers a decent selection of deli goods and a supermarket-ful of stuff to go with it. More deli stuff can be got at **New York Deli** *(585 Midland Ave., Staten Island, (718) 987-0062)* where Italian and American subs are made to order. **La Roca's**—a genuine restaurant with a sit-down dining area—serves pizza, ice cream, and more *(489 Midland Ave., Staten Island, (718) 979-8833)*.

Or, if you don't get seasick, grab a lunch and take it on the free **Staten Island Ferry.** Travelling between Whitehall terminal on the southern tip of Manhattan and St. George on Staten Island, the ferry provides great views of the harbor and may be one of the best (certainly the cheapest) of New York's traditional tourist attractions. There's a lunch counter on board if you forget to pack your own.

There are plenty of other places you can go that feel as far away from the bustle of lower Manhattan as the commute will make it seem anyway. **Pelham Bay Park**, in the northeast corner of The Bronx, is one of the city's biggest, encompassing woodland, golf courses, and beach. It guards the approach to **City Island**, another weird and appropriately insular community that's renowned for its seafood restaurants. **Ward's Island**, across the Hell Gate from Astoria Park but much easier to access (for pedestrians) by the footbridge at 102nd St. in Manhattan, offers a commanding view of New York's maze of waterways, along with ample picnic grounds and athletic fields. Don't be surprised to find hundreds of barbecues burning at once come summer. **Jacob Riis Park**, on the Rockaway Peninsula, gives expression to some of the ambitious dreams of Moses (Robert, that is). Grab your food in **Belle Harbor** or further up the peninsula, though—**Breezy Point** doesn't welcome strangers.

You get the idea!

—*Joe Cleemann*

Figures from New York City 5 Borough Atlas, Fifth Large Scale Edition (Hagstrom Map Company, Maspeth, NY, 1998.

Empire Szechuan

Who says you can't tell take-out joints apart?
This is one of the best.

$$

4041 Broadway, Manhattan 10032
(at 170th St.)

Phone (212) 568-1600/1611/1616

CATEGORY	Chinese/Pan-Asian/Eat-in/Take-out/ Delivery
HOURS	Daily: 10:30 AM–midnight
SUBWAY	A, C, 1 to 168th St.
PAYMENT	VISA MasterCard AMERICAN
POPULAR FOOD	All your favorites: chicken *lo mein, moo shu* pork, fried or boiled dumplings; Empire does right by every gourmet's favorite military-hero-cum-celebrity-chef, the great General Tso—try his chicken or his chicken and prawn duet
UNIQUE FOOD	Empire is just that, uniting Asian cuisine under one glorious banner; my born-and-bred Japanese girlfriend eats and enjoys their sushi (most platters under $10, half price if you eat in)
DRINKS	Beer, wine, liquor, water, soda
SEATING	Seats about 50
AMBIENCE	There's a comfortably low-rent dining area in the back: you get table service and you're shielded from the take-out counter
OTHER ONES	• Upper West Side: 2574 Broadway, Manhattan, 10025, (212) 663-6006

—*Joe Cleemann*

Exclusive Pizza

(see p. 149)
Pizzeria
810 W. 181st St., Manhattan 10033
Phone (212) 795-0550

Falafel Cart

No name, but the food is distinctive.

$

NW corner of 168th St. and Ft.
Washington Ave., Manhattan 10032

CATEGORY	Falafel Cart
HOURS	Supposedly 24/7, but the cart occasionally disappears on Sundays and holidays
SUBWAY	A, C, 1 to 168th St.
PAYMENT	Cash only
POPULAR FOOD	Falafel sandwich; the chicken sandwich— a spicy pita wrap—is amazing and amazingly cheap; budget breakfasts also available (prices vary depending on what you get, but don't expect to pay more than $5)
UNIQUE FOOD	A refreshing approach to the ubiquitous meat platter: the meat (chicken, beef, or

both) seems fresher and healthier than what you'd get at your average falafel cart, the lettuce is greener and crisper and (unlike some purveyors of falafel) these guys don't skip on the tomatoes; besides rice, the platter comes with good home fry-style potatoes, a piece of pita, and of course falafel; the sauces—white, hot, and *tahini*—all do the job

DRINKS	Soda, juice, coffee
SEATING	None—it's a cart!
AMBIENCE	Gets a lot of business from nearby Columbia-Presbyterian hospital, but also from the surrounding neighborhood
EXTRAS/NOTES	Between the quality of ingredients, the generous portions, the loving preparation, and the superb taste, this tragically unnamed falafel cart rises above the competition.

—Joe Cleemann

Fort Washington Deli Bakery

(see p. 149)
Deli/Bakery
808 W. 181ˢᵗ St., Manhattan 10033
Phone (212) 795-1891

Mike's Bagels

Bagel bar serves them up hot (or to order).
$
4003 Broadway, Manhattan 10032
(at 168ᵗʰ St.)
Phone (212) 928-2300 • Fax (212) 928-2300

CATEGORY	Bagels
HOURS	Mon–Thurs: 6 AM–6 PM Fri–Sun: 6 AM–5 PM
SUBWAY	A, C, 1 to 168ᵗʰ St.
PAYMENT	Cash only
POPULAR FOOD	As often as not the bagels here are still warm from the oven, and they're the taste and consistency you want; a good variety of regular and low-fat cream cheeses available, such as vegetable, chives, etc.
UNIQUE FOOD	Mike's does a top-notch job of turning a bagel into a deli sandwich: stack up the honey turkey, lettuce, tomato, and more and go home happy
DRINKS	Soda, juice, water
SEATING	No seats, but some bar space available if you want to eat standing up
AMBIENCE	Most eat on the go, and the line moves briskly, so you're not going for the company, or for the atmosphere, which is as plain as white bread

—Joe Cleemann

THE BRONX /
WAY UPTOWN

THE BRONX

Banao

Filipino all-you-can eat buffet in a Bronx mini mall? Gloria, Cori—perhaps even Imelda—would surely approve.

$$

5677 Riverdale Ave, The Bronx 10471
(between W. 258th and W. 259th Sts.)
Phone (718) 601-9900/9660

CATEGORY	Filipino Buffet
HOURS	Tue–Thurs: 11 AM–9 PM Fri/Sat: 11 AM–10 PM Sun: 9 AM–9 PM
SUBWAY	1 to 231st and Broadway, then B7 bus to W. 258th St.
PAYMENT	VISA MasterCard AMERICAN EXPRESS Discover
POPULAR FOOD	Among the 15 different entrees available, the most popular are the Filipino national dish, *adobong manok at baboy* (pork and chicken stewed in soy sauce, vinegar, garlic, peppercorn, and bay leaf), pork barbecue (grilled marinated pork on skewers), *tilapia* in sesame (flash-fried *tilapia*, sesame seeds, tamarind sauce), and *sinigang* (tamarind soup with beef, fish, or pork)
UNIQUE FOOD	*Paksiw na bangus* (milkfish cooked in vinegar and spices), *binagoongan baboy* (pork cutlets stewed in shrimp paste and vinegar), *adobong pusit* (squid stewed in vinegar and spices), *dinuguan* (pork pieces and green papaya in beef and pork blood), *laing* (taro leaf with shrimp paste and pork in coconut milk), *turon* (plantain and jack fruit in spring roll wrapper), cassava cake (ground cassava in sweet coconut milk)
DRINKS	*Calamanci* (Filipino style lemonade—*calamansi* is difficult to find in the states, so *calamansi* juice from concentrate is used for this beverage), mango juice, cantaloupe juice, guava juice, soda, coffee, tea, and hot chocolate
SEATING	Twenty-five at tables
AMBIENCE	An all-you-can-eat breakfast, lunch and dinner buffet in a cozy dining area with wooden artifacts and textiles native to the Philippines
EXTRAS/NOTES	Banao's buffet also includes a number of dishes that will satisfy the pickiest of picky vegetarians: vegetarian curry (wheat gluten, carrots, potato, and peppers in a curry coconut sauce); *pinakbet* (eggplant, squash, okra, string beans sautéed in garlic, onion, and tomatoes); *ensaladang ampalaya* (bitter melon with tomato and onion in vinegar dressing); *ensaladang talong* (broiled eggplant, tomatoes, onion,

in sweet and sour dressing); eggplant omelette; *lumpiang sariwa* (mixed vegetables wrapped in crepe with sweet sauce); sautéed string beans; and Bicol Express (green chillies and coconut milk). Gracious owners Victoria and Marc Greenberg named the restaurant after a town in Iriga City, Philippines, the hometown of Victoria's father. Located in the Skyview Shopping Center. Karaoke on Tuesday nights after 8 PM.

—Marie Estrada

El Malecón

(see p. 146)
Dominican
5592 Broadway, The Bronx 10463
Phone (718) 432-5155

Edy's

Eclectic home away from home.
$
5901 Riverdale Ave., The Bronx 10471
(corner of W. 258th St.)
Phone (718) 549-8938

CATEGORY	Ice Cream Parlor/Soup Shop
HOURS	Mon–Sun: 10 AM–2 AM
SUBWAY	1 to 231st and Broadway, then B7 bus to 258th
PAYMENT	Cash only
POPULAR FOOD	Potato leek soup, seafood gumbo with a generous amount of shrimp and lobster; soups change daily and with the whim of the owner, but there's always one vegetarian option available; soups come with fresh bread
UNIQUE FOOD	Custom theme and character ice cream cakes
DRINKS	Espresso, cappuccino, milkshakes
SEATING	Tables for 12
AMBIENCE	Ultra pretty—long, open, and narrow, brightly lit, with potted plants and fresh flowers mingling with stuffed animals, ballerina figurines, children's artwork, tin tables, and yellow vinyl seats
EXTRAS/NOTES	You'll feel completely at ease chatting with the owner, a songwriter of Dutch origin, who started Edy's with his wife (she's the artist behind the gorgeous ice cream cakes). But, if you're on the move, Edy's has the perfect indulgences to carry out: gourmet soup, freshly cut flowers, Italian cappuccino, and decadent ice cream dessert—yum.

—Marie Estrada

Belmont's Little Italy of The Bronx

Drive, ride, strap-hang, and hoof-it out to this beautifully preserved relic of what the borough once was…

Anyone familiar with the history of New York's outlying neighborhoods—in the outer boroughs and in Upper Manhattan—knows the story. Prosperous working class suburbs witnessed a decades-long decline during the Post-War Years as insensitively placed highways and interstates paved over bustling commercial districts. And no other borough suffered more than The Bronx, where the Model City of mid-century decayed into the expansive slums of the 1970s, where the Grand Concourse's diminished challenge to the Champs-Elysées challenged only the good taste of those who joked about it, and where the name Robert Moses is still greeted with dread. But certain Bronx enclaves held the line against decline. And of these unlikely success stories, none is more fondly noted than that of Belmont, where a collection of Italian (and now also Albanian) businesses on and around Arthur Avenue are still known collectively as Little Italy of The Bronx.

Here, trench-coated men and a scattering of limousines—some credit these, or what they imagine these represent, with the neighborhood's survival—patrol freely along the storefronts. And the pizzerias, cafes, rated restaurants, and an extraordinary array of specialty shops draw customers from across the five boroughs. Nowhere near as commercial or touristy as its Manhattan counterpart, Little Italy of The Bronx hides hundreds of gourmet bargains.

A hunk of cheese all by itself can make a good and inexpensive meal. If you're in the mood, check out bare-bones **Calandra's Cheese** *(2314 Arthur Ave., (718) 365-7572. Mon-Sat: 8 AM–6 PM)*, where artisans have crafted their medium into shapes as strange as those of elephants, and into snacks as tasty as a mozzarella and sausage roll. More picturesque than Calandra's, and offering a more comprehensive array of goods, **Casa Della Mozzarella** *(604 E. 187th St., (718) 364-3867. Mon-Sat: 7:30 AM–6 PM, Sun 7:30 AM–1 PM)* boasts a full deli case, 110 lb. hunks of provolone hanging from the ceiling, and a window through which you can watch the cheese-makers themselves ladling gooey mozzarella from their enormous pots. In addition to the cheese (including a mozzarella and provolone roll), choose from meats, olives, and assorted antipastos.

But you need not stop at cheese. A few more feet, in fact, and you'll have a whole

sandwich. **Calabria Pork Store** *(2338 Arthur Ave.,
(718) 367-5145. Mon–Sat: 7 AM–5:30 PM)* begs a
visit from the staunchest vegetarian. Enter and
you're greeted by the enticing pungency of a
thousand salamis. Hanging from the ceiling and in
various states of aging (don't be put off by the
occasional spot of mold, that's part of the game),
these amazing salamis represent what may be one
of the objectively coolest culinary offerings in New
York. They're joined in the case by various fresh
pork sausages, and elsewhere by big wheels of
fresh cheese. Then grab a loaf of bread—*pane
de casa* is the most popular kind—at nearby
G. Addeo & Sons Bakery *(2352 Arthur Ave.,
(718) 367-8316. Mon–Sat: 7:30 AM–6:30 PM.* And if
you're ready for dessert, grab some biscotti.

If not, try the clams at **Randazzo's Seafood**
(2337 Arthur Ave., (718) 367-4139). A full-service
seafood store, Randazzo's operates a clam cart out
front from which the willing may purchase and
consume ice-cold, freshly killed raw clams at six for
$4. They'll pull the shells apart; you add lemon and
sauce and eat. If that doesn't come naturally to you,
go inside and choose some fresh fish to take home
and cook. And if you plan to cook anyway,
celebrated **Biancardi's** butcher shop, across the
street, bears checking out *(2350 Arthur Ave., (718)
733-4058. Mon–Sat: 8 AM–6 PM).* It's hard to miss,
anyway: their specialties—baby lambs, kid goats,
rabbits—hang fully-furred by their hind legs in the
front window. But it's a full service butcher and you
can obtain tamer fare as well from the helpful staff.

For dessert, try a cannoli with a cup of
espresso at **De Lillo Pastry Shop** *(606 E. 187th St.,
(718) 367-8191. Daily: 8 AM–7 PM).* In business
since 1925, De Lillo offers several cases full of eye-
catching confections, along with a small eating area.

Arthur Avenue Retail Market

There is a short-cut, though, for those who
want to run the whole gamut in 20 minutes to
half-an-hour. The **Arthur Avenue Retail Market**
(2344 Arthur Ave., Mon–Sat: 8 AM–6:30 PM.) was
commissioned and built under the LaGuardia
administration in 1940. An outdoor market placed
indoors, this cavernous, sky-lit, cement floored,
feline-patrolled retail space houses a small
collection of first rate specialty booths, selling wares
ranging from the ceramic to the horticultural, to the
hand-rolled cigar. There's plenty to eat, as well.

Three produce stands compete for floor space
with a few distinct seating areas. For those planning
to cook at home, these offer decent varieties of
reasonably fresh fruits and vegetables. There's also
an exotic selection of pastas, organic foods, rice,
oils, and vinegar, at **Mt. Carmel Gourmet Foods**
(718) 933-2295. Joining them is **Peter's Meat Market**

(718) 367-3136, "Arthur Avenue's Favorite 'Meating' Place," which offers a stunning variety of meats, plain and prepared (but uncooked) including—but by no means limited to—calf brains. More appetizing are the prepared meatballs, pinwheel steaks, and veal rolls that join choice cuts of more conventional meats in the main case.

But if you plan to eat there—and there are plenty of spots to do so, on the main floor among the red, white and green pennants and red, white, and blue flags, and (more romantically, seriously) upstairs near the bathrooms—you have a couple excellent options. **Café del Mercato** (718) 364-7681 is one: it offers a straightforward selection of hero sandwiches (one's even called the Fire Man's Special) and very crisp-crusted rectangular pizzas. **Mike's Deli** (718) 295-5033 is the other. Mike's sells deli meats, cheeses, antipastos, stromboli, etc., along with cheap and delicious sandwiches on focaccio or baguette. Try the *caponara* on toast: for about $5 you get five small slices piled high with the eggplant salad and topped with fresh mozzarella, all on a generous heap of lettuce and olives.

It's not easy to get to Little Italy of The Bronx. The closest train stop is Fordham Station, which serves Metro-North's Harlem Line. If you want to take a subway, your best bet is the D to Fordham Road: walk east on E. 188th St until you hit Arthur Ave. Then turn right. It's a pretty long walk, and it takes you through some neighborhoods that may frighten you. If you're driving, there's probably a highway nearby.

—*Mayu Kanno & Joe Cleemann*

Little Bit of Jam

Tasty Jamaican alongside a fine and famous slice.

$$

3033 Tibbett Ave., The Bronx 10471
(at W. 231st)
Phone (718) 549-8893

CATEGORY	Jamaican Pizzeria
HOURS	Mon–Sat: 6 AM–midnight Sun: noon–midnight
SUBWAY	1 to 231st St.
PAYMENT	Cash only
POPULAR FOOD	Go entirely Jamaican and have the treat of your life; the popular dishes are the oxtail, stewed chicken and goat, and Tuesday's curried shrimp—all come with rice, peas, and choice of carrot, cabbage, or plantains; wash it all down with a slice of Jamaican rum cake and a shot of Irish Moss

UNIQUE FOOD	Have the Ital Stew and a side of yellow rice and peas or make your own vegetable platter from the 12 vegetable, bean, and starch options including Middle Eastern-style okra, macaroni and cheese, spinach and garlic, dumplings, and yams
DRINKS	Various seasonal juices such as cane, fruit punch, vegetable, and a variety of smoothies; Caribbean drinks include Irish Moss, carrot and beet, Agony, Double Trouble, and Root
SEATING	Seats eight at two-person tables
AMBIENCE	Bright and welcoming railroad style space with an impressive mural painted by the artist known as Regal, "stone-cold" speaker system, and 35-inch TV; friendly staff and customers
EXTRAS/NOTES	If you're not in the mood for Jamaican fare, try the utterly simple but divine slice of pizza made with fresh dough and fresh stewed tomatoes—prepared by none other than acclaimed King and Creator of the first Shamrock-shaped Pizza.

—*Marie Estrada*

Sam's Soul Food Restaurant & Bar

The only reason to ever visit this part of The Hub.

$$

596-598 Grand Concourse, The Bronx 10471
(between 150th and 151st St.)

Phone (718) 665-5341 • Fax (718) 665-1409

CATEGORY	American Soul Food
HOURS	Mon–Wed: 11 AM–10 PM Thurs–Sat: 11 AM–11 PM Sun: 2 PM–8 PM
SUBWAY	2, 3 to 149th Grand Concourse
PAYMENT	
POPULAR FOOD	The catch of the day with two sides is always a pleasantly tasty surprise; also try the hickory smoked barbecue pork ribs, home made Southern-style meat loaf, smothered pork chops, oven baked Virginia ham (made with cloves, cinnamon, pineapple), and last but not least, jerk chicken
UNIQUE FOOD	Cajun burger, stewed chicken (chunks of chicken prepared with root vegetables in a savory tomato herb sauce)
DRINKS	Full bar
SEATING	Tables for over 100
AMBIENCE	Huge and expansive space with several different rooms—empty in the afternoon, hopping during dinner and late night when the bar crowd kicks in
EXTRAS/NOTES	There are three parts to Sam's—Sam's Take Out, Sam's Bar, and Sam's the Dining Room Restaurant. Sam's Take Out includes

a sit-down counter that seats about eight comfortably in front of the grill, and is open Thurs–Sat until 1 AM. Sam's Bar is open Mon–Wed: 11 AM–2 AM, Thurs–Sat: 7 AM–4 AM, and Sun: 2 PM–10 PM. Live Blues, Jazz, Reggae, and Karaoke in the evening dining room and bar.

—*Marie Estrada*

Tibbett Diner

Feel miles away from the urban grind at this homey secluded diner.

$$

3033 Tibbett Ave., The Bronx 10471
(just south of W. 231st St.)
Phone (718) 549-8893

CATEGORY	Diner/American
HOURS	Daily: 11 AM–10:30 PM
SUBWAY	1 to 231st St.
PAYMENT	VISA MasterCard AMERICAN DISCOVER
POPULAR FOOD	Daily specials: Friday's chicken pot pie, Saturday's lamb shank, Sunday's prime rib; also chicken caesar salad
UNIQUE FOOD	Utterly decadent Disco Fries: french fries with melted cheese and thick brown gravy
SEATING	Thirteen booths with plenty of seats and 10 at the counter
DRINKS	Egg creams, coffee, herbal and black tea, hot chocolate, fountain soda, mineral water, and milk
AMBIENCE	Flowered curtains with pink and mauve dominated décor; older neighborhood folk, friendly and helpful staff
EXTRAS/NOTES	Huge portions—you'll have leftovers to last at least another two meals.

—*Marie Estrada*

QUEENS

ASTORIA

The Bagel House

Queens' Dark Horse Contender for Citywide Bagel Title.

$

38-11 Ditmars Blvd., Queens 11105
(at 38th St.)
Phone (718) 726-1869

CATEGORY	Bagel Shop
HOURS	Daily: 5:30 AM–7:30 PM
SUBWAY	N, W to Ditmars Blvd.
PAYMENT	Cash only
POPULAR FOOD	Sticks faithfully to the basics: plain, sesame, salt, pumpernickel, everything, garlic, whole wheat, and poppy—all are exceedingly fresh, with a slightly hardened crust surrounding the perfectly chewy, gummy dough that makes up a bagel's heart and soul; various flavors of homemade cream cheese include veggie, walnut raisin, and olive pimiento—add it to your bagel for an extra buck or so
UNIQUE FOOD	Mini-bagels, with fillings like *sorpressata* and Swiss cheese; a selection of focaccia pizza: the Luna features mozzarella, oven-dried tomato, goat cheese, and zucchini, while the Frescha is topped with mozzarella, fresh tomato, and basil
DRINKS	Coolers stocked with everything from orange and tomato juice to Gatorade and Snapple; the coffee is consistently fresh
SEATING	Most patrons are in and out, but a six-seat counter offers a view of Ditmars Blvd.
AMBIENCE	While there's no real ambience in the traditional sense, during the fall and winter you may be asked for your thoughts on the weekend's Jets game while at the register
EXTRAS/NOTES	Clientele ranges from parents stopping by after church on Sundays to young singles fighting through their weekend hangovers. The Bagel House also offers a range of typical fare: egg sandwiches, muffins, and bagel sandwich choices like grilled chicken with roasted peppers and fresh mozzarella or smoked turkey, brie, sun-dried tomato and honey mustard.

—*John Hartz*

"Another trouble with leftovers is that their recipes
are almost impossible to write.
There is no way to capture again
the taste of a cupful of yesterday's sautéed mushrooms
put at the last minute unto a spinach soup
because two more people turned up for supper."
—*M.F.K. Fisher*

Blue Sea Café

*Some of the better breakfast
specials in Queens.*

$$

30-20 30th Ave., Queens 11102
(at 31st St.)

Phone (718) 274-7704

CATEGORY	Diner with Delivery/Greek/American
HOURS	Mon: 6 AM–midnight Tues–Sat: 24 hours Sun: midnight –10 PM
SUBWAY	N to 30th Ave.
PAYMENT	Cash only
POPULAR FOOD	All the baking is done on the premises, so try the pastries: French crullers, angel wings, and muffins are the favorites. American and Greek specials go over well with clientele: beef gyro platter, burgers and fries
UNIQUE FOOD	The breakfast special (5 AM–11 AM, on premises only): even the most expensive—corned beef hash with two eggs, home fries, toast, juice, and coffee—is cheap; the other six are cheaper, sometimes much cheaper, and are all filling like the American Breakfast: two eggs, any style, with bacon, ham, or sausage, and home fries, toast, juice, and coffee or tea—and the coffee is good
DRINKS	Coffee, tea, juice, milk, no booze
SEATING	Seats for 35–40, half of which line the wavy-shaped blue counter
AMBIENCE	As you might have guessed, whoever painted the Blue Sea Café didn't pinch pennies on the blue paint; local crowd

—*Joe Cleemann*

Bohemian Hall & Park

*New York City's last great
beer garden, featuring
hearty Czech specialties. Like beer.*
Since 1910
$$$

29-19 24th Ave., Queens 11105
(between 29th St. and 31st St.)

Phone (718) 728-9776 • Fax (718) 728-9278

CATEGORY	Czech
HOURS	Daily: noon–4 AM
SUBWAY	N, W to Ditmars Blvd.
PAYMENT	Cash only
POPULAR FOOD	A range of Czech and Eastern European staples, such as: homemade kielbasa, Hungarian beef goulash with dumplings, roast pork with dumplings and sauerkraut, and schnitzel with potatoes or fries

UNIQUE FOOD As an appetizer, the head cheese with bread and onions; not to be missed: the deep-fried cheese stuffed with ham and potatoes

DRINKS The Czechs are world renowned for their beer, and the Bohemian Hall delivers on two excellent examples via its taps: Staropramen and Pilsner Urquell, in sizeable beer hall-worthy steins

SEATING The bar is somewhat cramped, with five large booths, two or three smaller tables and about ten stools; the outdoor garden features 60–80 large picnic tables, arranged in rows beneath the leafy old-growth canopy

EXTRAS/NOTES Owned by the Bohemian Citizen's Benevolent Society, the beer garden is the last of its kind in New York City. It was going strong from its construction in 1910 until after World War II, when interest in the cultural activities offered at the hall dwindled. But Czechoslovakia's 'Velvet Revolution' in 1989 sparked a revival for both the Benevolent Society and the Bohemian Hall. Czech President Vaclav Havel paid a visit in the late 1990s, and the hall currently under consideration for inclusion on the National Register of Historic Places. (It has already been recognized as a Queens landmark through the Queensmark program). Bohemian Hall continues as a social venue for the local Czech and Slovak community, but it also draws from across the Queens (and at times, Manhattan) spectrum. The garden is open year-round, but it gets cold in the winter. During weekends in the spring and summer you can catch live entertainment, including various locally produced plays and musical events. Be warned: the quality of these events can vary widely, and sometimes you need to purchase a ticket to the show to get into the garden.

—John Hartz

Cevabdzinica Sarajevo
Bosnian-style Hungry-man sandwiches.
$$
37-18 34ᵗʰ Ave., Queens 11103
(at 37ᵗʰ St.)
Phone (718) 752-9528

CATEGORY Bosnian
HOURS Daily: 10:30 AM–11 PM
SUBWAY R, G to Steinway; N to Broadway
PAYMENT Cash only
POPULAR FOOD The specialty (and what just about everyone orders) is *cevapi*, grilled ground meat shaped to look like a sausage: hollow

out half a loaf of bread, stuff it with the *cevapi,* some onions, and a very light tomato sauce. . . and *that* is how you make a sandwich

DRINKS	Soda, juice
SEATING	A few tables, seats about 19
AMBIENCE	One of the newer eating places in Astoria, it's already filled with hardcore regulars looking for a taste of home (home being Sarajevo)
EXTRAS/NOTES	The owners are very friendly and always more than happy to give newcomers a rundown of the menu and make recommendations.

—Larry Ogrodnek

La Guli Pastry Shop

(see p. 149)
Soda Fountain/Bakery
29-15 Ditmars Blvd., Queens 11105
Phone (718) 728-5612

Last Stop Café
Home-style food at Mom's prices.
$$$
22-35 31ˢᵗ St., Queens 11105
(at Ditmars Blvd.)
Phone (718) 932-9419

CATEGORY	American/Diner
HOURS	Daily: 6 AM–midnight
SUBWAY	N, W to Ditmars Blvd.
PAYMENT	VISA MasterCard AMERICAN
POPULAR FOOD	Breakfast is served until 3 PM; breakfast special before 11 AM (two eggs; hash browns; toast; bacon, sausage, or ham; coffee; and juice for $3.50); real New York pizza—ask for it cooked well done; assortment of Italian dinners for under $10; soups made on the premises
UNIQUE FOOD	*Stracciatella* Soup—chicken broth, spinach and whisked eggs
DRINKS	Soda, Snapple, and one of the best bottomless cups of cheap-o coffee in NYC
SEATING	Small dining room is packed for breakfast and lunch, especially during the weekends
AMBIENCE	Two TVs (usually are tuned to CNN or trash talk shows during the day) distract from the cheesy subway murals on the walls; crowd is Astoria locals ranging from old to young, straight to gay, and everything in between—everyone gets treated like they've been longtime customers (though the wait staff definitely notices who tips well and who doesn't)

—Michael Connor

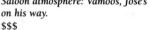

Los Amigos

Saloon atmosphere: Vamoos, Jose's on his way.

$$$

22-73 31ˢᵗ St., Queens 11105
(at 23ʳᵈ Ave.)
Phone (718) 726-8708 • Fax (718) 956-8855

CATEGORY	Mexican Eat-in/Take-out
HOURS	Daily: 11 AM–2 AM
SUBWAY	N, W to Ditmars Ave.
PAYMENT	
POPULAR FOOD	Seven different combination platters, served with rice and refried beans, include various combinations of burritos, tacos, *chimichangas,* enchiladas, and more; for something cheaper, choose from seven varieties of soft tacos; servings are generous
DRINKS	Full bar (beer, wine, liquor), juice and soda
SEATING	About 35 seats and six stools at the bar
AMBIENCE	Los Amigos draws the white middle class professionals who are in increasing numbers making Astoria their home, and real, live Mexicans who have done likewise; it's dark, decorated with old bullfighting advertisements and Pancho Villa recruitment posters

—*Joe Cleemann*

McCann's Pub & Grill

Old fashioned bar-and-grill standbys done right.

$$$

36-15 Ditmars Blvd., Queens 11105
(between 35ᵗʰ and 36ᵗʰ Sts.)
Phone (718) 278-2621/2039 • Fax (718) 762-5126
www.mccannspub.com

CATEGORY	Irish Pub
HOURS	Mon–Sat: 10 AM–4 AM Sun: noon–4 AM
SUBWAY	N, W to Ditmars Blvd.
PAYMENT	Cash only, but there's an ATM downstairs
POPULAR FOOD	Food is outstanding and extremely fresh, if basic: the deluxe hamburgers, served with steak fries, lettuce, tomato, onion, and pickle range from a straightforward burger to the bacon cheeseburger; the grilled chicken salad is outstanding
UNIQUE FOOD	McCann's offers some excellent food and drink combination specials; to wit: on Tuesdays, any burger with a pint goes for ten bucks; Thursdays bring an order of wings with a pitcher of beer for the same

DRINKS	All the usual alcoholic suspects, highlighted by a well-pulled pint of Guinness
SEATING	Fairly small as far as floor space goes, McCann's manages to squeeze in five large tables along the wall, plus a couch in the rear, and about 15 stools at the bar
AMBIENCE	Primarily a younger Astoria crowd, particularly on weekends, but McCann's also draws a fair share of middle-aged visitors
EXTRAS/NOTES	There are many great things about McCann's, but perhaps the greatest is that it is what it says it is: a BAR and GRILL. It comes complete with Irish bartenders and waitresses, and a decent selection of draught beer. But unlike so many bars, the grill is not an afterthought. The big screen (eight-foot) television, and its 20 or 25-inch cousins, come in handy during sports seasons, since McCann's is a sports bar at heart. It can become a very passionate (and crowded) place during big games that involve the local squads. Also, there are a couple of pool tables in the back room.

—John Hartz

Neptune Diner

A dominant diner in the heart of Greek America.

Since so long ago no one remembers.

$$

31-05 Astoria Blvd., Queens 11102
(between 33rd and 31st Sts., where the Grand Central Pkwy. approaches the Tri-boro)
Phone (718) 278-4853

CATEGORY	Diner/Greek/American
HOURS	24/7: "We threw away the key," they tell us
SUBWAY	N, W to Astoria Blvd.
PAYMENT	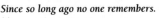
POPULAR FOOD	It's a diner, so pretty much everything under the sun (and under the sea) is available: grab a full breakfast for around $6—pay more and you can skip lunch; heaping Greek specials like *souvlaki* won't break the bank either; nearly a dozen varieties for burger range from a plain ⅓-pound hamburger to a Deluxe Twin Cheeseburger
DRINKS	Full bar
SEATING	Seats 150 (about 15 at the counter)
AMBIENCE	A diner right down to its fieldstone façade; inside, you get booths, a bar (backed by a long mirror), big plate glass windows, personal jukeboxes (brings lots

167

of quarters if you groove on the sultry sounds of Kenny G); drawing the usual truckers, oldsters, and hipsters, each at their designated time

—*Joe Cleemann*

Sal, Kris & Charlie Deli

The "Sandwich King of Astoria" consolidates his awesome power!

$

33-12 23rd Ave., Queens 11105
(between 33rd and 35th Sts.)
Phone (718) 278-9240

CATEGORY	Deli
HOURS	Mon–Sat: 5 AM–5 PM Sun: 5 AM–4 PM
SUBWAY	N, W to Ditmars Ave.
PAYMENT	Cash only
POPULAR FOOD	Real simple, real cheap: get a gigantic deli sandwich, usually for less than $5
DRINKS	Pull what you want out of the refrigerated case
SEATING	Carry out
AMBIENCE	Small, but well staffed; great deals on great sandwiches draw all kinds: if the cops and the taxi drivers like it, it ought to be good; you'll find both at Sal, Kris & Charlie Deli, and not a few prison guards on lunch break from nearby Riker's Island
EXTRAS/NOTES	During lulls, this old-timer used to hand out free samples—surprisingly delicate combinations of (usually) sweet peppers and cheese that revealed the artist's understanding of how delicatessen flavors work together. I was sad to hear he's gone. But that artistry still goes into each sandwich.

—*Joe Cleemann*

Shish Kabob Cart Under Hellgate Bridge

Nothing but shish kabob from a true Greek grillmaster.

$

North side of 23rd Ave., Queens 11105
(between 33rd and 35th Sts.)

CATEGORY	Cart
HOURS	Mon–Fri: 1 PM–8 PM Sat/Sun: noon–7 PM
SUBWAY	N, W to Ditmars Blvd.
PAYMENT	Cash only
POPULAR FOOD	Just one thing for the getting here—shish kabob—but the getting is great: six or seven morsels of pork, charcoal grilled to moist perfection, slightly charred and speared onto a wooden stick, doused with

	lemon juice (squirted from an old Evian bottle), dusted with salt, and accompanied by a hunk of hearty bread from Sal, Kris & Charlie's Deli across the street (see p. 168)
UNIQUE FOOD	You can also have the grilled meat included in a pita sandwich, with dressing and some lettuce and tomatoes, but why bother?
DRINKS	Head to the deli across the street for a full selection of drinks
SEATING	No seating
AMBIENCE	Almost underneath the approach to the Hellgate Bridge—a.k.a. "Pee and Poo Bridge," thanks to the pigeons that make their homes in its superstructure; hang around the cart and eat while the proprietor converses with the regulars—older Greek men, all—or take it with you wrapped in aluminum foil

—John Hartz

Uncle George's Greek Tavern

Good, greasy, sloppy Greek food.
$$
33-19 Broadway, Queens 11106
(at 33rd St.)
Phone (718) 626-0593

CATEGORY	Greek
HOURS	24/7
SUBWAY	R, G to Steinway; N to Broadway
PAYMENT	[VISA] [MasterCard] [American Express] [Card]
POPULAR FOOD	*Dolmades* (stuffed grape leaves), lamb stew with spinach (Thurs and Sun), *pastitsio,* baby shark, *spanakopita*
DRINKS	Soda, beer, wine by the kilo
SEATING	Plenty of seating at tables
AMBIENCE	The cheap, tasty Greek food and wine by the kilo (served in '70s shiny metal pitchers) draws big crowds at all hours of the evening: dinnertime, there's typically a neighborhood family crowd and Uncle George's is filled with talking, laughing, and Greek music from the jukebox
EXTRAS/NOTES	When your order arrives, it won't be much more than an enormous mess of food piled as high as one plate can withstand. The relaxed atmosphere and great Greek food are what keep people coming back to Uncle George's. Even though Uncle George's is open 24/7, at off-peak times the menu is limited. This is the most requested place to eat when my parents come to visit.

—Larry Ogrodnek

Viva El Mariachi

An authentic, friendly, and festive Mexican hangout.

$$

33-11 Broadway, Queens 11105
(at 34th St.)
Phone (718) 545 4039

CATEGORY	Mexican Diner
HOURS	Daily: 8 AM–midnight
SUBWAY	R, G to Steinway; N to Broadway
PAYMENT	VISA MasterCard AMERICAN
POPULAR FOOD	*Tinga* (spicy chicken) tostada, chorizo taco (sausage taco), *huevos con chorizo* (eggs with sausage), enchiladas *verdes,* but nothing settles a hangover like a plate of eggs, rice, and beans
DRINKS	Mexican sodas, shakes, coffee, tea, beer, fresh juices
SEATING	A counter with about a dozen seats and ample table seating too
AMBIENCE	Viva El Mariachi is a choice spot for that long weekend breakfast in Astoria; customers will be busy talking about the previous night's escapades, current events, or just reading the paper; staff is very friendly and more than willing to make recommendations to help you try out the entire menu
EXTRAS/NOTES	If you are in serious chow-down mode, head straight to the counter. It comes right up to your chin for those times when your hands are just slowing you down. The extra height also helps those who are more enthusiastic about eating than keeping track of napkins.

—*Larry Ogrodnek*

Zygos (Libra) Taverna

"Home style" Greek food: delicious, greasy, Greek!

$$

22-55 31st St., Queens 11105
(between Ditmars Blvd. and 23rd Ave.)
Phone (718) 728-7070

CATEGORY	Greek *Taverna*
HOURS	Daily: 11 AM–midnight
SUBWAY	N,W to Ditmars Blvd.
PAYMENT	VISA MasterCard AMERICAN
POPULAR FOOD	The gyro (don't get cute, just say JAI-rho), the *souvlaki,* or the *donner*—they're great and cheap; upgrade to "platter" size and you more than double the price in exchange for french fries and salad
UNIQUE FOOD	*Tzatziki* (a yogurt, garlic, and cucumber sauce, served with toasted pita) isn't

unique to Zygos, but you get a good bowl of it here; check out the "dishes of the day" on the menu: leg of lamb with potatoes is fantastic; *mousakas* comes highly recommended

DRINKS   Wine (try the *retsina* for a change), soda, beer, coffee

SEATING   Seats around 50

AMBIENCE   Authentic taverna style: snug and not-too-light, with various Greek odds and ends on display (including photos of Greek-American über-celebrity Telly Savalas); the centerpiece of the dining area is three-dimensional mural of downtown Athens; "blinker" Christmas lights simulate the energy consumption habits of Greek homeowners and shopkeepers

EXTRAS/NOTES   This kind of food—greasy and mouthwatering—usually gets passed off as "home style," but one wonders whether this is really the style of food that Greeks, a Mediterranean seafaring people, would prepare in their homes on a day-to-day basis. Maybe on special occasions. Eat-in, take-out, and free deliveries over $10.

—Joe Cleemann

RIDE THE 7

Barrio Fiesta

(see p. 122)
Filipino
65-14 Roosevelt Ave., Queens 11233
Phone (718) 429-4878

Ihawan

(see p. 122)
Filipino
40-06 70ᵗʰ St., Queens 11233
Phone (718) 205-1480

Jackson Diner

Legendary: put Jackson Heights on the Indian culinary map.
$$
37-47 74ᵗʰ St., Queens 11372
(at 37ᵗʰ Ave.)
Phone (718) 672-1232 • Fax (718) 396-4164

CATEGORY   Northern Indian/Buffet

HOURS   Sun–Thurs: 11:30 AM–10 PM
Fri/Sat: 11:30 AM–10:30 PM

SUBWAY   E, F, V, G, R to Roosevelt Ave.; 7 to 74ᵗʰ St./Broadway

PAYMENT   Cash only

POPULAR FOOD	Diners salivate over the Tasting of Three (fish, chicken *malabar,* and *samosa*), the *murg* (chicken) *tikka makhanwala,* and luscious lamb dishes like the *korma;* all-you-can-eat lunch buffet provides the best of all worlds (weekdays: 11:30 AM–4 PM)
UNIQUE FOOD	Most dishes are northern Indian standards; a little extra scratch buys goat curry
DRINKS	Full bar
SEATING	Seats 150 at long tables
AMBIENCE	Jackson hosts an eclectic crowd, reflective of the mind-boggling diversity of the greater neighborhood—culinary pilgrims come from all over, however, drawn by the Diner's reputation
EXTRAS/NOTES	The name is an artifact of the restaurant's early history. In 1983, the Indian owners took over an American-style restaurant, only gradually adding their native dishes to the usual hamburger-and-milk-shake fare. Needless to say, the tandoori really caught on, and while the newer, more colorful, and bigger location (since 1998) bears no resemblance to a diner, there was no sense in fooling with a lucky name.

—Esti Iturralde

Jaiya

(see p. 95)
Thai
81-11 Broadway, Queens 11373
Phone (718) 651-1330

Kabab King of New York

(see p. 74)
Mediterranean/Pakistani/Indian
73-01 37 Rd., Queens 11372
Phone (718) 457-5857

Krystal's Café and Pastry Shop

(see p. 122)
Filipino
69-02 Roosevelt Ave., Queens 11233
Phone (718) 898-1900

Sweet-n-Tart Restaurant

(see p. 18)
Chinese
136-11 38ᵗʰ Ave., Queens 11354
Phone (718) 661-3380

Flushing

On the far side of Flushing Meadow's Valley of Ashes, Flushing is vintage Queens: blocks and blocks of densely packed row houses giving way to the occasional condo complex or housing project, all straddling bustling commercial districts and astride mile-wide main drags. In recent decades, Flushing has witnessed the growth of an Asian population to rival Chinatown's. They've bathed acres of drab Queens architecture in garrish neon, rolled out their awnings, and pushed the Western alphabet out to the margins of (some) restaurant menus. Lacking the office workers, tourists, and gawkers that grace its downtown cousin, Flushing practically feels like a different country.

The question is: Which country? The far side of the Pacific Rim reveals its sparkling diversity on the streets of Flushing.

The buildings on 40th Road appear ready to collapse under the weight of their signage. Look for the sign that says **Curry Leaves Malaysian Cuisine.** It will lead you to what some connoisseurs claim is the best Malaysian food in Queens. And since you really have to try to find an entree over eight bucks, chances are you'll be eating with the lights on next time you dine at home. *135-31 40th Rd., Flushing, 11354, (718) 321-2078/2328. Daily: 6:30 AM–1 PM. Cash only.*

But wait, you say, money doesn't grow on trees, you want to know your alternatives. Well, if it's the best Malaysian you're after, be warned that a recent chowhound.com insurgency has taken up the banner of nearby **Penang,** where colorful murals brighten an already spicy experience. Most entrees run under ten bucks, and plenty go for much less. *38-04 Prince St., Flushing, 11354, (718) 321-2078 and (718) 321-2078/2828. Daily: 11 AM–11:30 PM. Cash only.*

While Flushing's luminosity is dimmed slightly on Prince (one block west of—and parallel to—bustling Main), this is not the case with its cuisine. The strip between 38th and 39th Avenues, across from the parking lot, is home to Penang along with a few other Flushing favorites. Look for names like **Happy Beef Noodle House** and **No. 1 People's & People Restaurant,** in front of which one or two of No. 1 People's and People's people may be grilling meat and corn on an outdoor barbecue. *38-10 Prince St., Flushing, 11354, (718) 661-3969.*

Laifood's Taiwanese cuisine wins unqualified praise from its faithful. Come for the lunch special. *38-18 Prince St., Flushing, 11354, (718) 321-0653. Daily: 11 AM–3 PM. Cash only.*

For Vietnamese, go to **Pho Vietnamese Restaurant**. Jockey for a table at this popular hangout and you're all but promised a superb dinner for under ten bucks. *38-02 Prince St., Flushing, 11354, (718) 461-8686. Daily: 11 AM–midnight. Cash only.*

If it's class you're after, head up to 38th Avenue, where you'll find some of the swankier joints in Flushing. Colorful, spacious, and clean, **Sweet-n-Tart Café** has critics swooning (see review p. 18). And after you've sampled its vast, adventurous, and eminently affordable menu, you may understand why. *136-11 38th Ave., Flushing, 11354, (718) 661-3380. Daily: 9 AM–midnight. Cash only.*

But if *shabu shabu's* more your thing, head next door to the equally sleek and modern **Minni's Shabu Shabu II & Hibachi II**. *Shabu shabu* is one of Japan's greatest contributions to international cuisine. First, you're presented a big plate of finely sliced raw meat, a bowl of veggies, some dipping sauces, and a pot of boiling water. Then you cook it yourself. There are only a few things to do with those ingredients without making a mess, so here's a hint: if you're generating sounds similar to this—*shabu shabu*—you're doing it right. Minni's *shabu shabu* starts at the unheard-of low price of $8.25. *136-21 38th Ave., Flushing, 11354, (718) 762-6277. Daily: 11 AM–2 PM. Visa MC.*

For cheap, great food and simple, utilitarian surroundings (not to mention throngs of locals) get one last fix of Chinese at **Flushing Noodle Shop**. It comes highly recommended and the menu—as usual—doesn't see many double-digits left of the decimal. *135-42 Roosevelt Ave., Flushing, 11354, (718) 353-1166. Daily: 9 AM–10 PM. Cash only.* It's also close to the **subway station**, which is at the intersection of Roosevelt Ave. and Main St.

—*Joe Cleemann*

Ten Ren
(see p. 11)
Tea House
135-18 Roosevelt Ave., Queens 11354
Phone (718) 461-9305

"As I looked out over the stained cloth,
past the half-empty wine bottles and the
flushed conversation of the strangers I dined with,
I knew that I was, from that moment on,
a thinking human being instead of a
healthy young animal."

—*M.F.K. Fisher*

CENTRAL QUEENS

Alba Pizza

Crispy crusts make the detour worthwhile.

Since 1965

$$

137-67 Queens Blvd., Queens 11432
(at Main St.)
Phone (718) 291-1620

CATEGORY	Pizzeria
HOURS	Sun–Thurs: 11 AM–11 PM
	Fri/Sat: 11 AM–11:30 PM
SUBWAY	F to Van Wyck Blvd.
PAYMENT	Cash only
POPULAR FOOD	All manner of calzones and pasta meals, but the real treats are the slices and the garlic knots; brisk business ensures freshness, and thinly kneaded crusts are crispy right out of the oven, raising undiscovered Alba to a special status among NYC pizzerias
UNIQUE FOOD	Sausage, chicken, and vegetable rolls
DRINKS	Soda and iced tea
SEATING	Booth seating for 40, many just eat on the run
AMBIENCE	As new immigrants arrive from Russia, the Caribbean, Asia, and Latin America, Alba remains a fixture in Forrest Hills; always crowded with local school kids and commuters coming back from the subway
EXTRAS/NOTES	In early 2002, Alba was planning a move to a larger location next door (137-65) that would consolidate Alba with Jack & Pete and offer delivery. The same family owns Jack & Pete, one block away down Queens Blvd.

—Esti Iturralde

Austin House

Colossal menu packed with old-time Queens neighborhood flavor.

$$

72-04 Austin St., Queens 11375
(at 72nd Ave.)
Phone (718) 544-2276

CATEGORY	Diner
HOURS	Daily: 7:30 AM–10 PM
SUBWAY	E, F, G, R to 71st St. and Continental Ave.
PAYMENT	VISA MasterCard AMERICAN ☐
POPULAR FOOD	Great big buttery pancakes, lox, eggs, and onion omelette; sandwiches galore; broiled steaks and fish
UNIQUE FOOD	When asked to suggest something on the menu, waiters scratch their heads and point to the abundant rotating specials—it

would be hard not to find something
there, even chopped liver

DRINKS Egg creams and milk shakes; beer and
wine, too, "but this is a family place"

SEATING Seats 60 in booths, 10 at counter

AMBIENCE Breakfast through dinner, chatty older
women whose dye jobs match their
turquoise jewelry discuss, among (a very
few) other things, their grandchildren

EXTRAS/NOTES Greek and Italian dishes are on the menu,
too. Good luck finding a seat during
Sunday brunch, a testament to its quality.

—Esti Iturralde

Baluchi's Indian Food

*A citywide opportunity for feasting on
spicy Indian.*

$$$

113-30 Queens Blvd., Queens 11375
(at 76th Rd.)
Phone (718) 520-8600
www.baluchis.com

CATEGORY Northern Indian

HOURS Mon–Fri: noon–3 PM, 5 PM–11 PM
Sat/Sun: noon–11 PM

SUBWAY F to 75th Ave.

PAYMENT VISA ⬡ AMERICAN

POPULAR FOOD *Tikka masala* is reportedly the "number
one seller," but powerfully spicy dishes
like the *vindaloo* and complex ones like
the *saagwala* deserve special praise

UNIQUE FOOD Baluchi's shrimp curry is a specialty

DRINKS Full bar

SEATING About 100 at tables

AMBIENCE Baluchi's wins points in the details, from
the earthy colors to the gorgeous wall
hangings; no garish Christmas lights
reminding you of the less couth Indian
joints on E. Sixth St.

EXTRAS/NOTES The 50 percent discount on all in-house
menu prices applies to lunch and
sometimes even to dinner (depending on
location), making Baluchi's an incredible
steal. Take-out and delivery available.
Lunch prices until 3 PM.

OTHER ONES • Downtown Fancy: 193 Spring St.,
Manhattan, 10012, (212) 226-2828

• Around Washington Square Park:
361 Sixth Ave., Manhattan, 10014,
(212) 929-0456

• East Village: 104 Second Ave.,
Manhattan, 10003, (212) 780-6000

• Midtown West: 240 W. 56th St.,
Manhattan, 10019, (212) 397-0707

• Upper West Side: 283 Columbus Ave.,
Manhattan, 10023, (212) 579-3900

- Upper East Side: 1431 First Ave.,
  Manhattan, 10021, (212) 396-1400
- Upper East Side: 1565 Second Ave.,
  Manhattan, 10028, (212) 288-4810
- Upper East Side: 1724 Second Ave.,
  Manhattan, 10128, (212) 996-2600
- Upper East Side: 1149 First Ave.,
  Manhattan, 10021, (212) 371-3535

—Esti Iturralde

Linda's Natural Kitchen

(see p. 99)
Vegetarian/Vegan
81-22 Lefferts Blvd., Queens 11415
Phone (718) 847-2233

Nick's Pizza

Simplicity, elegance, taste—pizza as art.
$$
108-26 Ascan Ave., Queens 11375
(at Austin St.)
Phone (718) 263-1126

CATEGORY	Pizzeria
HOURS	Mon–Thurs: 11:30 AM–9:30 PM
	Fri: 11:30 AM–11:30 PM
	Sat: 12:30 PM–11:30 PM
	Sun: 12:30 PM–9:30 PM
SUBWAY	E, F, G, R to 71ˢᵗ St. and Continental Ave.
PAYMENT	Cash only
POPULAR FOOD	No lengthy menu here to distract from the masterpiece: exquisite gourmet pizza pies on thin crusts caressed with fresh basil
UNIQUE FOOD	They've got ricotta pizzas, too, and for those who can't decide, half-whites and half-reds
DRINKS	Beer and wine
SEATING	A cozy capacity of 40, seated at tables
AMBIENCE	Behind a vintage storefront and lined with black-and-white photos of the neighborhood in the olden days, Nick's beckons families at dinnertime and young hipsters late on weekends
EXTRAS/NOTES	Their motto seems to be "No slices!" for why partition such a perfect canvas? Choice toppings serve to enhance rather than bury. A large serves two perfectly. Salads are big enough to split. No delivery, no slices, but whew, there's take-out. And if you're in the neighborhood, there's another bigger restaurant in Long Island.
OTHER ONES	• Long Island: 272 Sunrise Hwy., 11570, (515) 763-3278

—Esti Iturralde

Peking Duck Forest

Excellent taste and value for a sit-down Chinese meal.

$$$

107-12 70 Rd., Queens 11375
(at Austin St.)
Phone (718) 268-2404 • Fax (718) 268-7431

CATEGORY	Chinese
HOURS	Mon–Thurs: 11:30 AM–11 PM Fri/Sat: 11:30 AM–midnight Sun: noon–11 PM
SUBWAY	E, F, G, R to 71st St. and Continental Ave.
PAYMENT	VISA MasterCard American Express
POPULAR FOOD	Usual favorites are done with extra freshness and taste: chicken *lo mein;* beef with broccoli—never oily or bland, and served in filling portions
UNIQUE FOOD	The chef's pride, a crispy Peking duck heads the specialty list; other noteworthy dishes include fresh lobster and sea bass
DRINKS	Full bar
SEATING	Seats 60 at tables
AMBIENCE	Frequented by couples on a casual date gearing up for a movie at the Midway; adults and families enjoying a quiet dinner
EXTRAS/NOTES	With free delivery, Peking Duck Forest keeps a large local clientele. But given its soft music, ambient lighting, diligent waiters, and free parking, why not sit down and stay awhile?

—Esti Iturralde

BROOKLYN

WILLIAMSBURG / GREENPOINT

Bliss

(see p. 98)
Vegetarian
191 Bedford Ave., Brooklyn 11211
Phone (718) 599-2547

Ciao Bella

*Swanky Mediterranean-style bistro
featuring palm trees as well as hearts of
palm.*
$$$
138 N. Eighth St., Brooklyn 11211
(between Bedford Ave. and Berry St.)
Phone (718) 599-8550/8551 • Fax (718) 599-8633

CATEGORY	Italian Bistro
HOURS	Daily: 11:30 AM–11:30 PM
SUBWAY	L to Bedford Ave.
PAYMENT	VISA
POPULAR FOOD	*Carpaccio* dishes, Caesar salad with chicken, fresh pasta
UNIQUE FOOD	Salmon with vegetables, rack of lamb
DRINKS	Beer and wine
SEATING	About 10 barstools, dining room seats about 70, outdoor café dining beginning summer 2002
AMBIENCE	Mediterranean decor with spacious dining room and a modern-style bar and lounge area, supremely colorful; frequented by young and jovial gourmands (with small pocket books) who enjoy leisurely meals
EXTRAS/NOTES	The owner has great musical taste, which sets the tone for tranquil dining and amorous glances. Marco moved to the states from Milan, Italy 15 years ago, and Ciao Bella's success can be attributed to both the quality of the food and Marco's personality.

—*Rebecca Wendler*

L Café

*A harbinger of Williamsburg's revival
stays true to its roots.*
$$
187 Bedford Ave., Brooklyn 11211
(at N. 11th St.)
Phone (718) 302-2430 • Fax (718) 302-2428

CATEGORY	Diner/Bistro
HOURS	Daily: 10 AM–midnight
SUBWAY	L to Bedford Ave.
PAYMENT	VISA
POPULAR FOOD	Really creative sandwiches and burgers (like the Johnny Cash, Joni Mitchell, and Edi Gourmet) especially at lunchtime, soup, salads, and platters

UNIQUE FOOD	Chicken Shepherd's Pie, sweet potato fries
DRINKS	Beer and wine, juice, tea, coffee
SEATING	Seats 34 inside and 18–24 outside (in a heated tent in the winter)
AMBIENCE	Young locals looking for a relaxing place to catch up with friends, homework, or themselves, or to just to stare at the walls
EXTRAS/NOTES	L Café claims to be the first café on Bedford Ave. It changed owners five years ago, but not much has changed. Business is always booming. Look out: the menu changes; different entrees are available at breakfast, lunch, and dinner (and on Saturday and Sunday, at brunch).

—Rebecca Wendler

Loco Burrito

California-style south-of-the-border, eat-in or take-out.

$$

345 Graham Ave., Brooklyn 11211

(at Metropolitan Ave.)

Phone (718) 388-8215

CATEGORY	*Taquería*/Burrito Bar
HOURS	Daily: 11 AM–10 PM
SUBWAY	L to Graham Ave.
PAYMENT	Cash only
POPULAR FOOD	Salads, plain and not-so-plain (with chicken, grilled veggies, or beef), burritos (beef, chicken, vegetarian), nachos (chicken, veggie), *fajitas* (chicken, veggie, or beef)
UNIQUE FOOD	Add soy cheese or tofu sour cream to your meal for an extra buck or try the soups (Traditional Tortilla Soup or Chili)
DRINKS	Beer, soda, juice
SEATING	Seats about 30
AMBIENCE	Young, mostly local clientele; particularly vegetarians
EXTRAS/NOTES	Open for about a year, business has been so fruitful that Loco Burrito expanded next door, making room for one of the most interesting band and bumper sticker collections I've seen since my head-banger days.

—Rebecca Wendler

Lomzynianka

Authentic Polish food in a setting cozy as Grandma's kitchen.

$$$

646 Manhattan Ave., Brooklyn 11222

(between Lorimer St. and Nassau Ave.)

Phone (718) 389-9439

CATEGORY	Polish and Eastern European
HOURS	Daily: noon–9 PM

SUBWAY	G to Nassau; L to Lorimer (and a bit of a hike, consider the B61 and B43 buses)
PAYMENT	Cash only
POPULAR FOOD	Traditional food is the best seller here: the Polish Platter (three pierogies, kielbasa, stuffed cabbage, *bigos,* and potatoes), and the Hungarian Pie (beef goulash sandwiched between two potato pancakes)
UNIQUE FOOD	The plates of coleslaw, cabbage, and marinated tomatoes that start you off are light enough to leave room for what's to come: sweet cheese blintzes wrapped in golden brown crepes and dusted with powdered sugar (order them with fruit filling only if you're in a sweets mood); fried pierogies filled with sweet farmer cheese and served with onions and sour cream; crispy potato pancakes, also served with sour cream, hot and deep fried to that perfect point right before burning; authentic Polish kielbasa topped with sweet onions is crispy on the outside and served with homemade mashed potatoes
DRINKS	Juices, Polish and American sodas
SEATING	Seats 24
AMBIENCE	Incredibly charming, despite, or maybe because of, the fake "brick" walls, artificial plants, fading oil paintings, dusky pink tablecloths covered in sticky clear plastic, and white organza curtains and blinking Christmas lights in the front window; golden oldies on the sound system and football on TV complete the picture; twentysomethings rub elbows (almost literally) with the neighborhood crowd
EXTRAS/NOTES	Four people can eat for under $25, including drinks: order your food family style so you can try a little bit of everything. The owner's not lying when she bills Lomzynianka as "fine Polish Cuisine" (the menu is in Polish on the left side, English on the right) and "home cooking in the heart of Greenpoint." Eating here truly makes you feel like you could be in someone's house. The one and only waiter brings your food on a brown plastic tray from a back area that could be your grandmother's kitchen, complete with an off-white fridge and a silver metal stove. On cold nights, the glass door and windows fog up from the heat. Dimmer light in the back of the restaurant makes it cozier than the front area near the door. If you're looking for light and healthy, this is not your place. The traditional Polish food is heavy by definition (not by fault of the cook), but well worth the indulgence. As it says on the door, *Zapraszamy!* (Polish for bon appétit).

—*Sarah Winkeller*

How Do You Say HUNGRY?

1. Amheric or Amarënya (Ethiopia): *rabeny t'emany!* Pronounce the 'e' as in her and 'ny' as in canyon

2. Arabic: *ænæ gæ'æn!* Sounds like: jaw'aan.

3. Basque: *gose naiz!*

4. Cantonese: *nogH touH nogH!* Sounds like: Naw (deeper sound, like "bog') toe naw! Literally means: My stomach's hungry! Idiomatically, this is more common than just saying "I'm hungry." (You may notice that the Cantonese version is very difficult, especially since "I" and "hungry" are very close (but actually sound very different). Don't ask me why there are capital H's everywhere—that's how Yale does it.

5. Croatian: *gladan sam.*

6. Czech: *mam hlat.* Sounds like: mom lot.

7. Danish: *jeg er sulten.* Sounds like: yai air SOOL-ten.

8. English: *I'm hungry. I need to eat. I'm famished. I'm starved. I need some grub. Feed me!*

9. French: *J'ai faim.* Sounds like: zhay feh (as in family).

10. German: *Ich bin hungrig or (Ich habe hunger.).* Sounds like: Ick (as in icky) bin hoongrig.

11. Greek: *Ego peenao!* (accent on the 'o' in Ego and on the 'a' in 'peenao'; the g in Ego is gutteral)

12. Haitian Creole: *Grangoo.* Sounds like: Ghrawngoo (g is gutteral on both counts)

13. Hausa (Northern Nigeria, Niger):
    I'd like breakfast: *ina son karin.* Sounds like: eena sawn carin.
    I'd like lunch: *ina son kumallo.* Sounds like: eena sawn coomawloh.
    I'd like dinner: *ina son abincin.* Sounds like: eena sawn abinchin.

14. Hawaiian: *pōloli au.* Sounds like: PUH low li.

15. Hebrew: *ani raev (reeva)*

16. Hindi: *aap ko bhook lagi hai.* Sounds like: awppkoh booklawgeehey)—'g' is gutteral.

17. Hokkien: *gua ya iyao!*

18. Hungarian: *éhes vagyok.*

19. Ilocano: *Mabisin nak.* Sounds like: muBEEsin knock.

20. Italian: *Sono affamato.* Or: *mio haves famo.*

21. Japanese: *onaka ga suki mashita.*

22. Korean: *bego pawyo.* 'e' in pego is pronounced like e in leg. bae-ko-p'a-yo

23. Kriolu: Capeverdian Creole: *N sta ku fomi.*

24. Mandarin: *wo en le!* Sounds like: Waw (rhymes with raw) uh luh! Literally means: I'm hungry already!

25. Maori (or Te Kōrero Maori) (New Zealand): *e hia kai ana ahau!*

26. Maylay or Bahasa Indonesia or Bahasa Melayu (Brunei, Indonesia, Singapore): *Saya mau makan.* Literally means: I want to eat!
27. Farsi: *goshnameh* or *gorosneh-am.*
28. Polish: *Jestem glodny.*
29. Portuguese: I'd like breakfast: *Queria tomar o pequeno almoço.*
    I'd like lunch: *Queria tomar o almoço.*
    I'd like dinner: *Queria tomar o jantar.*
    (The letters f, l, p, t, y of the Portugese alphabet is pronounced as in English.)
30. Russian: *ya hochu est.*
31. Spanish: *Tengo hambre.*
32. Swahili (Kenya, also Tanzania and Uganda): *nina njaa!*
33. Swedish: *Jag är hungrig.* Sounds like: Yag (as in father eyr long as in bear hoongrg.)
34. Tagalog: *Nagugutom ako.*
35. Tibetan: *nga throgaw-tog giy du.*
36. Wolof (Senegal, Coastal Gambia): *da ma xiif.* Sounds like: daw maw kif.

Mama B's Juice Bar Café

Fragrant shards of wistfully organic grass call to the carrot, "Orange you glad to 'C' me?"

$$

351 Graham Ave., Brooklyn 11211
(at Metropolitan Ave.)
Phone (718) 599-4572

CATEGORY	Juice Bar
HOURS	Mon–Fri: 7:30 AM–8 PM
	Sat/Sun: 10 AM–6 PM
SUBWAY	L to Graham Ave.
PAYMENT	Cash only
POPULAR FOOD	Super-duper juices, smoothies, and bagels
UNIQUE FOOD	Hummus sandwich, veggie burger: try them with any combination of about eight additional toppings, like ginger and green algae
DRINKS	Coffee and tea
SEATING	No seats, except for those provided for the wait for your food
AMBIENCE	The health savvy and vegetarians who resemble the Beat poets
EXTRAS/NOTES	T-shirts for sale with great designs from a local duo.

—*Rebecca Wendler*

Oznot's Dish

(see p. 46)
Brunch
79 Berry St., Brooklyn 11211
Phone (718) 599-6596

Val Diano

Just like Grandma used to make.
$$$
659 Manhattan Ave., Brooklyn 11222
(at Bedford Ave.)
Phone (718) 383-1707

CATEGORY	Pizza Parlor
HOURS	Daily: 11 AM–9:30 PM (kitchen closes 9 PM on Sun)
SUBWAY	L to Bedford Ave.
PAYMENT	Cash only
POPULAR FOOD	You'll never want another mozzarella stick once you've tried the delicious mozzarella in *carrozza* (a fresh mozzarella sandwich dipped in a light egg batter and fried; served with a marinara dipping sauce); simple pasta dishes shine, like the homemade *cavatelli* in fresh tomato sauce with basil and rigatoni with broccoli *rapa* in garlic and oil
UNIQUE FOOD	Penne *all'arrabbiata* is a spicy pasta dish rich with green chilies; lightly sautéed broccoli rapa, a sharp-tasting relative of turnip greens popular in southern Italian cooking, adds bite to many dishes
DRINKS	Beer (including Peroni), wine (a steal at $2.50 per glass for the house red or white), San Pellegrino, soda, coffee
SEATING	Seats 10–12 at tables
AMBIENCE	Away from the trendy Williamsburg strip, this is a refreshingly casual and friendly neighborhood spot
EXTRAS/NOTES	If you're not in the mood for pasta, the meat and fish dishes are good, but get pricey. Top off your meal with one of their homemade dessert specials and a frothy cappuccino.

—Julia Pastore

"When you wake up in the morning, Pooh," said Piglet at
last, "What's the first thing you say to yourself?"
"What's for breakfast?" said Pooh.
"What do you say, Piglet?"
"I say, I wonder what's going to happen exciting today?"
said Piglet.
Pooh nodded thoughtfully. "It's the same thing," he said.
—A.A.Milne, 'The House at Pooh Corner

Downtown Brooklyn Diner

Eat burgers and wash your dirty clothes anytime you want!

$$

515 Atlantic Ave., Brooklyn 11217
(at Third Ave.)
Phone (718) 243-9172

CATEGORY	Diner
HOURS	24/7
SUBWAY	Q, 1, 2, 4, 5 to Atlantic Ave.; M, N, R, W to Pacific St.; A, C, G to Hoyt-Schermerhorn
PAYMENT	VISA MasterCard AMERICAN DISCOVER
POPULAR FOOD	Extensive king-size omelette menu—try the plain omelette which comes with home fries and toast—yummy add-ons include salami, broccoli, spinach, feta, bacon, sausage, and pepper
UNIQUE FOOD	Feta burger—six oz. burger grilled and topped with generous amount of feta, lettuce, and tomato—pungent and tasty—be sure to get it with the crispy-on-the-outside, soft-on-the-inside fries
DRINKS	Lots of fruit juices, coffee, tea, soda, herbal tea, egg cream, milkshakes, full bar in the connected tavern closes at 4 AM
SEATING	About 20 booths and tables and eight counter seats seat around 35; the backyard opens in summer
AMBIENCE	Cute Brooklyn ambience with Brooklyn street signs affixed next to each booth to flaunt that local flair; and there's an old-school soda fountain feel to the place; and as with most 24/7 joints, the clientele varies heavily according to the time of day you choose to eat; service is faster late at night; crowds slow things down on Saturday and Sunday mornings
EXRAS/NOTES	There's no better place in Brooklyn for steak tips over rice with mushrooms or some simple fried chicken fingers at four in the morning. The service can be a tad surly at times, especially "after hours," but that just makes it a more authentic Brooklyn experience. Brooklyn diner is connected to Brooklyn Tavern. When the bar is open, you can order bar food from the diner menu. One more perk: The diner and tavern are one block from a gigantic 24-hour laundromat.

—*Lindy Settevendemie*

DOWNTOWN BROOKLYN WEST

Amin

(see p. 30)
Indian
140 Montague St., Brooklyn 11201
Phone (718) 855-4791

Bagel World

Bustling gourmet bagel shop offers top-quality, generous portions at rock-bottom prices.

$

181 Court St., Brooklyn 11201
(between Dean and Bergen Sts.)
Phone (718) 624-3972
www.bagelworldnyc.com

CATEGORY	Bagel Shop
HOURS	Mon–Fri: 6 AM–10 PM
	Sat: 6 AM–8 PM
	Sun: 6 AM–7 PM
SUBWAY	F to Bergen St.; A, C to Jay St./ Borough Hall
PAYMENT	Cash only
POPULAR FOOD	Bacon, egg, and cheese on an everything bagel—fans of this popular choice say that BW's Everything bagels have a perfect distribution of herbs and spices, and the sandwich has just the right amount of bacon, egg, and cheese in every bite
UNIQUE FOOD	Owner Scott Rossillo says that everything in his shop is unique because "everything is made here, and everything is made daily;" lots of organics, tofu spreads, wraps, soups (seasonal), pastries, many salads, and a huge meats deli—if you go away unsatisfied, it's your own fault!
DRINKS	Lots of good gourmet coffee drinks, teas, bottled smoothies, sodas, and juices
SEATING	Ten at five tables, seasonal outdoor seating
AMBIENCE	No frills, homey ambience, Brooklyn paraphernalia, including new decorations every few months depending on what's happening in the neighborhood; customer service is outstanding—a cheerful, well-oiled machine
EXTRAS/NOTES	If it's a nice day and there aren't any seats available, check out the park one block away on Clinton St. at Congress St.—there are plenty of benches, picnic tables, and green, green grass. Daily specials on coffee, cream cheese, and general lunch items. After 2 PM on weekdays, buy a dozen bagels and get six free (two free on weekends). Coffee mugs and T-shirts for sale. Catering available.

—*Lindy Settevendemie*

Brooklyn Ice Cream Factory

Eight cool flavors with a view.

$

1 Old Fulton St., Brooklyn 11201

(at Water St.)

Phone (718) 246-3963

CATEGORY	Ice Cream Shop
HOURS	Tue–Sun: 1 PM–10 PM
SUBWAY	A, C to High St./Brooklyn Bridge
PAYMENT	Cash only
POPULAR FOOD	The antithesis of ubiquitous chains, this small shop offers just eight flavors: vanilla, chocolate, strawberry, vanilla chocolate chunks, chocolate chocolate chunks, butter pecan, peaches and cream, and coffee
UNIQUE FOOD	The key here is quality, not quantity—this is just about the pinnacle of ice cream, right up there with Ciao Bella—silky and strongly flavored; wonderful breads and sandwiches from the nearby River Café are also served
DRINKS	Soda (Coke in bottles) and coffee
SEATING	Tables for 40
AMBIENCE	Located in a historic fireboat house at the Fulton Ferry landing; overlooks the Brooklyn Bridge and offers sweeping views of the Manhattan skyline
EXTRAS/NOTES	Champagne corks litter the parking space around the landing, a popular spot for wedding photos. Some brave couples even manage some artful poses here in the winter. Watching them is more entertaining than a movie, and it's free. Manager and ice cream guru Mark Thompson often mans the counter himself and likes to chat.

—Melissa Contreras

Buddy's Burrito and Taco Bar

Generous chefs assemble healthy, mouth-watering Mexican standards.

$$

260 Court St., Brooklyn 11231

(at Butler St.)

Phone (718) 488-8695

CATEGORY	Tex-Mex
HOURS	Mon–Sat: 11:30 AM–11 PM Sun: 11:30 AM–10 PM
SUBWAY	F to Bergen St.; A, C to Jay St./ Borough Hall
PAYMENT	Cash only
POPULAR FOOD	Try the HUGE Brooklyn Burrito served with your choice of chicken, beef, or pork

and beans, rice, salsa *fresca,* and cheese; or two fish tacos, with rice and beans

UNIQUE Buddy's Burger—taken nine years to perfect, a charbroiled burger on sesame egg bun with salsa *fresca,* lettuce, tomato, and American cheese served with corn chips; add guac for extra change, and you have the perfect Tex-Mex burger

DRINKS Mexican and American beer, fresh and bottled sangria, wine, *aguas frescas* (tamarind, lime, etc.), Buddy's Famous Root, various domestic sodas, iced tea

SEATING Inside table seating for 30, seasonal outdoor seating for eight

AMBIENCE Cafeteria-style, low-key decor; the only music you hear is the cooks' Spanish, locals of all kinds, and many come for take-out; tasty food and char-broiled aromas make up for the lack of decorating

EXTRAS/NOTES Though Buddy's serves only the basics, the substantial dishes are competent enough for anyone looking for healthy and fresh Mexican on the go. Any selection can be made vegetarian. Fresh salsa and sangria. T-shirts for sale.

—Lindy Settevendemie

Café LULUc

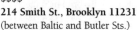

Euro-feel, Brooklyn style—terrific space, good food, friendly staff, great prices.

$$$$

214 Smith St., Brooklyn 11231
(between Baltic and Butler Sts.)
Phone (718) 625-3815

CATEGORY French Bistro and Bar

HOURS Mon–Thurs: 7:30 AM–midnight
Fri/Sat: 7:30 AM–2 AM

SUBWAY F to Bergen St.; A, C to Jay St./ Borough Hall

PAYMENT Cash only (ATM across the street)

POPULAR FOOD Pancakes and berries with maple syrup; grilled chicken sandwich with avocado, arugula, *asiago* cheese, and roast tomato vinaigrette on sourdough bread is well-rounded midday fuel

UNIQUE FOOD Delightful soups du jour and regularly French onion—always fancy and nourishing; and where else in Brooklyn can you get pan-roasted frog legs with lemon, butter, garlic, and parsley for about seven bucks?—*Vas-y,* just try 'em!

DRINKS Full bar, wine list

SEATING Seats about 60 at two- and four-person tables; bar seats about six

AMBIENCE You'll definitely get a cozy, European café feel sans existential cigarette smoke—nice old-looking bar, small wooden tables squeezed together like they do in Paris; predominantly childless crowd, Cobble Hill inhabitants, perhaps some Manhattanites who've come out to do Smith St.

EXTRAS/NOTES The evening menu offers entrées as well, though most are over $10—but fear not, no need for French dramatics and exclamations of *"c'est quelle dommage!"* You won't go hungry—there's plenty else to choose from. Check out the nighttime scene and crowded weekend brunches— there might be a wait.

—*Lindy Settevendemie*

California Taqueria

LA-style Mexcellent, massive burritos.

$$

187 Court St., Brooklyn 11201

(at Bergen St.)

Phone (718) 624-7498

CATEGORY	Mexican *Taqueria*
HOURS	Sun–Thurs: noon–10 PM Fri/Sat: noon–11 PM
SUBWAY	F, G to Bergen; 1, 2, 4, M, N, R to Court St./Borough Hall; A, C to Jay St./Borough Hall
PAYMENT	Cash only
POPULAR FOOD	A variety of Mexican treats, but the main attraction is the burritos: go for the Outrageous California (the beef is considerably more flavorful than the chicken) or the Vegetarian; get a good grip before you start and don't put it down, or everything will spill out
DRINKS	*Jarritos* (Mexican soda), iced tea
SEATING	Table seating for 30
AMBIENCE	Fast, no-frills service—eat in or, if the aggressive neon bothers you, take out
EXTRAS/NOTES	Free delivery.

—*Andrew Eastwick*

Fortune House

Yes, that says lamb on the menu.

$$

82 Henry St., Brooklyn 11201

(between Pineapple and Orange Sts.)

Phone (718) 855-7055

CATEGORY	Chinese
HOURS	Mon–Thurs: 11 AM–10 PM Fri/Sat: 11:30 AM–11 PM Sun: 12:30 PM–10 PM
SUBWAY	1, 2 to Clark St.
PAYMENT	VISA MasterCard AMERICAN EXPRESS
POPULAR FOOD	Sautéed broccoli in garlic sauce; chow mein; whatever else you usually find on a Chinese restaurant menu

UNIQUE FOOD	The menu here is more wide-ranging and eclectic than those at many Chinese restaurants, offering shredded turnip cake; lamb (with brown sauce and mushrooms, broccoli, and scallions); and mango chicken with vegetables; the lunch specials on weekends are an especially good bargain—try the filet sea bass, but skip the roast duck
DRINKS	Tea, soda, and beer
SEATING	Seats 40–50
AMBIENCE	The bright pink walls can be a bit disconcerting, but the wait staff is so friendly you won't care—popular with Jehovah's Witnesses (whose worldwide headquarters are in the neighborhood) on weekends
EXTRAS/NOTES	The wait for delivery on weekends can take up to an hour. You've been warned. A pity they no longer bring you pineapple chunks on the house for dessert (you have to pay), though you still get a free fortune cookie.

—*Melissa Contreras*

The Greens

(see p. 99)
Chinese/Vegetarian
128 Montague St., Brooklyn 11201
Phone (718) 246-1288

Grimaldi's

*Best pizza in New York AND a
public feud worthy of the other
Grimaldis.*
$$
19 Old Fulton St., Brooklyn 11021
(at Front St.)
Phone (718) 858-4300
www.grimaldis.com

CATEGORY	Pizza
HOURS	Mon–Thurs: 11:30 AM–11 PM
	Fri: 11:30 AM–midnight
	Sat: noon–midnight
	Sun: noon–11 PM
SUBWAY	A, C to High St.
PAYMENT	Cash only
POPULAR FOOD	Widely acclaimed as the best pizza joint in New York—so try the pizza, it's good, really, really good
DRINKS	Beer, wine, soda, water
SEATING	Seats about 70
AMBIENCE	Grimaldi's reputation is not a secret; you'll find all kinds dining amidst the Sinatra memorabilia in the cramped dining area.
EXTRAS/NOTES	Grimaldi's was established in 1990. But the spiritual legacy of the original "Patsy's

Pizzeria," founded in 1933, is still disputed. Okay, Grimaldi's is notable for at least four reasons:

1. The pizza really is as good as people say it is.
2. Among the people saying as much were a few characters on TV's *Law & Order*, during an episode in which the guy who played Lenny on *Laverne & Shirley* appears as a creepy, controlling father.
3. The owners' dispute with a real estate company that controlled rights to the restaurant's original name—Patsy's—made the papers. Not to mention the take-out menus at Grimaldi's.
4. Grimaldi's exalted status among pizza parlors means they call the shots. From the take-out menu: "NO SLICES * NO CREDIT CARDS * NO DELIVERY * NO RESERVATIONS" and, on a happier note: "OPEN 7 DAYS A WEEK".

OTHER ONES • Hoboken: 133 Clinton St., New Jersey, 07030, (201) 792-0800

—Joe Cleemann

Hale and Hearty Soups

(see p. 125)
Soup Shop
32 Court St., Brooklyn 11202
Phone (718) 596-5600

Harvest Restaurant

(see p. 45)
Brunch
218 Court St., Brooklyn 11201
Phone (718) 624-9267

Henry's Restaurant

Delicious, diverse home-cooking for breakfast, lunch, and an early dinner.
$$
333 Henry St., Brooklyn 11201
(between Atlantic Ave. and Pacific St.)
Phone (718) 222-0708

CATEGORY	Diner
HOURS	Mon–Fri: 4 AM–5 PM
	Sat: 4 AM–3 PM
	Sun: 4 AM–noon
SUBWAY	F, G to Bergen; 1, 2, 4, M, N, R to Court St./Borough Hall; A, C to Jay St./ Borough Hall
PAYMENT	Cash only (ATM on premises)
POPULAR FOOD	The grilled chicken platter is a hit, but "everything" is popular, and there's a lot to choose from for any meal: from burgers and seafood dishes to hot and cold

sandwiches made with Boar's Head Brand deli meats (you can create your own)— Italian, Hungarian, and Cajun specialties add variety

UNIQUE FOOD　Quality grits aren't easy to come by this far north, but all Henry's offerings are unique thanks to its special recipes; I recommend French toast with two eggs for breakfast and the pastrami or the gyro for lunch

DRINKS　Coffee (several flavors available), tea, frozen yogurt, egg creams, milk shakes, hot chocolate, soda, Snapple, juice

SEATING　Table seating for 36

AMBIENCE　The friendly, multi-ethnic crew knows many of the "best customers in the world" by name (and will learn yours after a few visits); the small area bustles with take-out patrons, but many locals stay to read the newspaper or chat; convenient for employees of Long Island College Hospital across the street

EXTRAS/NOTES　Catering for all occasions. Free delivery.

—Andrew Eastwick

Iron Chef House

Even the water's fresh at this elegant newcomer.

$$$

92 Clark St., Brooklyn 11201

(at Henry St.)

Phone (718) 858-8517/8537

CATEGORY　Japanese Sushi

HOURS　Mon–Thurs: 11:30 AM–2:45 PM; 4:30 PM–11 PM
Fri: 11:30 AM–2:45 PM; 4:30 PM–11:30 PM
Sat: 1 PM–11:30 PM
Sun: 4 PM–10:30 PM

SUBWAY　1, 2 to Clark St.

PAYMENT　VISA　MasterCard　AMERICAN EXPRESS　DISCOVER

POPULAR FOOD　Tempura, teriyaki, sushi, and sashimi platters

UNIQUE FOOD　Modern tuna *tataki* (chopped tuna with scallion and potato chips), Snow Ball (fresh scallop and caviar wrapped with squid)

DRINKS　Sake, beer, wine, soda, coffee, and tea

SEATING　A few tables and a small counter

AMBIENCE　Don't let the hokey name fool you— tranquil, chic, and tiny, the space sprang improbably from a dingy pizza joint yet has quickly become a neighborhood favorite

EXTRAS/NOTES　The fish is flown in fresh daily, the waitress says—and you can taste the difference. The sashimi is so good that *wasabi* and *shoyu* almost seem a distraction. Surprisingly, the tiramisu is as luscious as anything on Mulberry St. Even the water is meticulously prepared in chilled cobalt blue glass carafes.

—Melissa Contreras

Joya

Huge servings of basic Thai dishes at ridiculously low prices.
$$

215 Court St., Brooklyn 11201
(between Wyckoff and Warren Sts.)
Phone (718) 222-3484

CATEGORY	Thai
HOURS	Sun–Thurs: 5 PM–11 PM
	Fri/Sat: 5 PM–1 AM
SUBWAY	F, G to Bergen St.; 1, 2, 4, 5, N, R to Borough Hall/Court St.
PAYMENT	Cash only
POPULAR FOOD	Choose from a multitude of curry dishes, prices range from about $7 to $9 depending on ingredients; the spicy green curry will really get your nose running!
UNIQUE FOOD	*Pla muk kraprow* (sautéed squid with peppers, cabbage, carrots, and onions in a chili basil sauce)
DRINKS	Beer, wine, mixed drinks
SEATING	Table seating, more accommoding to groups of five or fewer (outdoor seating in warm weather)
AMBIENCE	High ceilings, a tile floor, brick walls, and dim lighting give a deceptively large, warehouse feel; however, the crowds (older couples and those with children dine early, after 8 PM a younger crowd takes over) remind you of the size— luckily the music (DJ), bar area, and the open kitchen (complete with stools for those who want to watch the chefs at work) will drown out the droning of your fellow diners
EXTRAS/NOTES	Daily specials (appetizers, entrées, and desserts) are always moderately priced. Take-out and delivery Mon–Thurs 5 PM–10 PM; take-out and pick-up daily 5 PM–closing.

—Julie Mente

New Golden City

Quick, quality Chinese take-out—golden.
$$

402 Henry St., Brooklyn 11201
(at Baltic St.)
Phone (718) 625-8583

CATEGORY	Chinese Take-out
HOURS	Mon–Thurs: 11 AM–11 PM

	Fri/Sat: 11 AM–midnight Sun: noon–11 PM
SUBWAY	F, G to Bergen; A, C to Jay St./ Borough Hall
PAYMENT	Cash only
POPULAR FOOD	Standard Cantonese, Szechuan, and Hunan—try the orange flavored chicken—especially good and crispy and also available as one of three surprisingly tasty "vegetarian meat" dishes; combos are a little larger (but the extra bulk is mostly rice) and include an egg roll; also recommend the steamed vegetable dumplings with excellent sauce
DRINKS	Soda
SEATING	None—take it to go
AMBIENCE	Time it: phone orders are ready in five minutes (maybe less)
EXTRAS/NOTES	Catering available. Free delivery, but it's a short walk from anywhere in Cobble Hill.
	—Andrew Eastwick

Nino's

A little slice of Italy where everyone knows your name.

Since 1968

$$$

531 Henry St., Brooklyn 11231

(at Union St.)

Phone (restaurant): (718) 858-5370

Phone (pizzeria): (718) 834-0863

CATEGORY	Italian
HOURS	Mon–Sat: 11 AM–10 PM Sun: noon–10 PM
SUBWAY	F, G to Bergen St.; 1, 2, 4, 5 to Borough Hall
PAYMENT	Cash only at pizzeria; VISA at restaurant
POPULAR FOOD	Outstanding Sicilian pizza (whole pies and by the slice) and a popular Italian buffet —pastas, chicken, veal, and eggplant dishes
UNIQUE FOOD	Specialty chicken or veal is especially good
DRINKS	Soda, beer, wine
SEATING	Seats 50 (along with a jukebox)
AMBIENCE	Definitely a neighborhood favorite; the bright lights, tile floors, and wood tables comfortably combine Italian cafeteria and Mom's kitchen table
EXTRAS/NOTES	The bar and the pizzeria are operated together, but one part takes credit cards, one part doesn't, and they have two distinct phone numbers. Stop by during the holidays for Nino's festive Christmas lighting.
	—Jill Sieracki

Park Plaza Diner

Everything you can think of to eat—except hot fudge sundaes.

$$$

220 Cadman Plaza West, Brooklyn 11201

(at Clark St.)

Phone (718) 596-5900

CATEGORY	Diner/Greek
HOURS	Sun–Thurs: 6 AM–2 AM Fri/Sat: 24 hours
SUBWAY	A, C to High St./Brooklyn Bridge
PAYMENT	VISA [MasterCard] [AMERICAN EXPRESS]
POPULAR FOOD	Huge portions of burgers, omelettes, pasta, pancakes, ice cream, cake, pie, and anything not good for you, plus a whole lot of other stuff that is
UNIQUE FOOD	Gigantic baklava and other Greek pastries (the owners are Greek); stuffed grape leaves; "lite" diner food—vegetables sautéed in olive oil, pasta salad; tasty salmon and turkey burgers (you can have them with fries and onion rings, too); wonderful fried calamari; specialty sandwiches like the China Town (roast pork on a toasted bun)
DRINKS	Cocktails, soda, juice, coffee, tea
SEATING	Plenty of seating at tables and booths
AMBIENCE	This neighborhood favorite is a humongous space with booths that have individual CD jukeboxes; also popular with those who have business to conduct at nearby City Hall and the courts and said to be the hangout of choice for defendants and their clients—the prosecutors supposedly favor the more genteel diner across the street
EXTRAS/NOTES	For some reason, there are never any hot fudge sundaes, though they're still on the menu. Not a few mourned when the revolving pie display was dispensed with about a year ago. Everything is baked on the premises. Skip the rubbery-crusted pies in favor of any and all cakes—chocolate fudge, towering strawberry shortcake, and cute chocolate mice (a favorite with the neighborhood kids, whose parents have them delivered). On hearing an order for "Two mice," the manager once replied, "That sounded like a problem." Take a mint or three from the rolling dispenser as you leave.

—*Melissa Contreras*

REMEMBER THE NEEDIEST!

Sam's Italian Cuisine

In the thick of tidied-up Court Street, a long-established Italian American restaurant charms locals and visitors with down-home Brooklyn cookin' and attitude.

Since 1930

$$$

238 Court St., Brooklyn 11201

(at Baltic St.)

Phone (718) 596-3458

CATEGORY	Italian
HOURS	When asked, Sam's said that there aren't any specific hours—"When I get up, I come here. When I get tired, I close." It's probably safe to assume that they have regular lunch and dinner hours. Open daily except for Tuesday.
SUBWAY	F to Bergen St.; A, C to Jay St./ Borough Hall
PAYMENT	Cash only
POPULAR FOOD	Brick oven pizza (subtract $1 for takeout, takes about 10–15 minutes to prepare); prepared in a traditional brick oven, these pies are the talk of Cobble Hill
UNIQUE FOOD	Pasta with various sauces (mushroom, meat, or clam)
DRINKS	Beverage list is as long as the food menu, and includes classics like a Side Car, Rob Roy, and a Sloe Gin Fizz; very full bar with coffee, tea, cappuccino, demitasse, and standard soda choices
SEATING	Approx. 75–100 at booths and tables
AMBIENCE	Reminiscent of a 1970s basement rec room, Sam's is replete with red plastic tablecloths, a basic tiled floor, wood paneled walls, and random interior decoration—but hear this: you go to Sam's for the courteous service, the lip-smackingly good Italian American cuisine, and maybe a little people-watching
EXTRAS/NOTES	This is the old Brooklyn—waiters have genuine accents to prove it—and often you vaguely feel as though you might be an extra in an old movie (albeit a welcome extra) given the way locals come and go with greetings and neighborhood updates. These guys know what they're doing—they've been at it over 70 years. Having grown up with authentic Italian American cooking, I always loathe to eat red "sauce" in restaurants. In Sam's I've found my grandmother's cooking—the meat sauce reached taste buds I didn't even know I still had. Great with the cheese ravioli. Extensive menu includes heroes, calzones, salads, veggies, soups, and appetizers.

Meat, fowl, and seafood are a little pricier.
Complimentary bread and butter with
dinner. A family-owned Brooklyn fixture.

—*Lindy Settevendemie*

Taco Madre
Mexican Kitchen

*Fast, friendly hole in the wall for your
chicken* mole *fix.*

$$

118 Montague St., Brooklyn 11201
(between Henry and Hicks Sts.)
Phone (718) 858-6363

CATEGORY	Mexican Café
HOURS	Daily: noon–11 PM
SUBWAY	N, R to Court St.
PAYMENT	VISA MasterCard AMERICAN
POPULAR FOOD	Tacos, burritos, quesadillas
UNIQUE FOOD	Barbecued Hidalgo chicken with black beans, rice and tortillas; 17-spice chicken with *mole* sauce; humongous combination platters as well as non-spicy kiddie portions
DRINKS	Mexican fruit waters, soda
SEATING	Five tables and a small counter seats 25
AMBIENCE	Taco Madre brings some much-needed earthiness to a bland, touristy strip of the Heights; the egg yolk-yellow walls and wooden furniture lend a festive, homey air to the cramped basement space
EXTRAS/NOTES	Regulars greet the staff by name and get what they want without having to ask. Free soda refills from the fountain at the counter.

—*Melissa Contreras*

Thai Grille

Flavorful Thai and desserts too good to miss.

$$$$

114 Henry St., Brooklyn 11201
(at Clark St.)
Phone (718) 596-8888

CATEGORY	Thai
HOURS	Mon–Thurs: noon–3 PM, 4 PM–10 PM Fri: noon–3 PM, 4 PM–11 PM Sat/Sun: 4 PM–11 PM
SUBWAY	1, 2 to Clark St.
PAYMENT	VISA MasterCard AMERICAN
POPULAR FOOD	*Pad* Thai, *satay* chicken, beef, shrimp, or vegetable appetizers and various coconut-based curries
UNIQUE FOOD	Sweet and spicy wok-charred sausage; roast duck in curry sauce (special); fried ice cream
DRINKS	Thai iced tea, beer, wine, coffee, soda
SEATING	Tables for 65, seats for 10 at bar

AMBIENCE	Black-and-white photos of Thailand on the walls, orchids and candles on the table; neighborhood bar crowd can get boisterous on weekends
EXTRAS/NOTES	Leave room for dessert—especially the fried ice cream and a gooey, oozing chocolate volcano cake that's worth every bit of the 15-minute wait (or order it in advance).

—*Melissa Contreras*

Tutt Café

*These "pitzas" don't need pepperoni
to shine.*

$$

47 Hicks St., Brooklyn 11201

(at Middagh St.)

Phone (718) 722-7777

CATEGORY	Middle Eastern
HOURS	Daily: 11 AM–11 PM
SUBWAY	A, C to High St./Brooklyn Bridge
PAYMENT	Cash only
POPULAR FOOD	Falafel; *lambajin* (10-inch *pitza* with lamb, onion, tomato, parsley, and various spices); lentil soup made fresh everyday and served with a warm fresh pita
UNIQUE FOOD	*Pitzas* (pita topped with a light, zesty tomato sauce, mozzarella, and a choice of chicken, sun-dried tomatoes, shrimp, or veggies); all the homemade breads—try *zaatar* bread, pita topped with thyme, sesame seeds, and olive oil
DRINKS	*Loomi* (Middle Eastern citrus drink), Turkish coffee, juices, tea, soda, BYOB
SEATING	About 30 at tables
AMBIENCE	*Kilims* and papyrus panels on the walls, Egyptian music wafting from the stereos; popular with students, as much for the wallet-friendly prices as for the relaxed, hippie-ish atmosphere
EXTRAS/NOTES	Tutt is a bit further out than the numerous other Middle Eastern eateries in the neighborhood, but its lentil soup is by far the best. The silky homemade pita pops out like large pillows from the brick oven in back. Occasionally, a free slice of moist semolina cake arrives with your bill.

—*Melissa Contreras*

"Alocholism I have never feared.
I love to drink,
but I've gone for months and years without doing so
because I've not liked the people
I had to drink with."

—*M.F.K. Fisher*

Yemen Café

*For those of us who have suffered with
uninspiring Jewish Yemenite food for
years in New York, an authentically hearty
Yemeni shot in the arm.*

$$

176 Atlantic Ave., Brooklyn 11201
(between Clinton and Court Sts.)
Phone (718) 624-6540 • Fax (718) 843-9533

CATEGORY	Yemeni
HOURS	Daily: 10 AM–10 PM
SUBWAY	F, G to Berfen; 1, 2, 4, M, N, R to Court St./Borough Hall; A, C to Jay St./Borough Hall
PAYMENT	Cash only
POPULAR FOOD	*Rashoosh* (eaten with every meal: huge pieces of lightly browned flat bread baked to order in the kitchen, the perfect scooper for a bowl of *salta* or a plate of hummus); shish kabob with rice pilaf; *glaba* (sautéed lamb in tangy cinnamon and tomato sauce served over rice pilaf); curry lamb over rice; delicious fish of the day (lightly marinated, broiled whole, and served with vegetables); hummus (while not a traditional Yemeni food, these guys make fantastic hummus, and with a little tomato and oil, and a piece of *rashoosh,* makes the perfect meal for some, snack for others)
UNIQUE FOOD	The cafe's two kitchens specialize in traditional Yemen fare; *marag* (a thin, zesty Yemeni vegetable soup perfect to start any meal); *shafota* (yogurt porridge mixed with garlic, cilantro, and *nigella* seeds); *salta* (the customary Yemeni mid-day meal—a stone caldron boiling over with a foamy stew of eggs, meat, vegetables, and green fenugreek pasty); *fatta* (*rashoosh* pieces soaked in clarified butter, Yemeni honey, then fried to a decadent, lightly crispy perfection)
DRINKS	Start and finish every meal by serving yourself a cup of piping hot, spiced Yemeni tea from the percolator in the back; also try the Yemeni coffee—the best in the world—as well as an assortment of iced tea and soft drinks
SEATING	Seating for approximately 30
AMBIENCE	If the fantastic assortment of rakish characters storming into Yemen Café every few minutes, cell phones blaring, wolfing down their food, and jumping back into their SUVs isn't enough to keep you entertained, the quaint decorations of this casual Atlantic Ave. eatery will be; adorning the soft peach walls is a charming collection of photographs,

posters, scarves, and *jambiyyas* (the ornamental Yemeni side weapon worn by most adult males) from the homeland

EXTRAS/NOTES In a throwback to the *mafraj* windows of the traditional Yemeni home, the tops of the restaurant's front windows have been colored, providing a soft lighting to the sometimes frenetic dining room. This restaurant comes closer than any I've seen to capturing the flavors, aromas, and excitement of a midday meal in Sanaa's old city. Throw in one *baladi* of *Qat* and the picture will be complete. Yemen Café is situated in the heart of Atlantic Ave.'s bountiful Arab shopping district. Make sure to stop next door at the Oriental Pastry and Grocery Co. and at Malko Karkanni Brothers next to that, for the widest variety of canned and dry goods, dried fruit, fresh ground coffee, teas, *halvah,* spices, pastries, olive oil soaps, music, and decorative items from the Middle East and North Africa. Completely halal and provides carry-out only during Ramadan.

—*Scott Gross*

AROUND PROSPECT PARK

Aunt Suzie's Restaurant

Comfort food in a comfort setting—atmosphere is everything here.

$$$$

247 Fifth Ave., Brooklyn 11215
(between Carroll St. and Garfield Pl.)
Phone (718) 788-3377

CATEGORY	Southern Italian
HOURS	Mon–Sat: 5 PM–10 PM
	Sun: 3 PM–10 PM
SUBWAY	N, R to Union St.
PAYMENT	VISA MasterCard
POPULAR FOOD	The Really Cheap Menu is a big draw—for under $10 you can choose from five different meals, all of them substantial; Aunt Suzie's Combo consists of meatball, sausage, and eggplant parmigiana; choose the chocolate mousse, served in a glass dish and laden with whipped cream
UNIQUE FOOD	Not much here that's off the beaten path—it is, after all, traditional southern Italian Brooklyn food—but the pasta with broccoli in pink sauce is a delicious vegetarian choice, and cheap too
DRINKS	Small but decent selection of wines and beers

SEATING	Seats about 75
AMBIENCE	Food is good, but it's not the main draw— the feeling of coming home is: vintage wedding and family photos add to the effect; the lighting is dim, the wait staff friendly and informal; Aunt Suzie attracts an eclectic mix of Park Slope residents: lots of families (including small children) alongside older couples and various artsy Brooklynites of all ages
EXTRAS/NOTES	The portions vary from large to huge, so if you don't walk out with a doggy bag, you'll walk out with a *very* full belly. Keep an eye out for Aunt Suzie herself; she really exists and often stops by.

—*Teresa Theophano*

The Chip Shop

Delightful and obliging British folks offer simple and appetizing treats from across the Pond.

$$$$

383 Fifth Ave., Brooklyn 11215

(at Seventh St.)

Phone (718) 832-7701

www.chipshopnyc.com

CATEGORY	Fish 'n' Chip Joint
HOURS	Sun–Thurs: noon–10 PM Fri/Sat: noon–11 PM
SUBWAY	F to Fourth or to Seventh Aves.
PAYMENT	Cash only
POPULAR FOOD	Uh. . .fish and chips (of course!); the battered cod and chips (served with yummy tartar sauce) is marvelous, even more so to a Yank unacquainted with this stand-out in England's oft-maligned cuisine; also popular is the shepherd's pie, which is chock-full of mashed potatoes, meat, and veggies
UNIQUE FOOD	Various deep fried candy bars—e.g., Mars, Twix, etc., apparently, this is something veddy British, and surprisingly, they're quite tasty, but you mustn't think of your health whilst devouring one
DRINKS	Lots of funny English drinks like Typhoo Tea and Fizzy Ribena; the standard soda, coffee, tea, and a succinct listing of imported beer
SEATING	Seats 40 at two- and four-person tables
AMBIENCE	Minimal British paraphernalia adorns the bright yellow walls, punk is on the stereo, but not too loud, Park Slope hipsters and families alike are accommodated in this cozy establishment—there's even a $5 kids' menu
EXTRAS/NOTES	Blimey! Don't be an ugly American! There's a useful glossary on the menu that

helps decipher what exactly it is you've just ordered—and there's quite a lot to choose from. If you don't want fish, there's plenty to eat, even for vegetarians, including terrific mac 'n' cheese. And they'll allow you to substitute mashed potatoes for chips (for $3 less), but you may have your knuckles rapped in the process because, as the menu notes with some exasperation, "We are The CHIP SHOP and the chips are bloody lovely!" Free delivery in the Park Slope area.

—Lindy Settevendemie

Christie's Jamaican Patties

A taste of the islands in Brooklyn for a buck fifty.

$$

334 Flatbush Ave., Brooklyn 11238

(at Sterling Pl.)

Phone (718) 636-9746

CATEGORY	Jamaican Bakery
HOURS	Mon–Thurs: 9 AM–9 PM
	Fri/Sat: 9 AM–10 PM
SUBWAY	2, 3, 4, 5 to Bergen St.; W to Seventh Ave.
PAYMENT	Cash only
POPULAR FOOD	Try the tender, tasty patties (beef, chicken and vegetable), coco bread, cinnamon rolls, carrot cake, jerk chicken; vegetable patty (stuffed with peas, lentils, and cabbage) packs enough of a punch to erase from memory all those soggy, tasteless specimens you may have had in the past
UNIQUE FOOD	Currant bread (a cousin to the cinnamon roll)
DRINKS	*Sorrel,* ginger ale, sodas
SEATING	Take-out only
AMBIENCE	Heavenly aroma from this small storefront permeates an otherwise nondescript block of nail parlors and curio shops; some regulars like their patties sandwiched in coco bread
EXTRAS/NOTES	Skip the codfish cakes, which manage to be dry and oily at the same time. The bread pudding may sit in your stomach through your next two meals. Most of the baked goods are $1.50 each. Tour buses stop here on weekend mornings, so you're better off taking a short walk through nearby Prospect Park first than being besieged by a camera-toting throng.

—Melissa Contreras

Get the Fever for the Flavor of Flatbush Brooklyn

Church and Flatbush Avenues

Flatbush Brooklyn is home to the most ethnically diverse zip code in the United States. You don't have to be a Busta Rhymes fan to recognize that many of the colors and flavors that make the Flatbush and Church Avenue neighborhoods so exciting come from its West Indian residents and particularly the Jamaican and Trinidadian restaurants that dot the landscape. Here's a list of the bakeries, jerk shacks, and *roti* shops that have earned *Hungry?* high marks.

Four Seasons

This colorful spot bakes fantastic tarts, buns, and rolls. Choose from apple, currant, coconut, pineapple, strawberry, and cheese, to name a few, in both flour and whole wheat crusts. Also try their bread pudding. Catering available. *2281 Church Ave., Brooklyn, (718) 693-7996.*

Jimbo Jean

Broiled red snapper and kingfish served with onions and peppers. *Ackee* and codfish. Mackerel and plaintains. Homemade patties. All for under $10. Vegetarians be warned, Jimbo might turn you! Catering available. *2223 Church Ave., Brooklyn, (718) 469-7925.*

Sybil's Caribbean and American Cuisine

A neighborhood institution located right next to Brooklyn's Temptation's nightclub, Sybil's offers the full range of island fare, with plenty of seating for large parties. Try their *pouri* (stuffed with veggies, beef, goat, shrimp, oxtail, *channa*, codfish, or potato).Catering available. *2210 Church Ave., Brooklyn, (718) 469-9049.*

Paradise Eats

The ladies at Paradise claim that their gargantuan patties (veggies, chicken, or beef) are the best in town. One thing's for sure. Once you eat one, there won't be any room left to try someone else's! Also feast on succulent barbecue ribs and chicken. Catering available. *875 Flatbush Ave., Brooklyn, (718) 282-5000.*

Precious Restaurant and Bakery

At Precious the multi-tiered wedding and birthday cakes, and gorgeous puff pastries are just that. Careful, or you'll find yourself celebrating the same birthday every week. *772 Flatbush Ave., Brooklyn, (718) 940-8657.*

Bon Bon's

Yes they have beautiful wedding and birthday cakes with color photographs screen printed on them. Yes they have a huge cake with the flag of Jamaica in the front window. Yes this restaurant is impeccably clean, and staffed by very pretty, friendly girls in smart white and red outfits. But I go for the curry crab. *1081 Flatbush Ave., Brooklyn,(718) 282-8629/8602.*

Finger Lickin 'R' Us

Home of the best Ms. Pac-Man called "Super Zola Pac-Girl" cabinet I have ever played in eight years of living in New York City. Modified with alternate pages full of heart-shaped pellets, custom fruits, and the speed cranked way up. This machine is so good it probably hurts business. *14 Duryea Pl., Brooklyn, (718) 692-7927.*

J and W Image Restaurant

One of several Trinidadian restaurants in the area, J and W highlights the mixed Indian/African culinary tradition of this island. Try their *roti* or *parathas* stuffed with chicken, beef, goat, pumpkin, *channa, kutchella, bhaggi,* vegetables, or conch. *825 Flatbush Ave., Brooklyn, (718) 826-2280.*

Roti Shack

These guys are keeping it real. Doubles, *allou* pies, *ackee* and saltfish, kingfish with CooKoo and *callaloo.* And if you're man enough, broiled (or curried) shark! *738 Flatbush Ave., Brooklyn, (718) 856-5956.*

—*Scott Gross*

Geido

A unique sushi joint with fresh, affordable food.
$$$
331 Flatbush Ave., Brooklyn 11217
(at Seventh Ave.)
Phone (718) 638-8866

CATEGORY	Japanese/Sushi
HOURS	Tue–Thurs: 5:30 PM–11 PM
	Fri/Sat: 5:30 PM–11:30 PM
	Sun: 5:30 PM–10:30 PM
SUBWAY	Q to Seventh Ave.; 1, 2 to Grand Army Plaza
PAYMENT	VISA MasterCard AMERICAN
POPULAR FOOD	Shrimp tempura rolls
UNIQUE FOOD	*Okonomiyaki,* a Japanese pancake advertised as "very healthy" despite the quantity of mayo atop it—vegetable and seafood versions available

DRINKS	Sake, beer, plum wine, sodas, juices, green tea
SEATING	Seats about 50, several at stools along the sushi bar
AMBIENCE	Small and funky, with colorful, amusing graffiti on the walls, Geido offers a laid-back, snob-free sushi experience
EXTRAS/NOTES	Geido's location on Flatbush Ave. (at the crux of the Park Slope and Prospect Heights neighborhoods) puts it right in the middle of the action and makes it easy to access by train or bus (B67 to Flatbush/Seventh Ave.). Yet, because it's not quite in Park Slope proper, the prices are better than any you'll find further down on Seventh Ave. Cute Geido T-shirts are available, so you can take your own home instead of wistfully admiring the one your waitress wears. Jazz music wafts through the speakers, and service is pleasant and usually fairly quick.

—*Teresa Theophano*

The Islands

The spice of island life combines with the warmth of home living.

$$$

803 Washington Ave., Brooklyn 11238
(between Eastern Pkwy. and Lincoln Pl.)
Phone (718) 398-3575

CATEGORY	Jamaican
HOURS	Sun–Thurs: 11:30 AM–10:30 PM Fri/Sat: 11:30 AM–midnight
SUBWAY	1, 2 to Eastern Pkwy.
PAYMENT	VISA [cards]
POPULAR FOOD	Any chicken dish: it's so tender that the meat just falls off the bone, and so good that customers have been known to gnaw on the ends (literally!) for more; try the orange island chicken, the sweet and spicy rice, plantains, or a dumpling—or have it all, it's cheap!
UNIQUE FOOD	Curried goat or oxtail with beans; but rather than going by the menu, just ask what they've got that day
DRINKS	Caribbean sodas, fruit punch, coffee, tea
SEATING	Six counter seats, small seating section upstairs and outdoor seating in warm weather
AMBIENCE	Immaculate (which is amazing considering how tight the space is); walking in is like being hugged—warm and comfortable; the ladies running The Islands are sweet and genuinely happy to see you: makes you just want to hang out all afternoon
EXTRAS/NOTES	Run by two jolly ladies, one of whom is a Jamaican native. Go here once and they'll know you by name. The place is tiny, but

that just seals in the heavenly aromas. Sit at the counter and watch the cooks sauté green bananas in a huge, black iron skillet.

—*Jill Sieracki*

The Olive Vine

Intimate neighborhood joint with Middle Eastern standards served piping hot.

$$$

131 Sixth Ave., Brooklyn 11215
(between Sterling and Park Pls.)
Phone (718) 636-4333
www.olivevine.com

CATEGORY	Middle Eastern/Greek
HOURS	Daily: 11 AM–11 PM
SUBWAY	1, 2 to Bergen St.
PAYMENT	Cash only
POPULAR FOOD	Falafel is a perennial favorite among the many vegetarians who frequent the Olive Vine; fresh-baked and sold for the bargain price of $1, the homemade pita bread comes out of the oven ballooned full of air and the soft dough melts in your mouth—especially good for dipping in the hummus or lentil soup
UNIQUE FOOD	Greek-influenced Middle Eastern food: the Olive Vine pizza is served on a thin and crispy pita crust; spinach pie (spinach, onions, and light mozzarella cheese, baked calzone-style); chicken platter (served in a sandwich with romaine lettuce, plum tomatoes, and *tahini,* with a side of green salad, fresh pita, and *baba ganoush* or hummus); or the chicken pizza with scallions (to add a little zing)—tender with a wonderful lemon flavor
DRINKS	*Loomi* (sun-dried Middle Eastern citrus steeped slowly overnight with a hint of cloves), Turkish coffee, house tea, fruit juice (orange, mango orange, kiwi, apple grape orange), or BYOB
SEATING	Forty-four seats in front, more in the garden and in back
AMBIANCE	Woven red tapestries—in various stages of fading—cover most of the exposed brick walls; Arabic music plays in the background (if you stay until closing, you might see the staff crank up some 1970s Arabic pop music and groove to the beat as they clean up); in summer, the front windows open to let in the breeze
EXTRAS/NOTES	A hidden garden in back is decorated with Christmas lights and hanging lanterns: it's a perfect place for a romantic dinner on a warm spring or summer night. A back room off the garden offers an intimate space for larger private parties.

OTHER ONES
- Around Prospect Park: 362 15th St., Brooklyn, 11215, (718) 499-0555
- Around Prospect Park: 81 Seventh Ave., Brooklyn, 11215, (718) 622-2626

—Sarah Winkeller

Ozzie's Coffee

Great coffee and more at a community hot spot.

$$

57 Seventh Ave., Brooklyn 11217

(at Lincoln Place)

Phone (718) 398-6695

www.ozziescoffee.com

CATEGORY	Coffee Shop
HOURS	Daily: 6 AM–11 PM
SUBWAY	1, 2 to Grand Army Plaza
PAYMENT	VISA MasterCard AMERICAN EXPRESS DISCOVER
POPULAR FOOD	Breakfast favorites on hand: muffins, croissants, etc.; and don't forget the soups, sandwiches, and sweets
DRINKS	Ozzie's doesn't mess around with coffee: 40 varieties of beans, roasted fresh daily, go into everything from hot cappuccino to Granida ("like frappuccino but better," served in summer)
SEATING	Seats 50
AMBIENCE	The Seventh Ave. location is housed in what was—a long time ago—a pharmacy, and they've kept a lot of the neat old junk intact (think "apothecary"), giving Ozzie's an inviting (and some say nostalgic) feel
EXTRAS/NOTES	Ozzie's offers Friday night poetry readings and occasional live music. Check web site.
OTHER ONES	• Around Prospect Park: 249 Fifth Ave., Brooklyn, 11215, (718) 768-6868

—Mayu Kanno

Park Café

Food stands out by being just what you expect.

$$$

82 Seventh Ave., Brooklyn 11217

(between Berkeley Pl. and Union St.)

Phone (718) 399-0957

www.parkcafe.net

CATEGORY	Diner
HOURS	Daily: 7 AM–10:45 PM
SUBWAY	Q to Seventh Ave.
PAYMENT	VISA AMERICAN EXPRESS DISCOVER
POPULAR FOOD	Cheeseburger deluxe; two eggs (served with potatoes and toast)
UNIQUE FOOD	Grilled chicken with mozzarella and grilled tomato; chicken kabob
DRINKS	Coffee, tea, hot chocolate (with whipped cream!), sodas, juices, egg cream

SEATING	Seats 54, including five at the counter
AMBIENCE	Bring a friend, your family, or the newspaper—you'll never feel rushed at this casual, no-frills diner that lends itself to long conversations or solitary contemplation; during holiday season, keep a weary eye on the dancing Santa above the counter
EXTRAS/NOTES	Named for its proximity to Prospect Park, the Park Café draws crowds of tired Park Slope residents seeking coffee and eggs on any given weekend morning. The two eggs are just that: served any way you please with potatoes and toast, they make a hearty breakfast that will leave you and your wallet feeling full and content. The tuna sandwich is generous with the tuna and tomato, and not too heavy on the mayonnaise.

—Emma Berndt

Purity Diner

*Down-home charm meets
New York style.*
Since 1929
$$

289 Seventh Ave., Brooklyn 11215
(at Seventh St.)
Phone (718) 840-0881 • Fax (718) 840-0882

CATEGORY	Diner
HOURS	24/7
SUBWAY	F to Seventh Ave.
PAYMENT	VISA MasterCard
POPULAR FOOD	Steak, seafood, diet menu, and a variety of burgers, sandwiches, salads, pastas, roast meats, and fish; international dishes include daily Spanish specials and Greek gyros, *spanakopita, moussaka*
UNIQUE FOOD	Full breakfast menu includes king-size three-egg omelettes
DRINKS	Herbal teas, coffee, cocoa, sodas, seltzers, egg creams, beer, and wine
SEATING	Booths and tables
AMBIENCE	Exposed brick walls and large windows give Purity the feel of a NY loft; serving Park Slope singles and families, and the staff of the hospital next door—you're never alone at the Purity, but you don't have to wait around long for a table either
EXTRAS/NOTES	Be sure to check out the black-and-white photos of old Brooklyn. The service is quick and always goes the extra mile to make your meal enjoyable. Want a newspaper to read while you eat? They got it! Want to chat for awhile? No problem!

—Jill Sieracki

Red Hot Restaurant

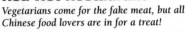

Vegetarians come for the fake meat, but all Chinese food lovers are in for a treat!

$$

347 Seventh Ave., Brooklyn 11215
(at Tenth St.)
Phone (718) 369-0700

CATEGORY	Chinese/Vegetarian
HOURS	Mon–Thurs: 11:30 AM–10:30 PM
	Fri/Sat: 11:30 AM–11 PM
	Sun: 1 PM–10:30 PM
SUBWAY	F to Seventh Ave.
PAYMENT	VISA MasterCard AMERICAN EXPRESS DISCOVER
POPULAR FOOD	Great versions of standards like scallion pancakes, *lo mein*, and chicken with broccoli join a bevy of sumptuous vegetarian specialties; try the Shanghai-style vegetarian wontons
UNIQUE FOOD	Vegetarian sweet and sour spare ribs, which don't really taste like pork, but are delicious nonetheless; big tureens of vegetarian wonton soup, loaded with fresh spinach—intended for two but could serve as an appetizer for three or even four; cashew bird's nest features wonderfully chewy wheat gluten cubes mixed with vegetables, cashews, and walnuts in a white sauce
DRINKS	Tea, soda, juice
SEATING	Seats about 50
AMBIENCE	Go there for the food rather than the atmosphere; Park Slope yuppies and youngish locals sit down to eat—often with children in tow—but just as often call in for delivery
EXTRAS/NOTES	Focusing on healthy cuisine, Red Hot's food is MSG free and less greasy than most Chinese. Everything's made with fresh vegetables and brown rice is available.

—*Teresa Theophano*

Rice Thai Kitchen

Lulled by the mood lighting and the spicy Thai, the stone reliefs begin to look real.

$$$

311 Seventh Ave., Brooklyn 11215
(at Eighth St.)
Phone (718) 832-5169 • Fax (718) 832-0939

CATEGORY	Thai
HOURS	Mon–Thurs: noon–11 PM
	Fri/Sat: noon–midnight
	Sun: 1 PM–11 PM
SUBWAY	F to Fourth or Seventh Aves.
PAYMENT	VISA MasterCard

POPULAR FOOD	The tofu soup is brimming with fresh sprouts and lots of tofu in a delicate broth; Thai spring rolls come with wonderfully tangy dipping sauce; fresh lime gives the better-than-average *pad* Thai—already chock full of baby shrimp—a burst of flavor
UNIQUE FOOD	Cooked with coconut milk, the curries are light, creamy, and packed with chunks of fresh vegetables
DRINKS	Soda, frozen fruit drinks, Thai tea and coffee, red and white wine
SEATING	Fifteen tables
AMBIENCE	A great place to relax after dodging baby carriages on Seventh Ave.; with fresh flowers and candles on every table, you'll never want to leave

—Julia Pastore

Roma Pizza

The capital of Pizza.

$$

85 Seventh Ave., Brooklyn 11217
(between Berkeley Pl. and Union St.)
Phone (718) 783-7334

CATEGORY	Pizza Parlor
HOURS	Daily: 11 AM–11 PM
SUBWAY	Q to Seventh Ave.
PAYMENT	Cash only
POPULAR FOOD	Salad slice, chicken cutlet parmesan, garlic knots
UNIQUE FOOD	Fresh mozzarella, made fresh every morning by the Roma Pizza staff
DRINKS	Soft drinks (including grape and orange soda!) and juice
SEATING	Nine large booths easily accommodate 36
AMBIENCE	A brightly lit, smoke-free, family-owned pizza parlor; attracts groups of friends, parents, and children, tired souls on their way home from work, and (rumor has it) even the occasional movie star; stop in for reliably good food served piping hot—stay and do your homework or take it to go
EXTRAS/NOTES	Why call it Roma Pizza? As the guys behind the counter will be happy to tell you: "Rome is the capital of Italy, and Roma Pizza is the capital of Pizza." Right on both counts. The crusts on Roma Pizza's pies are delightfully crisp. The salad pizza contains more vegetables than you can shake a stick at. Not in the mood for pizza? The eggplant in the eggplant parmesan is of the perfect consistency— not too firm or too mushy, but just right.

—Emma Berndt

Tom's Restaurant

A Brooklyn legend—and one of the borough's coziest diners.

Since 1936

$$$

782 Washington Ave., Brooklyn 11238
(at Sterling Pl.)
Phone (718) 636-9738

CATEGORY	Diner/Luncheonette
HOURS	Mon–Sat: 6 AM–4 PM
SUBWAY	1, 2 to Eastern Pkwy.
PAYMENT	Cash only
POPULAR FOOD	Tom's home fries, whether they're served alongside eggs or by themselves, have earned a sterling reputation; the delectable variety of pancakes like pumpkin walnut, harvest (cranberry and sweet corn), chocolate chip, and various fruit flavors, all served with delicious strawberry- and cinnamon-flavored butters and regular syrup, can't be beat
UNIQUE FOOD	Wonderful pumpkin walnut Belgian waffles
DRINKS	Iced coffee served with whipped cream, tea, brewed coffee, sodas, juices, egg creams, and a famous cherry-lime rickey
SEATING	About half a dozen stools at the counter plus two dining rooms (seats about 75)
AMBIENCE	Tchotchke-laden: reviews and photographs on every wall, along with the lyrics to Suzanne Vega's song "Tom's Diner" (it's about the unrelated Tom's Diner in Manhattan); brunch-crazed locals—many of them younger, artsy, and/or yuppie—come in on Saturday mornings, but all kinds of people show up regularly
EXTRAS/NOTES	A Brooklyn landmark since 1936, Tom's has as rich a history as this diverse neighborhood itself. In 1968, after the assassination of Martin Luther King, Jr., African-American neighbors linked arms to keep Tom's from being razed along with other white-owned businesses. And so it thrives today. Gus, the jovial owner, will throw a couple of peppermints and a smile your way after serving you coffee. Be patient while waiting in line for Saturday brunch. You'll be offered fresh orange wedges—and then handy wipes—by a bus person soon enough. If only this charming Mom-and-Pop joint was open for dinner and Sunday brunch…

—Teresa Theophano

REMEMBER THE NEEDIEST!

Uncle Moe's Burrito and Taco Shop

(see p. 79)

Mexican

341 Seventh Ave., Brooklyn 11215

Phone (718) 965-0006

Veggie Castle

Converted White Castle offers healthy, creative, and colorful vegan meals and baked goods.

$$

2242 Church Ave., Brooklyn 11226

(at Flatbush Ave.)

Phone (718) 703-1275

CATEGORY	Jamaican/Vegan
HOURS	Daily: 10 AM–11 PM
SUBWAY	Q to Church Ave.; 2, 5 to Church Ave.
PAYMENT	Cash only
POPULAR FOOD	Lunch specials for $5 include rice and beans, a choice of vegetables, and entrées ranging from baked tofu in a tangy barbecue pineapple sauce, to a curry or barbecue soy with stewed carrots and onions; also try their famous veggie burgers and vegan macaroni and cheese
UNIQUE FOOD	Veggie Castle bakes its own patties (soy, *callaloo,* veggie, soy chicken), cassava balls, and cakes (some made without eggs, lard, or yeast); apple cinnamon, pumpkin, and banana nut breads
DRINKS	Over 42 fresh juices and smoothies, each prescribed as its own remedy "to cure what ails ya" are what makes this restaurant unique; try the #1 Cold and Flu, the #10 Memory, the #16 Fatigue, or the #34 Green Juice—*Hungry?* can't vouch for their therapeutic powers, but we promise they'll work wonders for your taste buds
SEATING	Plenty of comfortable seating for parties ranging from two to 20
EXTRAS/NOTES	Veggie Castle operates out of an old White Castle—basically a 180-degree turnaround from its predecessor. After your meal, be sure to check out the Castle's natural foods and supplement section, stocked with everything from oat bran and unbleached wheat flour, to the very same protein powders and spirulina used in the restaurant's juice concoctions. The Castle also sells ginseng, sea moss, *baji,* and locally grown bee pollen, honey, and molasses.

—Scott Gross

SOUTH BROOKLYN

Chio Pio Inc.

*Fantastic, cheap Uzbek food in a
sparse Soviet setting.*
$$

3087 Brighton Fourth St., Brooklyn 11235
(at Brighton Beach Ave.)
Phone (718) 615-9221

CATEGORY	Uzbek Café
HOURS	Daily: 10 AM–10 PM
SUBWAY	Q to Brighton Beach Ave.
PAYMENT	Cash only
POPULAR FOOD	Poor command of Uzbek and Russian leaves me at a disadvantage communicating with the patrons, proprietor, and staff, but diners seem to eat the Uzbek bread with just about everything on the menu: for less than a subway token, you get half a wagon wheel of the delicious starchy stuff, almost a meal by itself
UNIQUE FOOD	The sign on the awning bears a picture of a cartoon chicken, so I guessed the chicken was the specialty and ordered the Chicken Fried in Uzbek Style: you get a whole bird, bigger than a Cornish game hen but smaller than your average chicken, grilled nicely, and topped with not a little garlic—it's outstanding
DRINKS	Snapple and assorted juices in the refrigerated case
SEATING	Seating for 22
AMBIENCE	The dining area is a tiny square of linoleum tiles, maybe 20 by 20, decorated with waterfall pictures, and packed with simple tables. . .at those tables, when I went, were enough patrons to fill the place—apparently from several corners of the former Soviet Union—dividing their attentions between the food in front of them and the occasional montage of people falling down on NTV International
EXTRAS/NOTES	I visited Chio Pio on the advice of my girlfriend and on that of various critics on chowhound.com. I've only been there once, but I plan to go back to try the very cheap kebabs (*Lyulya,* chicken, lamb, pork, lamb ribs). It bears mentioning that the french fries are excellent as well, clearly made from fresh-cut potatoes.

—*Joe Cleemann*

"Shallots are for babies.
Onions are for men.
Garlic is for heroes."

—*Anon*

Seaside Brooklyn

The nerdiest of our readers will already know that you don't necessarily find the best restaurant in a neighborhood by seeking out the cuisine that it's known for—or that its chamber of commerce would like it to be known for. These die-hard budget gourmets might insist that the finest Greek restaurant in the city sits on some side street in Chinatown, or that you'll find great haggis only at one particular location in Harlem. The nerds, as usual, know what they are talking about. So it's with apologies to them that we present this somewhat superficial culinary overview of inexpensive archetypes in Brooklyn's maritime neighborhoods: seafood in **Sheepshead Bay**, formerly Soviet specialties in **Brighton Beach**, and junk food in **Coney Island**.

•••

Sheepshead Bay:
Seafood for the Masses

Across the inlet from Manhattan Beach, and a short walk from Brighton Beach, is the neighborhood of Sheepshead Bay. In *My Father's Gun* (Plume, 1999), Brian McDonald's account of growing up in a New York City Police family, a chef at a Catskill cop resort tells one uppity officer's wife that if she wants oysters, she can go to Sheepshead Bay. The point? Well into the 20th Century, Sheepshead Bay remained one of the few places where blue-collar New Yorkers could get a taste of the ocean's harvest.

It retains that character today. The main bay-front drag, Emmons Avenue, is flanked by wharves on its south side. In the summer, a small fleet of huge boats is based here, offering twice-daily fishing excursions to the shoals off Long Island. If you're running short on Dramamine, just wait around. Professional fishermen sell their day's catch right off those docks in the afternoons. Or, if you don't feel like cooking, just skip across Emmons. Choose from among a dozen or so seafood joints.

Randazzo's Clam Bar calls itself "The Pride of Sheepshead Bay." It's probably the closest thing around to the kind of fast, no-nonsense seafood roadhouse you'd find attracting economical locals in less urbanized seaside communities. Nothing pretentious about this establishment: just one big open room with lots of seats and a bar, behind which the cooks boil, broil, grill, and deep fry any number of crustaceans and the occasional vertebrate. Manhattan and New England clam chowders in a cup or bowl are a steal. Clams can get expensive, but an order of ubiquitous steamers won't put on too much of a hurting on your wallet. Seafood sandwiches—fried filet, fried oysters, fried scallops, etc.—all remain comfortably under the ten buck mark. Typical of Sheepshead Bay, you can also order from any number of Italian specialties, but they run a little more expensive. *2017 Emmons Ave., (718) 615-0010. Sun–Thurs: 11 AM–12:30 AM, Fri/Sat: 11 AM–1:15 AM.*

Next door is **Mario & Luigi's.** Pay close attention to the "Housa Rules." Mario's Mom's words, posted throughout, admonish customers: "Smoking Makesa the Sauce Turn Sour So Pleasea No Smoke." Luigi's father's prohibitions on credit cards have been repealed, but, like the 18th Amendment or the signatures of the South Carolina delegation in our Constitution, they haven't been removed from the constitution, just superceded. Anyhow, the food here is overpriced, and the pasta dishes I tried were a bit heavy, but if you take advantage of the luncheon special, you can score a generously-proportioned seafood or pasta dish for, again, under $10. And the ambience is extraordinary in a masochistic way. *2007 Emmons Ave., (718) 891-4300/4343. Sun–Thurs: noon–10:30pm, Fri/Sat: noon–11:30. Lunch special: Mon–Fri: noon–4 PM, Sat/Sun: noon–5 PM.*

Also worth a look but not budget-friendly is **Lundy Brothers,** which has the undisputed rule of the roost in Sheepshead Bay. It's elegantly decorated and furnished, but don't confuse elegance with subtlety in this case. There is no disguising the size of this labyrinthine succession of dining areas. The Lundy Brothers founded the landmark in 1934, and it was at that time the second biggest restaurant in the world, according to its management. It's hard to contest that claim: there's seating for nearly 800 patrons! You're looking at entrees in the $20 range, though you can go a little lower. The Sunday brunch isn't cheap ($19.95, 11 AM–2 PM), but the food is prepared remarkably well and it is all you can eat seafood. But whether you stay or go, Lundy Brother's is definitely worth your time. *1901 Emmons Ave., (718) 743-0022. Sun: 11 AM–9 PM, Mon–Wed: 11:30 AM–9 PM, Thurs/Fri: 11:30 AM–10 PM, Sat: 11:30 AM–11 PM. Open later summer and holidays.*

And you can always head to the diner. **El Greco** offers all of a diner's usual suspects, and perhaps, in the words of the immortal Claude Rains, twice the usual number of suspects. With burgers around $5 it won't break the bank, either. *1821 Emmons Ave., (718) 934-1288. 24/7.*

•••

Internationale Flavors
at Brighton Beach

The jury is still out (probably literally) on the quality of water around New York City, so you're not likely to encounter a real dainty set splashing in the small breakers that wash up on Brighton Beach. The times I've visited, the most eye-catching bathers and sunbathers have been less notable for their sleek sexiness than for their heft and apparent lack of inhibition. Yes, there are some old, fat people on Brighton Beach, and they wear swimsuits that their American-born contemporaries would probably call European-style. Some of these bathing beauties represent the Soviet equivalent of our "Greatest Generation." They, as much as any other octogenarians in the world, have earned the right to wear bikinis on the beach. And by what twist of fate did so many of them end up in Brighton Beach, now hailed as one of America's biggest Russian communities? Who knows? But the fact is that Brighton Beach is the place to go in New York City for Russian cuisine. Or any formerly-Soviet cuisine.

The delis on Brighton Beach Avenue compete with Manhattan's gourmet emporiums. As often as not including some variation of the word "gastronomy" on their marquees, these big, clean, usually gorgeous establishments combine the best aspects of a full service deli—plenty of reasonably cheap Russian specialties, both hot and cold—with the stunning variety of exquisitely packaged sweets, crackers, etc. that you'd find in a duty-free shop. A few worth mentioning for their size and their splendor: **Taste of Russia, Gastronom Jubilee**, and **M&I International**. But don't stop there, and don't by any means neglect Brighton Beach's produce stands, among the best and cheapest in the city.

If you plan to stay for a meal, you have plenty of options. Russian restaurants line the boardwalk, but, for our money, some of the best and best-priced food can be found on the side streets. **Chio Pio** (see p. 214) offers very good, very cheap Uzbek specialties in what looks like a renovated barber shop.

If you decide you like Uzbek food, check out the more colorful ambience at **Eastern Feast.** Murals of the great mosques and markets of Samarkand contribute to a cozy, pizza parlor atmosphere, in which you can wash down your kebab (under $4 in most cases) with a cold beer or a glass of wine. **Varenichnaya** promises "Russian style ravioli." Another variation on what Poles call a *pierogi*, the *vareniki* can be eaten in the dining area for a song or taken home and cooked for a few notes ($2.95 for 25 pieces, many varieties).

- **Eastern Feast:** 1003 Brighton Beach Ave., (718) 934-9608/9605. Sun–Thurs: noon–10 PM, Fri: noon–10:30 PM, Sat: noon–11 PM.
- **Gastronom Jubilee:** 281-285 Brighton Beach Ave., (718) 743-3900. Daily: 8 AM–10 PM.
- **M&I International Food:** 249 Brighton Beach Ave., (718) 615-1011. Daily: 8 AM–10 PM.
- **Taste of Russia:** 219 Brighton Beach Ave., (718) 934-6167). Daily: 8 AM–10 PM.
- **Varenichnaya:** 3086 Brighton Second Street, (718) 332-9797. Daily: 10 AM –9 PM.

• • •

Coney Island
and the Unbelievable Takeru Kobayashi,
the Eighth Wonder of the World!

It's hard to deny that Coney Island is trashy. And that, its champions will tell you, is precisely its charm.

It's plenty entertaining: from the subway (F,Q,W to Coney Island/Stillwell Avenue of F, Q to West 8th St./NY Aquarium) you're within easy striking distance of Key Span Park (come see the New York Penn League 2001 Champions, the Brooklyn Cyclones, play from June through September; I'm assured it's a good time), an aquarium, the beach (naturally), and the rides. And what rides! Don't be fooled by the small size of the Cyclone, one of the world's oldest roller coasters: it's terrifying both because of and in spite of that fact. June offers the infamous Mermaid Parade, a cavalcade of transvestism and general freakishness. Winter offers another spectacle, the Polar Bear Club: beginning on the New Year, members psychotically plunge into the chilly Atlantic every Sunday. Get all the scoop at www.coneyislandusa.com.

Coney Island is most famous for junk food. You could probably call it the spiritual home of this decidedly American contribution to international cuisine (who decided? Probably the Frogs). And if it is the spiritual headquarters of one of the greatest transforming cultural institutions our nation has ever witnessed, where is the one-eyed mullah? Smart money's on 1310 Surf Avenue: the original **Nathan's** (see p. 112). A short block from the boardwalk and open even in the winter, Nathan's opens up its shutters in the summer months and expands into adjacent quarters. In it's outdoor eating area, gluttons compete every year on the Fourth of July for the title of world's fastest hot dog eater. It's an impressive institution, but don't expect to go home with the laurels: last year, 5'7", 131-pound Takeru Kobayashi, 23, of Japan doubled countryman Kazutoyo "The Rabbit" Arai's previous record, consuming an unbelievable 50 hotdogs in twelve minutes.

And hot dogs are what Nathan's is famous for. Get your basic dog for under two bucks, or splurge on the Chili Cheese Dog for just under three. But it doesn't end with hot dogs. Fronting for a few other franchises and offering more than your usual assortment of Nathan's hot dogs and fries, this landmark junk food stand advertises *chow mein*, roast beef, and even a clam bar.

And don't miss the world-famous Coney Island Boardwalk. This is a place where freak shows are still advertised in public (though most of the freaks seem to have freaky talents rather than crippling physical deformities). And where the many painted signs drop apostrophes, add quotation marks, and use words like "famous" and "original" to advertise goods and services that are neither.

Dominating the lesser competitors on the boardwalk is **Gregory & Phil's**, under the giant cantilevered rocket that marks the entrance to the Astroland amusement park. Gregory & Phil's *(Boardwalk, between W. 10th and W. 11th, closed in winter)* is liberally decked-out with paintings of the food it serves and outrageous boasts about its quality and/or notoriety. To give you a better idea of what that food looks like, check out the models by the counter. And it does, by the way, serve every kind of junk food you could think of: hot dogs, french fries, pizza, knishes, Italian sausage, gyros, etc. And of course—beer. It belongs to the same part of America that produced Route 66 kitsch, and Gregory & Phil's goes a long way toward ensuring that, like the great highway's legend, Coney Island's faded mystique, may never vanish from this earth.

—*Joe Cleemann*

Gino's Focacceria

Friendly staff, generous portions of delicious Italian classics.

$$$

7118 18th Ave., Brooklyn 11204
(between 71st and 72nd Sts.)
Phone (718) 232-9073

CATEGORY	Neighborhood Italian restaurant
HOURS	Mon–Thurs: 11 AM–8 PM Fri/Sat: 11 AM–9 PM
SUBWAY	N, W to 18th Ave.
PAYMENT	Cash only
POPULAR FOOD	You can't go wrong with any of the pastas served *al dente*—particularly with tender calamari in a marinara sauce or in a light vodka sauce; eggplant is prepared just how it should be—lightly breaded without a hint of grease

UNIQUE FOOD	For the adventurous: *vasdette* roll (boiled cow spleen on fresh-baked roll with ricotta and parmesan)
DRINKS	Mineral water, beer, wine, coffee
SEATING	Ample seating: six large booths and 10–12 tables
AMBIENCE	Chianti bottles and the Italian flag are a nice touch, but locals come for the food, not the ambience
EXTRAS/NOTES	Dinner entrées include salad bar and warm bread—a real bargain.

—*Julia Pastore*

Fond Farewell
Peter's Ice Cream Parlor
(a.k.a. Pete's)
Brooklyn Heights

Two crucial yardsticks of any decent neighborhood are a serviceable Laundromat and a good ice cream parlor. If yours has neither, move. Many people almost did after Pete's closed last March, before it could sweeten one last summer. A petition to stop the closing circulated, but the property's landlords won out, doubling the rent and allowing a day spa to take Pete's place along Atlantic Avenue. A day spa!

With its 12-foot tin-roof ceilings and the house cat that occasionally leapt onto the tables in the hopes of stealing a few licks of leftover ice cream, Pete's was, as so few places are these days, genuinely comfortable and full of character. It did not play smooth jazz or have its own soundtrack. It did not put anything weird in the coffee. It did not venture into merchandise. At Pete's, you could only get Pete's Ice Cream, along with a slice of pie or cake, or maybe a cookie, or a truffle, everything homemade and delicious. You took your pie—crust breaking away and ice cream melting into a pool around it—to a booth or a couch and lounged and maybe leafed through a newspaper or two while picking away at the gooey mess. Nobody looked at you funny or chirped "Have a nice day." In the Fall you could get pumpkin ice cream that really tasted like pumpkin. I still have dreams about Pete's endorphin-boosting Chocolate Decadence ice cream, which stuck to the roof of my mouth and was dark as mud. And the new Ben & Jerry's a few blocks away just can't make those dreams come true. There will be many unwitting ice cream orphans in the neighborhood in the years to come, who will never even get to dream about the homemade peanut butter ice cream in a chocolate-dipped waffle cone with sprinkles. And that may be the story's saddest part.

—*Melissa Contreras*

STATEN
ISLAND

STATEN ISLAND

DeNino's Pizzeria Tavern

(see p. 225)
Italian
524 Port Richmond Ave., Staten Island 10302
Phone (719) 442-9401

Go-Go
Souvlaki King

Go Greek or not at this
"something for everyone restaurant of the
'90s."
$$

2218 Hylan Blvd., Staten Island, 10306
(corner of Lincoln Ave.)
Phone (718) 667-0880

CATEGORY	Greek Diner
HOURS	Sun–Thurs: 7:30 AM–2 AM Fri/Sat: 7:30 AM–5 AM
BUS	S78, S79 buses
PAYMENT	VISA MasterCard AMERICAN DISCOVER
POPULAR FOOD	Fabulous gyros and kabobs with fresh meat and vegetables, great falafel with Go-Go's famous white sauce (which is more like mayo than *tahini*)
UNIQUE FOOD	If you love grease, go for the Mexi-Special tacos, burritos, or nachos with spicy cheese, or any of the fried fish dishes
DRINKS	Draft beer in large or jumbo, lemonade, milk shakes, soda
SEATING	Ten booths and one large table that seats 18
AMBIENCE	Friendly, chatty service—clientele keep to themselves—maybe because of the amazing Pac-Man to play or endless sports on the tube
EXTRAS/NOTES	With over 20 burger options, various fish sandwiches, Italian specialties, cold salad platters, Southern food, and even quiche choices—see for yourself if Go-Go's has the "largest menu on the East Coast."

—*Laura Russo*

"If I go down for anything in history,
I would like to be known as the
person who convinced the
American people that catfish is one of
the finest eating fishes in the world."

—*Willard Scott (The Today Show)*

Island Roti Shop and Bakery

Delish Trinidadian with an East Indian flare.

$$

65 Victory Blvd., Staten Island 10301

(at Bay St.)

Phone (718) 815-7001

CATEGORY	Trinidadian West Indian
HOURS	Mon–Sat: 10 AM–9 PM
BUS	S48, S61, S62, S66, S67 buses to Victory Blvd. or Bay St.
PAYMENT	Cash only
POPULAR FOOD	*Roti* (here, it's prepared as a large spicy sandwich made with flat Indian *naan*) with beef, chicken, shrimp, and veggies; potato and channa; the tasty sides that come with the spicy dishes: spinach, *dal* (soupy lentils), fried plantains
UNIQUE FOOD	*Roti* with goat, chewy conch, mild pumpkin, spinach (*aka bhaji*), or shrimp; *accra* codfish cake; Trinidad's answer to the knish, the *aloo* pie; fresh turnovers in apple, strawberry, and pineapple, coconut tarts, currant rolls, and drops (cookies)
SEATING	Standing room/carry-out only
DRINKS	Variety of Trinidadian and American sodas
AMBIENCE	The ambience encourages you to find a bench in the tiny park a block away, where Victory meets Bay
EXTRAS/NOTES	Until recently, the proprietor offered Trinidad-style Chinese food; ask with a smile and he might oblige you with a taste.

—*Jessica Nepomuceno*

Jimmy Max

(see p. 226)

Italian

280 Watchogue Rd., Staten Island 10314

Phone (718) 983-6715

La Roca's

(see p. 150)

Pizza/Ice Cream

489 Midland Ave., Staten Island 10306

Phone (718) 979-8833

Lakruwana

The best of the new Sri Lankan eateries on S.I.

$$

3 Corson Ave., Staten Island 10301

(south of Victory Blvd. and Bay St.)

Phone (718) 876-9870

CATEGORY	Sri Lankan
HOURS	Daily: 10 AM–10:30 PM

BUS STOP S48, S61, S62, S66, S67 buses to Victory Blvd. or Bay St.

PAYMENT Cash only

POPULAR FOOD The most popular dishes showcase the Dutch and Portuguese influences on what would otherwise be an entirely East Indian influenced cuisine—try fish or vegetable cutlets (croquettes); hoppers (delicate bowl-shaped rice flour crepes, to dip and drape with curry); lamb black curry (toasting the spices before cooking provides a deep, rich, lingering hotness); *kotthu roti* (*naan* sandwiches) with chicken, pork, beef, or fish; *biryani* rice dishes come with vegetable, chicken, beef, lamb, or shrimp—ideal for the less adventurous eater

UNIQUE FOOD Try the *lamprais*, (*basmati* rice with meat curry, veggies and spices steamed in a banana leaf); squid curry; kingfish curry; vegetable curry (depends on what is in season: a recent veggie curry included cashews, yucca, turnip, and lentil in a fragrant sauce)

DRINKS Delicious Ceylon black tea with nickel-sized chunks of ginger, soda

SEATING Tables for 20–25

AMBIENCE Much more elegant than one expects for the area—walls are accented with white and rich red, decorated with brass Buddhist statuary; chairs are harder than you'd like, but the overall effect is warm and homey; service is attentive and the clientele includes adventurous Staten Islanders looking for an alternative to Italian or Chinese, as well as members of the growing Sri Lankan community in the area—I would (and will) bring my parents here without thinking twice

EXTRAS/NOTES The kitchen will make your food as spicy or mild as you like. Menu is very friendly to vegetarians. Lakruwana has a sister restaurant on 44th and Ninth in Manhattan; it's had glowing reviews in the *New York Times, The New York Post,* and *Zagat.* Its owner lives on Staten Island, hence this tiny outpost of the older, more established eatery. The chef at the Staten Island location, Sanjay, also takes an occasional turn at the burners at the sister restaurant in Manhattan.

OTHER ONES • Midtown West: 358 W. 44th St., Manhattan, 10036, (212) 957-4480

—*Jessica Nepomuceno*

When it Comes to New York Pizza and "The Slice," Everyone's Got an Opinion.

New York pizza is world-famous, and with good reason. A decent New York slice, warm but not too hot, with a reasonable ratio of dough to sauce to cheese, almost effortlessly trumps other cities' best offerings. But that doesn't mean you're guaranteed great pizza with your rent—or your toll. On the contrary, many marginal purveyors serve marginal pizza made with marginal ingredients. In places like this, you, the consumer, can end up with a tasteless, greasy slice (dreaded by some, loved by others) that you'll need to mop off with napkins before biting.

But forewarned is forearmed. And the informed pizza aficionado need never be disappointed while trekking through the Big Apple's endless parlors. Adding flavor and variety to the outstanding traditional options, the city's global hodge-podge has made an impact on this Italian favorite. And experimentation with every type of dough, sauce, and toppings has made some interesting combinations—if you have the stomach for them.

The *best* pizza in New York? It's an eternal and ultimately fruitless debate. In fact, just about everybody has a (fiercely held) opinion.

Here, then, are just a few of the landmarks that dot this vibrant intellectual landscape:

Alba Pizza

Great garlic knots and thinly kneaded pizza crusts. See review p. 175.

- *Central Queens: 137-67 Queens Blvd., Queens, 11415, (718) 291-1620.*

DeNino's Pizzeria Tavern

Lush tomato sauce and creamy mozzarella on a hearty thick crust.

- *Staten Island: 524 Port Richmond Ave., 10302, (719) 442-9401.*

Famous Famiglia

Comfortable and tasty New York semi-chain pizza joint. See review p. 109.

- *From Chelsea to West Houston: 61 Chelsea Piers, Manhattan, 10011, (212) 803-5552.*
- *Midtown West: 686 Eighth Ave., Manhattan, 10036, (212) 382-3030.*
- *Midtown West: 1630 Broadway, Manhattan, 10019, (212) 489-7584.*
- *Upper East Side: 1284 First Ave., Manhattan, 10021, (212) 288-1616.*
- *Upper East Side: 1398 Madison Ave., Manhattan, 10029, (212) 996-9797.*

- *Upper West Side: 734 Amsterdam Ave.,
  Manhattan, 10025, (212) 749-1111.*
- *Upper West Side: 2859 Broadway, Manhattan,
  10025, (212) 865-1234.*
- *Way Uptown: 4007 Broadway, Manhattan,
  10032, (212) 927-3333.*

Grimaldi's

Thin-crust critic's favorite. See review p. 191.

- *Downtown Brooklyn West: 19 Old Fulton St.,
  Brooklyn, 10021, (718)-858-4300.*

Jimmy Max

Rescues prepubescent pizza lovers from
creepy animatronic rodents with cool make-your-
own pizza parties and Kindergarten Pizza Seminars.

- *Staten Island: 280 Watchogue Rd.,
  10314, (718) 983-6715.*

Joe's Pizza

Get the fresh mozzarella, plain cheese, or
pepperoni and walk with it. See review p. 49.

- *Around Washington Square Park:
  233 Bleecker St., Manhattan, 10014,
  (212) 366-1182.*
- *Around Washington Square Park: 7 Carmine
  St., Manhattan, 10014, (212) 255-3946.*

John's Pizzeria

Baked to perfection in traditional stone
floor ovens.

- *Upper East Side: 408 E. 64th St., Manhattan,
  10021, (212) 935-2895.*
- *Around Washington Square Park:
  278 Bleecker St., Manhattan, 10014,
  (212) 243-1680.*
- *Upper West Side: 48 W. 65th St., Manhattan,
  10019, (212) 721-7001.*
- *Midtown West: 260 W. 44th St., Manhattan,
  10036, (212) 391-7560.*

Koronet's Pizza

Top value: huge slices for a buck-fifty.

- *Upper West Side: 2848 Broadway, Manhattan,
  10025, (212) 222-1566.*

Nick's Pizza

Exquisite gourmet pizza pies on a thin crust
caressed with fresh basil. See review p. 177.

- *Central Queens: 108-26 Ascan Ave., Queens,
  11375, (718) 263-1126.*

Nunzio's Pizzeria

Friendly pizzeria demonstrates what 60 years
of experience can do for a pie. See review p. 229.

- *Staten Island: 2155 Hylan Blvd., 10306,
  (718) 667-9647.*

Ray's Pizza
Fame can be a mixed blessing, but the faithful whisper that this one's the original.

- *From Chelsea to West Houston: 465 Sixth Ave., Manhattan, 10011, (212) 243-2253.*

Roma Pizza
The staff makes the mozzarella fresh every morning. See review p. 211.

- *Around Prospect Park: 85 Seventh Ave., Brooklyn, 11217, (718) 783-7334.*

Slice of Harlem and Slice of Harlem II
The best (and perhaps the only) place to grab a slice in Harlem. See review p. 138.

- *The Harlems: 2527 Eighth Ave., Manhattan, 10030, (212) 862-4089.*
- *The Harlems: 308 Lenox Ave., Manhattan, 10027, (212) 426-7400.*

Totonno Pizzeria Napolitano
A Coney Island legend since 1924.

- *South Brooklyn: 1524 Neptune Ave., Brooklyn, 11224, (718) 372-8606.*
- *Upper East Side: 1544 Second Ave., Manhattan, 10028, (212) 327-2800 (called Totonno's Manhattan).*

Val Diano
Great Pizza and sit-down Italian specialties. See review p. 185.

- *Williamsburg & Greenpoint: 659 Manhattan Ave., Brooklyn, 11222, (718) 383-1707.*

Viva Herbal
The pizza Ray would make if he were a healthy hippie. See review p. 67.

- *East Village: 179 Second Ave., Manhattan, 10003, (212) 420-8801.*

—Trevor Soponis

Los Lobos

Authentic Mexican alongside utterly forgettable pizza.

$$

194 Bay St., Staten Island 10301
(at Victory Blvd.)
Phone (718) 420-9472

CATEGORY	Mexican/Pizzeria
HOURS	Daily: 11 AM–10:30 PM
BUS	S48, S61, S62, S66, S67 buses to Victory Blvd. or Bay St.
PAYMENT	
POPULAR FOOD	*Huevos revueltos* with red or green salsa (scrambled eggs with hot or hotter sauce)

comes with beans and fresh corn tortillas or fluffy bread; soft corn tortilla tacos, three per order: choice of *suadero* (beef shoulder), *cecina* (salted beef), *al pastor* (pork in tangy barbecue sauce), or *pollo* (chicken)—each has a satisfying mound of meat, choice of red or green salsa, and a pile of freshly chopped and fragrant cilantro; the *chuleta a la mexicana* is excellent for dinner (meaty pork chops with tomato, onions, and jalapeños, accompanied by the savor of long-simmered beans and rice)

UNIQUE FOOD Join the weary hordes over their bowls of *panzila y pozole,* a hearty beef tripe soup made with hominy and shredded pork— guaranteed to cure any lingering hangovers—which is good, since it's served Saturdays and Sundays only

DRINKS Chase the eats with a tall frosty *licuado* (milk shake) made with blended fruits like guanabana, papaya, guava, and mango; during warmer months, cool off with an *agua fresca,* potent fresh fruit juice dependent on what's in season; soda and jarringly (some might say) sweet Mexican sodas; Mexican and American beer, as well

SEATING Eight bare bones tables seat around 30

AMBIENCE Brightly lit and linoleum underfoot— while waiting for your tacos, gaze at the cultural cacophony on the walls: Mexican kitsch straight from chichi's fame mixed with movie stills from Mafia movies; TV will most likely be tuned to Telemundo Channel 47—good fun when the variety shows are on; count on the jukebox to be blasting mournful Mexican pop and *rancheros*

EXTRAS/NOTES There used to be a sign on the wall that said "Two beer minimum"—evidently, off duty workers found Los Lobos to be the perfect happy hour joint. The situation has since calmed down. Free delivery.

—*Jessica Nepomuceno*

Mommie Marcy's Place, Inc.

Stick-to-your-ribs home cooking that showcases the influence of East Indians on West Indian cuisine.

$$

11 Corson Ave., Staten Island 10301
(one block south of Victory Blvd. and Bay St.)
Phone (718) 815-1507

CATEGORY West Indian

HOURS Mon–Thurs: 10:30 AM–9 PM
Fri/Sat: 10:30 AM–10 PM

BUS S48, S61, S62, S66, S67 buses to Victory Blvd. or Bay St.

PAYMENT	Cash only
POPULAR FOOD	Beef, chicken, vegetable, shrimp patties; macaroni and cheese, jerk chicken, stew fish (available Fridays only), stew oxtails; chicken, vegetable, beef, goat, oxtail *roti* (made with flat bread)
UNIQUE FOOD	Chewy, spicy curry goat; cow heel soup—hearty!; *roti* skin; potato and chick pea sandwich; bake and saltfish—similar to *bacalao* (salt cod soaked in water and cooked again); *callaloo* (Fridays), mildly sweet and nutty coconut bread
DRINKS	Try the Jamaican and Trinidadian soda—but there's also *mauby,* and *sorrel,* virility-boosting sea moss, tangy carrot juice, and peanut punch
SEATING	Carry out
AMBIENCE	Tiny, dimly lit—get the local scoop from the Caribbean-American community newspaper; music from the islands on the boombox; usually full of locals getting their *roti* and patty fixes

—*Jessica Nepomuceno*

New York Deli

(see p. 150)
Italian/American Deli
585 Midland Ave., Staten Island 10306
Phone (718) 987-0062

Nunzio's Pizzeria

"Over 60 years of specializing in pizza!"
Since 1942
$$
2155 Hylan Blvd., Staten Island 10306
(between Midland and Zwicky Aves.)
Phone (718) 667-9647

CATEGORY	Italian/Pizza
HOURS	Mon–Sat: 11 AM–11 PM Sun: 11 AM–8 PM
BUS	S78, S79, S51, S81 buses
PAYMENT	Cash only
POPULAR FOOD	Nunzio's Neapolitan made with whole plum tomatoes, mozzarella, grated pecorino romano, and olive oil over an incredible thin crust
UNIQUE FOOD	You can get hero sandwiches here such as potato and egg, pepper and egg, mozzarella omelette, sausage and peppers, eggplant, or veal pattie
DRINKS	Small 7 oz. bottle of old fashioned Coke, Stewart's Rootbeer, orange and cream soda, and beer (Budweiser, Molson, Coors Light, Heineken)
SEATING	About 15 seats in the back
AMBIENCE	Even youngsters will feel a sense of nostalgia in this old and friendly

pizzeria—there's nothing strange about getting the wrong order here; fantastic old photos of the pizzeria and an autographed one of Bruno Kirby

EXTRAS/NOTES   Pizza sold by the slice or by the pie.

—*Laura Russo*

Shop Smart

(see p. 150)
Market/Deli
590 Midland Ave., Staten Island 10306
Phone (718) 987-4940

STILL
HUNGRY?

Our glossary covers many of those dishes that everyone else seems to sort of know but we occasionally need a crib sheet. As for ethnic dishes—we've only covered the basics.

adobo (Filipino)—a stew of chicken, pork, or fish traditionally flavored with garlic, soy sauce, white vinegar, bay leaves, and black peppercorns.

aduki beans—small, flattened reddish-brown bean; sometimes used as a confectionery.

affogato (Italian)—literally poached, steamed, or plunged; actually scoops of assorted ice-cream "plunged" in espresso, often topped with whipped cream.

agua fresca (Latin America)—(also *agua natural*) flavorful drink that's somewhere between a juice and a soda. We like *horchata* and *tamarindo!*

albondigas (Latin American)—meatballs. In Mexico it's popular as a soup.

antojitos (Latin American)—appetizers (means "little whims").

ayran (Middle Eastern)—yogurt based drink, like *lassi* but flavored with cardamom.

au jus (French)—meat (usually beef) served in its own juices.

baba ganoush (Middle Eastern)—smoky eggplant dip.

bansan (Korean)—see *panchan*.

bao (Chinese)—sweet stuffed buns either baked or steamed; a very popular dim sum treat!

basbousa (Middle Eastern)—a Semolina cake of yogurt and honey.

bean curd (Pan-Asian)—tofu.

beignets—New Orleans-style donuts (sans hole) covered in powdered sugar.

bigos (Polish)—winter stew made from cabbage, sauerkraut, chopped pork, sausage, mushrooms, onions, garlic, paprika, and other seasonings. Additional veggies (and sometimes red wine!) may be added.

bibimbap (Korean)—also *bibibap,* served cold or in a heated clay bowl, a mound of rice to be mixed with vegetables, beef, fish, egg, and red pepper sauce.

biryani (Indian)—meat, seafood, or vegetable curry mixed with rice and flavored with spices, especially saffron.

black cow—frosty glass of root beer poured over chocolate ice cream.

blintz (Jewish)—thin pancake stuffed with cheese or fruit then baked or fried.

borscht (Eastern European)—beet soup, served chilled or hot, topped with sour cream.

bratwurst (German)—roasted or baked pork sausage.

bul go gi (Korean)—slices of marinated beef, grilled or barbecued.

bun (Vietnamese)—rice vermicelli.

café de olla (Mexican)—coffee with cinnamon sticks and sugar.

callaloo—a stew made with dasheen leaves, okra, tomatoes, onions, garlic, and meat or crab, all cooked in coconut milk and flavored with herbs and spices.

calzone (Italian)—pizza dough turnover stuffed with cheesy-tomatoey pizza gooeyness (and other fillings).

caprese (Italian)—fresh bufala mozzarella, tomatoes, and basil drizzled with olive oil and cracked pepper—a lovely salad or fixins' for a sandwich.

carne asada (Latin American)—thinly sliced, charbroiled beef, usually marinated with cumin, salt, lemon, and for the bold, beer; a staple of the Latin American picnic (along with the boom box).

carnitas (Mexican)—juicy, marinated chunks of pork, usually fried or grilled. Very popular as a taco stuffer.

carpaccio (Italian)—raw fillet of beef, sliced paper thin and served with mustard sauce or oil and lemon juice.

Cel-Ray—Dr. Brown's celery-flavored soda. Light and crisp—a must at any deli.

ceviche (Latin American)—(also cebiche) raw fish or shellfish marinated in citrus juice (the citrus sorta "cooks" the fish), usually served with tostadas. Crunchy, tart delight that happens to be low in fat and cholesterol. It's rumored that ceviche is a new favorite with models. While ceviche may not give you Kate Moss' looks, you can at least eat like her. Note: If you are looking to reap the low fat benefits of ceviche steer clear of the tostadas that accompany it; they are deep fried and most certainly fattening.

challah—plaited bread, sometimes covered in poppy seeds, enriched with egg and eaten on the Jewish sabbath.

cheese steak—see Philly cheese steak.

chicharrones (Mexican/Central American)—fried pork rinds, knuckle lickin' good.

chicken fried steak—it's STEAK—floured, battered, and fried à la fried chicken.

chiles rellenos (Mexican)—green poblano chiles, typically stuffed with jack cheese, battered and fried; occasionally you can find it grilled instead of fried—*¡que rico!*

chili size—open-faced burger covered with chili, cheese, and onions.

chimichangas (Mexican)—fried, stuffed tacos.

chow fun (Chinese)—wide, flat rice noodles.

chorizo (Latin American)—spicy sausage much loved for its versatility. Some folks like to grill it whole and others prefer to bust it open, fry it up, and serve it as a side dish. Another favorite incarnation finds the chorizo scrambled with eggs for breakfast.

churrasco—charcoal grilled meat or chicken, usually served on a skewer.

cochinita pibil (Mexican)—grilled marinated pork, Yucatán style.

cocido (Spanish)—duck confit, chorizo, sausage, and preserved pork combined.

congee (Chinese)—(also jook) rice-based porridge, usually with beef or seafood.

corn dog—hot dog dipped in cornbread batter, usually served on a stick.

croque-madame (French)—grilled cheese sandwich, sometimes with chicken—no ham!

croque-monsieur (French)—sandwich filled with ham and cheese then deep-fried (occasionally grilled). Cholesterol heaven!

Cuban sandwiches (Cuban)—roasted pork sandwich pressed on Cuban rolls (which have a crusty, French-bread-like quality). Also see *medianoche* sandwiches.

cuitlacoche (Mexican)—Central Mexico's answer to truffles; technically, black corn fungus, but quite a delicacy!

dal (Indian)—lentil-bean based side dish with an almost soupy consistency, cooked with fried onions and spices.

dim sum (Cantonese)—breakfast/brunch consisting of various small dishes. Most places feature servers pushing carts around the restaurant. You point at what you want as they come by. Literally translated means: "touching your heart."

dolmades (Greek)—(also *warak enab* as a Middle Eastern dish) stuffed grape leaves (often rice and herbs or lamb and rice mixture).

döner **kebab**—thin slices of raw lamb meat with fat and seasoning, spit roasted with thin slices carved as it cooks.

dora wat (Ethiopian)—chicken seasoned with onions and garlic, sautéed in butter and finished with red wine.

dosa (South Indian)—(also *dosai*) oversized traditional crispy pancake, often filled with onion and potato and folded in half; bigger than a frisbee!

edamame (Japanese)—soy beans in the pod, popularly served salted and steamed as appetizers. Pop 'em right out of the end of the pod into yer mouth.

eggs Benedict—poached eggs, typically served with Canadian bacon over an English muffin, with hollandaise sauce.

empanada (Argentinian)—flaky turnover, usually stuffed with spiced meat; a favorite appetizer at an *asado*. Other Latin American countries also make their own versions of this tasty treat.

escovietch (West Indian)—cooked small whole fish in a spiced oil and vinegar mixture, served cold.

étouffe (Creole)—highly spiced shellfish, pot roast, or chicken stew served over rice.

falafel (Middle Eastern)—spiced ground chickpea fava bean balls and spices, deep fried and served with pita.

feijoada (Brazilian/Portuguese)—the national dish of Brazil, which can range from a pork and bean stew to a more complex affair complete with salted beef, tongue, bacon, sausage, and more parts of the pig than you could mount on your wall.

filo (Turkish and Mediterranean)—(also phyllo) thin pastry prepared in several layers, flaky and good.

flautas (Mexican)—akin to the taco except this puppy is rolled tight and deep fried. They are generally stuffed with chicken, beef, or beans and may be topped with lettuce, guacamole, salsa, and cheese. They resemble a flute, hence the name.

focaccia (Italian)—flatbread baked with olive oil and herbs.

frites (Belgian/French)—also *pommes frites,* french or fried potatoes or "french fries".

gefilte fish (Jewish)—white fish ground with eggs and matzo meal then jellied. No one—and we mean no one—under fifty will touch the stuff.

gelato (Italian)—ice cream or ice.

gnocchi (Italian)—small potato and flour dumplings served like a pasta with sauce.

gorditas (Mexican)—fried puffy rounds of corn meal dough topped with beans, *chipotle* sauce, and cheese.

goulash (Hungarian)—a rich beef stew flavored with paprika, originally based on Hungarian *gulyás,* a meat and vegetable soup; often served with sour cream.

grits—staple breakfast side dish of grainy white mush topped with butter or (in joints where they really know what they're doing) a slice of American cheese.

gumbo (Creole)—rich, spicy stew thickened with okra (often includes crab, sausage, chicken, and shrimp).

gyros (Greek)—spit-roasted beef or lamb strips, thinly sliced and served on thick pita bread, garnished with onions and tomatoes.

har gow (Chinese)—steamed shrimp dumplings.

head cheese—(not cheese!) a sausage made from bits of calf or pig head.

hijiki (Japanese)—a sun-dried and coarsely shredded brown seaweed.

hoagie—(also, Italian sandwiches, sub, grinder) huge flat oblong roll stuffed with deli meats and cheeses, pickled veggies, and onions.

horchata (Mexican/Central American)—cold rice and cinnamon drink, sweet and heavenly. One of the tastiest *aguas frescas* this side of the border.

huevos rancheros (Mexican)—fried eggs atop a fried tortilla with salsa, *ranchero* cheese, and beans.

humita (Chile/Argentina)—tamale.

hummus (Middle Eastern)—banded garbanzo beans, *tahini,* sesame oil, garlic, and lemon juice; somewhere between a condiment and a lifestyle.

hush puppies (Southern U.S.)—deep fried cornmeal fritter, in small golf ball size rounds. Originally used to be tossed to dogs to hush 'em up.

iddly (South Indian)—small steamed rice flour cakes served with coconut dipping sauce.

injera (Ethiopian)—flat, spongy, sour unleavened bread. Use it to scoop up everything when you eat Ethiopian food, but be forewarned: it expands in your stomach.

jamaica (Mexican/Central America)—hibiscus flower *agua fresca.*

jambalaya (Creole)—spicy rice dish cooked with sausage, ham, shellfish, and chicken.

jollof (West African)—a stew or casserole made of beef, chicken, or mutton simmered with fried onion, tomatoes, rice, and seasonings.

galbi (Korean)—(also *kal bi*) marinated barbecued short ribs.

kabob (Middle Eastern)—(also shish kabob) chunks of meat, chicken, or fish grilled on skewers, often with vegetable spacers.

kamonan (Japanese)—noodles with slices of duck.

katsu (Japanese)—pork.

kielbasa (Polish)—smoked sausage.

kimchi (Korean)—pickled vegetables, highly chilied- and garlicked-up. Some sweet, some spicy, some unbelievably spicy. Limitless variations.

knockwurst (German)—(also knackwurst) a small, thick, and heavily spiced sausage.

korma (Indian)—style of braising meat or vegetables, often highly spiced and using cream or yogurt.

kreplach (Jewish)—small pieces of noodle dough stuffed with cheese or meat, usually served in soup.

kutya (Ukrainian)—traditional pudding made with wheat-berries, raisins, walnuts, poppy seeds, and honey.

lahmajune (Armenian/Turkish)—a meat (most often lamb) pizza.

larb (Thai)—minced chicken or beef salad spiced with lemon juice, sweet onion, mint leaves, and toasted rice powder, served in a lettuce cup or with cabbage.

lassi (Indian)—yogurt drink served salted or sweetened with rose, mango, or banana.

lychee—red-shelled southeast Asian fruit served in desserts and as a dried snack (known as lychee nuts).

machaca (Northern Mexican)—shredded meat jerky, scrambled with eggs, tomatoes, and chiles.

macrobiotic—diet and lifestyle of organically grown and natural products.

makdoos (Middle Eastern)—miniature eggplant stuffed with walnuts and garlic, marinated with olive oil.

mandoo (Korean)—dumplings.

marage (Yemen)—vegetable soup.

mariscos (Pan-American)—seafood.

masala (Indian)—blend of ground spices, usually including cinnamon, cumin, cloves, black pepper, cardamom, and coriander seed.

matzo brie (Jewish)—eggs scrambled with matzo.

medianoche **sandwich** (Cuban, also midnight sandwich)—roast pork, ham, cheese, and pickles pressed on a sweet roll.

mee krob (Thai)—salad appetizer covered in fried noodles.

menudo (Mexican)—soup made of tripe, hominy, and chile, stewed with garlic and spices. A hangover remedy, and what Mexican families eat before or after Sunday mass.

mofongo (Dominican)—mashed green plantains with pork skin, seasoned with garlic and salt.

mole (Mexican)—thick poblano chile sauce from the Oaxacan region served over chicken or other meats. Most popular is a velvety black, *mole negro* flavored with unsweetened chocolate and raisins. Also available in a variety of colors and levels of spiciness depending on chiles and other flavors used (*amarillo,* or yellow, for example, uses cumin).

Monte Cristo sandwich—sliced turkey, swiss cheese, mustard, and ham sandwich, on French toast, fried, and dusted with powdered sugar. Served with sides ranging from syrup to jam to pickles.

moussaka (Greek)—alternating layers of lamb and fried aubergine slices, topped with Béchamel sauce, an egg and cheese mixture, and breadcrumbs, finally baked and brought to you with pita bread.

muffuletta—New Orleans-style hero sandwich stuffed with clod cuts and dripping with a roasted pepper and olive salad.

muj chien don (Vietnamese)—crispy squid in a little salt and pepper.

mulitas (Mexican)—literally, little mules; actually, little *quesadillas* piled up with meat, veggies, and other goodies.

mung bean—small green bean, eaten as a vegetable or used as a source of sprouts. May also be candied and eaten as a snack, or used to make bean curd.

musubi (Japanese)—rice ball, sometimes filled with bits of salmon or seaweed, or a sour plum. Hawaiian version features SPAM. Delicious grilled.

naan (Indian)—flat bread cooked in a tandoor oven.

niçoise salad (French)—salad served with all the accoutrements from Nice, i.e. French beans, olives, tomatoes, garlic, capers, and of course, tuna and boiled egg.

pad Thai (Thai)—popular rice noodle stir-fry with tofu, shrimp, crushed peanuts, and cilantro.

paella (Spanish)—a rice jubilee flavored with saffron and sprinkled with an assortment of meats, seafood, and vegetables, all served in a sizzling pan.

panchan (Korean)—the smattering of little appetizer dishes (*kimchi*, etc.) that magically appear before a meal of *soontofu* or barbecue; vinegar lovers rejoice.

pastitsio (Greek)—cooked pasta layered with a cooked meat sauce (usually lamb), egg-enriched and cinnamon flavored Béchamel, grated cheese, and topped with a final layer of cheese and fresh breadcrumbs.

patty melt—grilled sandwich with hamburger patty and melted Swiss cheese.

pescado (Spanish)—literally means fish; can be served in a variety of ways, baked in hot rock salt (*a la sal*), coated in egg batter and fried (*a la andaluza*), pickled (*en escabeche*), and even cooked in wine with onions and chocolate and served with mushrooms (*a la asturiana*).

Philly cheese steak—hot, crispy, messy sandwich filled with thin slices of beef and cheese from…where else?…Philadelphia.

pho (Vietnamese)—hearty rice noodle soup staple, with choice of meat or seafood, accompanied by bean sprouts and fresh herbs.

pico de gallo (Mexico)—(also *salsa cruda*) a chunky salsa of chopped tomato, onion, chile, cilantro. In Jalisco it's a *jicama* and orange salad sprinkled with lemon juice and chile powder.

pierogi (Polish)—potato dough filled with cheese and onion boiled or fried.

pigs-in-a-blanket—sausages wrapped in pastry or toasted bread then baked or fried; or, more informally, breakfast pancakes rolled around sausage links. Dip in syrup for extra fun!

plantain (Central American)—cooking banana from tropical regions. When ripe and yellow it's often served fried as a breakfast side dish. While it's green and unripe it's used to make yummy chips available at neighborhood markets.

po' boy—New Orleans-style hero sandwich with seafood and special sauces, often with lemon slices.

pollo a la brasa (Central/South American)—rotisserie chicken.

porgy—various deep-bodied seawater fish with delicate, moist, sweet flesh.

pozole (Mexican)—pork soup with corn, onions, hominy, and dried chiles. Sliced and diced cabbage and radishes are also used as garnish. Very popular come the Christmas season—so good it makes you wish it was Xmas everyday.

pulpo enchilado (Spanish)—octopus in hot sauce.

pupusa (Salvadorean)—round and flattened cornmeal filled with cheese, ground porkrinds, and/or refried beans, which is cooked on a flat pan known as a *comal*. The indigenous term literally means "sacred food." No doubt ancient civilizations concur with modern opinion that the *pupusa* is a sublime treat.

quesadilla (Mexican)—soft flour tortilla filled with melted cheese (and, sometimes, fancier fare).

raita (Indian)—yogurt condiment flavored with spices and vegetables (often cucumber) or fruits—the necessary core component to balance hot Indian food.

ramen (Japanese)—thin, squiggly egg noodle, often served in a soup.

Reuben (Jewish)—rye bread sandwich filled with corned beef, Swiss cheese, and sauerkraut and lightly grilled.

roti (Indian)—round flat bread served plain or filled with meat or vegetables.

S.O.S.—creamed beef on toast and a staple of all U.S. military mess halls; affectionately called shit on shingles.

samosa (Indian)—pyramid shaped pastry stuffed with savory vegetables or meat.

sashimi (Japanese)—fresh raw seafood thinly sliced and artfully arranged.

satay (Thai)—chicken or shrimp kabob, often served with a peanut sauce.

sauerkraut (German)—chopped, fermented sour cabbage.

schnitzel (English/Austrian)—thin fried veal or pork cutlet.

seitan (Chinese)—wheat gluten marinated in soy sauce with other flavorings.

shabu shabu (Japanese)—hot pot. Cook thin sliced beef and assorted vegetables in a big hot pot at your table—served with a couple of dipping sauces and rice.

shaved ice—Hawaiian snow cone. Ice with various juices/flavorings (from lime or strawberry to sweet green tea and sweetened condensed milk). Non-Hawaiian incarnations are called *raspado* and slush.

shawarma (Middle Eastern)—pita bread sandwich filled with sliced beef, tomato, and sesame sauce.

shish kabob—see kabob.

sloppy joe—loose, minced meat sandwich with sauce on hamburger bun.

soba (Japanese)—thin buckwheat noodles, often served cold with sesame oil-based sauce.

som tum (Thai)—green papaya salad.

soontofu (Korean)—boiling hot soup with soft tofu, your choice of protein elements (mushroom or *kimchi* for vegetarians, seafood, pork for non) served with a variety of *kimchis* and rice.

sopes (Mexican)—dense corn cakes topped with beef or chicken, beans, lettuce, tomato, and crumbled cheese.

souvlaki (Greek)—kebabs of lamb, veal or pork, cooked on a griddle or over a barbecue, sprinkled with lemon juice during cooking, and served with lemon wedges, onions, and sliced tomatoes.

sorrel (Caribbean)—sweet hibiscus beverage served cold.

spanakopita (Greek)—filo triangles filled with spinach and cheese.

spelt—ancient type of wheat, commonly used to make flour without traditional wheat flavor.

spotted dick (British)—traditional pudding.

sushi (Japanese)—the stuff of midnight cravings and maxxed out credit cards. Small rolls of vinegar infused sticky rice topped (or stuffed) with fresh raw seafood, sweet omelette, or pickled vegetables and held together with sheets of seaweed (*nori*).

Suzy Qs—(also Curly Qs) spiral-cut french fries (they look sort of like those confetti spirals).

tabouli (Middle Eastern)—light salad of cracked wheat (bulgur), tomatoes, parsley, mint, green onions, lemon juice, olive oil, and spices.

tahini (Middle Eastern)—paste made from ground sesame seeds.

tamale (Latin American)—Latin America's contribution to nirvana. Each nation has its own take on the tamale, but in very basic terms it is cornmeal filled with meat and veggies wrapped in corn husk or palm tree leaves for shape, then steamed. There are also sweet varieties notably the *elote,* or corn, tamale. A favorite during the holidays, the tamale is surely the sumptuous culprit of many a person's Yuletide bulge. Note: We understand that due to the tamales' versatility we cannot do it full justice in our definition. We can only encourage you to get your hands on some and indulge.

tamarindo (Mexican)—popular *agua fresca* made from tamarind fruit.

tandoori (Indian)—literally means baked in a tandoor (a large clay oven). Tends to be a drier form of Indian dish than, say, curries.

tapenade (Provençale italian)—chopped olive garnish; a delightful spread for a hunk of baguette.

taquitos (Mexican)—(also, *flautas*) shredded meat or cheese rolled in tortilla, fried, and served with guacamole sauce.

tempeh (Indian)—a substance made from soaking and boiling soy beans, inoculating with a fungus, packing into thin slabs and allowing to ferment. A great source of protein!

teriyaki (Japanese)—boneless meat, chicken, or seafood marinated in a sweetened soy sauce, then grilled.

thali (Southern Indian)—sampler meal comprised of several small bowls of curries and soup arranged on a large dish with rice and bread.

tikka (Indian)—marinated morsels of meat cooked in a tandoor oven, usually chicken.

tilapia—a white fish often served in the Tropics.

toad in the hole (British)—herb sausages baked in thick savory Yorkshire pudding mix.

tom yum gung (Thai)—lemongrass hot-and-sour soup.

tong shui (Chinese)—medicinal soups.

torta (Mexican)—Spanish for sandwich or cake.

tostada (Mexican)—traditionally a corn tortilla fried flat; more commonly in the U.S. vernacular the frilly fried flour tortilla that looks like an upside down lampshade and is filled with salad in wannabe Mexican restaurants.

tzatziki (Greek)—the best condiment to come out of the Greek isles; fresh yogurt mixed with grated cucumber, garlic, and mint (or corriander, or both).

udon (Japanese)—thick white rice noodles served in soup, usually *bonito* broth.

vegan/vegetarian—"Vegan" dishes do not contain any meat or dairy products; "Vegetarian" dishes include dairy products.

warak enab (Middle Eastern)—see *dolmades*.

Welsh rarebit (British)—(also Welsh rabbit) toast topped with melted cheese cream, and ale, usually served with Worcestershire sauce (very hot and spicy).

wet fries—french fries with gravy on top.

wet shoes—french fries with chili and cheese on top.

yakitori (Japanese)—marinated grilled chicken skewers.

zeek (Southern U.S.)—catfish, shrimp, and tater salad.

CATEGORY INDEX

CATEGORY INDEX

ABOUT THE CONTRIBUTORS

Emma Berndt looks forward to the day when she will finish reading *The Power Broker*. In the meantime, she finds solace in Brooklyn and cheeseburgers.

Joe Cleemann agreed to this assignment because he thought it would take his mind off anthrax. It didn't. But once he resumed acting like a man, he enjoyed researching, writing, and editing *Hungry?* He lives in Washington Heights.

Melissa Contreras is a vegetarian who consumes unnatural amounts of sugar to ward off her pork cravings. Sometimes confusion sets in and she does the reverse.

A transplant from the corn-fed Midwest, **Michael Connor** has funneled his insatiable appetites for food and drink into the quest to find the perfect (cheap) restaurant in New York. He writes and edits to pay for his bar tab and can be found asking random strangers if they would like to marry him—he's accepting applications.

Philip Curry gained 20 pounds after moving from London to New York in 1996. He enjoys the diverse ethnic food choices in the boroughs but is still searching for the perfect curry.

A philosopher trapped in the mind of a computer programmer, **Peter Davis** has thus far determined that food is an integral part of the meaning of life.

Andrew Eastwick is the world's least famous reclusive writer.

Marie Estrada has lived in New York for over a decade. When she's not scouring the city for the perfect rice pudding, she's editing books on New York's urban culture.

Laramie Flick really is hungry. He has no job.

Shannon Godwin is convinced that there's not a problem in the world a cold beer can't help solve. When she's not obsessing over tiaras and trying to convince her friends to make her queen, she can be found studying improv and mocking all things egotistical.

Jeff Gomez was born in South California and now lives in New York City; he is the author of four novels. You can visit his web site at www.dontcallhome.com.

A frequent contributor to the bohemian 125th and St. Nicholas corner deli scene, **Scott Benjamin Gross** has spent the last several years boosting Harlem in the minds and hearts of his Upper West Side contemporaries. Alas, his success has garnered little more than longer lines at Mannas on Sundays. Maybe he should have just kept his big mouth shut.

Matthew Gurwitz lives in Brooklyn, baby. He would like to thank Zen Master Yogi Berra for the following koan: "You've got to be careful if you don't know where you are going 'cause you might not get there!"

John Hartz lives in Astoria, Queens and works for a Manhattan public relations firm. His food preferences feature a distinct slant toward the countries of Eastern Europe.

Esti Iturralde has spent a lifetime fighting her surroundings, pronouncing words like "daughter" and "Long Island" correctly. Still, she can't resist that down-to-earth outer-borough vibe, proving that you can the take the Queens out of the girl, but you can't take the girl…

Joanna Jacobs will allow that New York pretty much has Tuscaloosa beat for restaurants. Even after four years, the jury's still out on the rest of it.

A native of Iwate prefecture and former resident of Tokyo, **Mayu Kanno** has spent the last three years developing a nose for bargain delicacies in New York. She studies film at Brooklyn College and lives in Washington Heights with her dogs, Riley and Joe.

Tanya Laplante has been ruined by the amazing, dirt-cheap food found only in NYC; she'll never be able to return to the painfully limited cuisine options of New Hampshire. She is fond of proclaiming that everything she eats is "the best [fill in the blank] ever", though she insists it is true of Corner Bistro's hamburgers.

Nemo Librizzi is an artist, adventurer, and closet gourmet. His wanderings have brought him across the globe, and culinarily speaking, from a youth spent following his mother through the world's five-star eateries to a present affinity for decent, down-to-earth vegetarian fare.

Anikah McLaren begins her life as a world traveler in Bahia, Brazil. She has threatened to go native.

Julie Mente was last seen with her sister scouring the dangerous streets of Staten Island for cheap eats. No sacrifice is too small when food bargains are concerned.

Sarah Mente jetted off to DC in February…and refuses to return.

A graduate of Barnard College, **Jessica Nepomuceno** is a native Staten Islander who defends her home borough whenever necessary. She writes, teaches, studies and eats all over New York City.

Larry Ogrodnek, slacker gourmet from Philadelphia, raised on cheesesteaks and hoagies, currently resides in Astoria, Queens. Represent!

Julia Pastore lives in Park Slope, Brooklyn.

Jeremy Poreca is a young gourmand who measures life in smiles. It just so happens most of his smiles come from ungodly portions of food and refreshing beverages fermented with malts and hops—at cheap prices, of course.

Steve Powers is an artist, an author, and a freelance breakdancer living in Manhattan.

Laura Ann Russo graduated from Tisch School of the Arts in May 2000. She lives in Brooklyn, New York.

Lindy Settevendemie, whose last name means "the seventh harvest of the vineyard", is always happy to write about food (or wine). She lives on a peaceful block in Brooklyn, New York.

Jill Sieracki is an overworked, underpaid New York writer/editor, lookin' for love in all the wrong places. She can often be found wandering Brooklyn, muttering thanks that chocolate, cheeseburgers, and beer are all still affordable.

Teresa Theophano is affectionately referred to by friends as "The Human Garbage Disposal," a nickname her gargantuan appetite has worked hard to earn her. When she's not eating, she's busy writing for various zines and Web sites, petting strangers' dogs on the street, and upsetting her mother by figuring out what to pierce next.

Rebecca Wendler was born and raised in Northern California. She studied most of the revolutionary thinkers, and is now a *librophile*.

Too poor to eat out very often, **Sarah Winkeller** has been known to try to leverage her review writing to get a free meal. It has never worked. However, she has managed to hit on a few good-looking waiters.

Brad Wood likes cute critters and scary monsters. Contrary to popular belief, he did not get gout from researching his hot dog sidebar.

Andrew Yang spends as much time unlearning as learning, pining as supining.

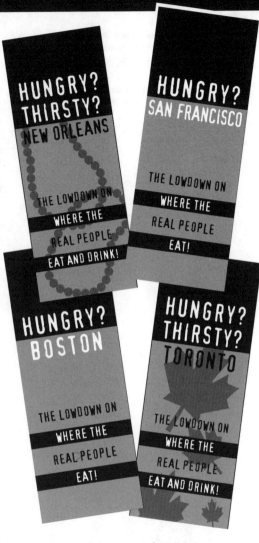

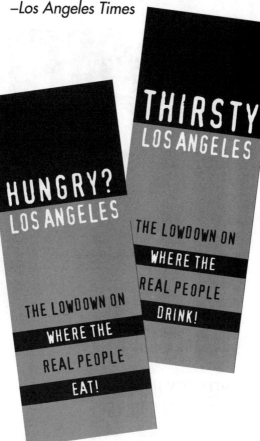

Glove Box Guides supports the ongoing efforts of City Harvest, the largest and oldest food rescue program in the country. As you explore the world of eating in New York City, please consider those who are still hungry.

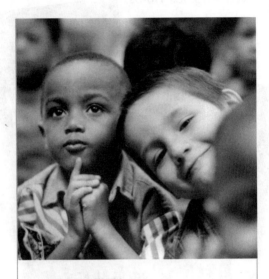

CITY HARVEST

RESCUING FOOD FOR NEW YORK'S HUNGRY

HELP CITY HARVEST FEED NEW YORK'S HUNGRY

One in five New Yorkers needed emergency food last year — and 500,000 of them were children. Since 1981, City Harvest has been collecting good, nutritious food that would otherwise go to waste and delivering it to community programs that feed the hungry.

You can join us in this vital work. Call 1-800 77 HARVEST or visit www.cityharvest.org

City Harvest, Inc. 575 Eighth Ave. NY, NY 10018 **tel** 917.351.8700 www.cityharvest.org

EAT WELL. BE COOL. DO GOOD.